Dear Philippe,

Our discussions on international justice brought us from Zhovkva and Lviv to Brussels. This book on minor experiments carries this exchange a little further.

Brussels, 22 February 2022

Pieter   Ornella

DEFEATING IMPUNITY

War and Genocide

General Editors: Omer Bartov, Brown University; A. Dirk Moses, University of Sydney

In recent years there has been a growing interest in the study of war and genocide, not from a traditional military history perspective, but within the framework of social and cultural history. This series offers a forum for scholarly works that reflect these new approaches.

The Berghahn series Studies on War and Genocide has immeasurably enriched the English-language scholarship available to scholars and students of genocide and, in particular, the Holocaust. —**Totalitarian Movements and Political Religions**

For a full volume listing, please see the series page on our website:
http://berghahnbooks.com/series/war-and-genocide

DEFEATING IMPUNITY

Attempts at International Justice in Europe since 1914

Edited by Ornella Rovetta and Pieter Lagrou

berghahn
NEW YORK • OXFORD
www.berghahnbooks.com

First published in 2022 by
Berghahn Books
www.berghahnbooks.com

Library of Congress Cataloging-in-Publication Data
Names: Rovetta, Ornella, editor. | Lagrou, Pieter, editor.
Title: Defeating impunity : attempts at international justice in Europe
  since 1914 / edited by Ornella Rovetta and Pieter Lagrou.
Description: First edition. | New York : Berghahn Books, 2022. | Series:
  War and genocide; 33 | Includes bibliographical references and index.
Identifiers: LCCN 2021028768 (print) | LCCN 2021028769 (ebook) | ISBN
  9781800732612 (hardback) | ISBN 9781800732629 (ebook)
Subjects: LCSH: Criminal liability (International law)--History--20th
  century. | Criminal justice, Administration of--Europe--History--20th
  century. | International criminal law--Europe--History--20th century. |
  War crimes--History--20th century. | Crimes against
  humanity--History--20th century. | Impunity--Europe--History--20th
  century.
Classification: LCC KZ7075 .D44 2021 (print) | LCC KZ7075 (ebook) | DDC
  345.4/04--dc23
LC record available at https://lccn.loc.gov/2021028768
LC ebook record available at https://lccn.loc.gov/2021028769

British Library Cataloguing in Publication Data
A catalog record for this book is available from the British Library.

ISBN 978-1-80073-261-2 hardback
ISBN 978-1-80073-262-9 ebook

CONTENTS

᪲

FIGURES AND TABLES

Figure

Tables

ACKNOWLEDGEMENTS

This volume is the outcome of two major research projects financed by the Belgian Federal Science Policy Office (Belspo): The Interuniversity Attraction Pole 'Justice & Populations: the Belgian Experience in International Perspective, 1795–2015' (2012–17) and the BRAIN-be (Belgian Research Action through Interdisciplinary Networks) project coordinated by the editors of this volume: '*Jusinbellgium*. A Century of Pioneering Case Law. A Digital Database of Belgian Precedents of International Justice, 1914–2014' (2014–19) at the Université libre de Bruxelles. This project has been conducted by researchers from the Université libre de Bruxelles, the State Archives, the KU Leuven University and the International Research and Documentation Centre for War Crimes Trials at the Philipps University in Marburg.

The research centre Mondes Modernes et Contemporains at the Université libre de Bruxelles has been our home base. This project would not have been possible without the partnership with the State Archives and with the International Criminal Court (Legal Tools project). The Fund for Scientific Research (FNRS) has supported scientific activities organized within the *Jusinbellgium* project.

The authors would like to thank the members of the follow-up committee of the project, Isabelle Delpla, Catherine Denis, Henry Rousso and Kim Priemel, for their support and feedback.

Finally, the authors would like to thank the colleagues who worked with them on these projects: Wolfgang Form, Thomas Graditzky, Delphine Lauwers, Hendrik Vandekerckhove, Marie-Anne Weisers, Jan Wouters and the students (Jonatan Agra, François Belot, Damien Deconinck, Morgane Degrijse, Margot Elmer, Lisa Van Hoogenbemt and Alys Koelman) and interns (Linn-Sophie Löber, Bettine Rau, Cecilia Toninato and Chloé Vullo) involved in the digitization process. Morten Bergsmo, Pierre-Olivier de Broux, Olivier Corten, Bais Devasheesh, Paul Drossens, Stanislas Horvat, Margo De Koster and Xavier Rousseaux have been precious partners in bringing the project to a good end.

ABBREVIATIONS

AAG	Archives of the Auditorat Général
ABMFA	Archives of the Belgian Ministry of Foreign Affairs
AGR	State Archives of Belgium
AID	Agency for Information and Documentation
CAS	Close Air Support
CEGES	Centre d'Etude et de Documentation Guerre et Société
CROWCASS	Central Registry of War Criminals and Security Suspects
DGJM	Directorate General Legal Support and Mediation of the Ministry of Defence
EU	European Union
GB MAT	German-Belgian Mixed Arbitral Tribunal
GBA	Federal Attorney General
GC	Geneva Conventions
ICJ	International Court of Justice
ICMP	International Commission for Missing Persons
ICRC	International Committee of the Red Cross
ICTR	International Criminal Tribunal for Rwanda
ICTY	International Criminal Tribunal for the Former Yugoslavia
ICWC	Internationales Forschungs- und Dokumentationszentrum Kriegsverbrecherprozesse (International Research and Documentation Centre for War Crimes Trials)
IHL	international humanitarian law
IHRL	international human rights law

IMT	International Military Tribunal
JTAC	Joint Terminal Attack Controllers
IMTFE	International Military Tribunal for the Far East
LEGAD	Legal Advisor
LIA	London International Assembly
LOAC	law of armed conflict
LPC	Legal Publications Committee
MAT	Mixed Arbitral Tribunal
MOD	Ministry of Defence
NAA	National Archives of Australia
NAACP	National Association for the Advancement of Colored People
NAB	National Archives of Belgium
NARA	US National Archives and Records Administration
NATO	North Atlantic Treaty Organisation
NFD	National Federation of Deportees of Belgium
NIOD	Nederlands Instituut voor Oorlogsdocumentatie (NIOD Institute for War, Holocaust and Genocide Studies)
NKVD	People's Commissariat for Internal Affairs
OLG	High State Court
POW	prisoners of war
RAF	Rote Armee Fraktion
ROE	Rules of Engagement
StGB	German Criminal Code
StPO	Procedural Criminal Law (Germany)
SVG	Service Victimes de Guerre
TNA	The National Archives
ULB	Université libre de Bruxelles
UN	United Nations
UNHCR	United Nations High Commissioner for Refugees
UNWCC	United Nations War Crimes Commission
WJC	World Jewish Congress
ZAB	Zivil Arbeiter Bataillonnen
ZdL	Zentrale Stelle der Landesjustizverwaltung zur Aufklärung nationalsozialistischer Verbrechen

CHRONOLOGY

<table>
<tr><td>1899</td><td>First Hague Peace Conference</td></tr>
<tr><td>1907</td><td>Second Hague Peace Conference</td></tr>
<tr><td>1919</td><td>Peace Treaty of Versailles</td></tr>
<tr><td>1919–20</td><td>Istanbul trials</td></tr>
<tr><td>1920</td><td>Peace Treaty of Sèvres</td></tr>
<tr><td>1920</td><td>Publication of the Allied Extradition List</td></tr>
<tr><td>1921–22</td><td>Leipzig trials</td></tr>
<tr><td>1923</td><td>Peace Treaty of Lausanne</td></tr>
<tr><td>1923–25</td><td>In absentia trials in France and Belgium</td></tr>
<tr><td>1924</td><td>Case of Belgian deportees before the German-Belgian Mixed Arbitral Tribunal</td></tr>
<tr><td>1943–53</td><td>Soviet war crimes trials</td></tr>
<tr><td>1945</td><td>Charter of the International Military Tribunal</td></tr>
<tr><td>1945–46</td><td>Nuremberg trial</td></tr>
<tr><td>1946–47</td><td>Tokyo trial</td></tr>
<tr><td>1946–1949</td><td>Nuremberg successor trials</td></tr>
<tr><td>1947</td><td>Belgian Law on War Crimes</td></tr>
<tr><td>1948</td><td>Genocide Convention</td></tr>
<tr><td>1948–52</td><td>Belgian war crimes trials</td></tr>
<tr><td>1949</td><td>Geneva Conventions</td></tr>
<tr><td>1961</td><td>Eichmann trial</td></tr>
</table>

1963–64	Frankfurt Auschwitz trial
1975	Majdanek trial
1993	Creation of the International Criminal Tribunal for the Former Yugoslavia
1993	Belgian law on universal jurisdiction
1994	Creation of the International Criminal Tribunal for Rwanda (ICTR)
1997	Extraordinary Chambers in the Courts of Cambodia
1998	Rome Statute (creating the International Criminal Court (ICC))
1998	First international decision based on the Genocide Convention (ICTR)
2000	Special Court for Sierra Leone
2002	Rome Statute (ICC) entry into force
2015	Closure of the ICTR
2019	Trial of Fabien Neretse before the Assizes Court in Brussels

DEFEATING IMPUNITY IN TWENTIETH-CENTURY EUROPE

Ornella Rovetta and Pieter Lagrou

In his documentary novel *The Seven Roses of Tokyo* relating everyday life in Tokyo during and immediately after the Second World War, Hisashi Inoue tells the story of the creation on 8 October 1945 of an 'Association to claim reparations from the United States, author of blind and massive barbaric bombings, including atomic bombs'.[1] The 'association' was the initiative of no more than ten middle-aged men who had lost family members in aerial bombing campaigns, some in Hiroshima, but mostly as a result of the incendiary bombs that reduced entire residential areas of Tokyo to ashes over the last months of the war. The association had conducted erudite discussions before the drafting of the protest motion it sent to General Douglas MacArthur, referring to the plenary session of the Geneva Disarmament Conference of July 1932, to the discussions in the British House of Commons on the shelling of Kagoshima by the Royal Navy in August 1863, and to Articles 22 and 23 of the annexe to the 1907 Hague Convention Respecting the Laws and Customs of War on Land. The association used strong wording, stating that the bombings constituted 'an unprecedented degree of atrocity', 'blind cruelty' and 'a new crime against civilization'. Usurping the voice of the Japanese government, it stated that: 'The imperial government, in its own name, in the name of the entire humankind and in the name of civilization, solemnly condemns the government of the United States and requests with the most vigorous determination that it instantly renounces to the further use of this barbaric weapon.'[2]

In a narrative oscillating between fiction and rigorous documentation, Inoue poignantly describes the distress and sorrow of bereaved fathers and husbands in postwar Tokyo and their thirst for justice. In the wake of the total and unconditional defeat, they seek to identify an authority to which they could address their claims: the imperial government that had initiated this war and kept on fighting beyond any reasonable hope for victory, the neutral countries, humankind, civilization and, probably most importantly, General MacArthur, head of the occupying forces. Amid utter destruction and mass death, they adhered to the language of international law and held the occupier up to its standards. Inoue even makes the Legal Service of the General Headquarters of the occupying forces respond to the motion of the association. In its reply, the Legal Service recalls, first, that only states can file a legal appeal under international law; second, that private persons, such as the members of the association, should address themselves exclusively to their national government; third, that even if the Japanese government would recognize the claims by private parties and even if it would have disposed of full sovereignty, no Japanese court could ever have jurisdiction over the actions of the US government; and, fourth, that the only option left open would be that of civil litigation over reparation before an American court. However, it is a fundamental principle of American law that the state cannot be legally challenged over the actions of its agents in the exercise of their functions.[3] The ten signatories ended up in an American military prison, having been charged with subversion.

Inoue's story is that of the discrepancy between the steady progress of the formulation of international law since the late nineteenth century, covering ever more areas of what constitutes lawful behaviour of states in times of war and peace, and the very unsteady trajectory of the attempts to make these new rules legally enforceable.[4] While it became increasingly clear between 1860 and 1949 what constitutes an international crime, it remained very unclear who is qualified to sue the offender, which jurisdiction is competent to investigate and judge the crime, how international rules translate into the language of national legal categories and which penalties apply. And yet, answers to these questions are crucial to any project of international justice. The cases under investigation in this volume explore this recurring debate in the European context after war and mass violence.

There is probably no storyline more universal than that of how an offender cannot, ultimately, escape some form of retribution for his or her offence. *Fiat Justitia, ruat Caelum* or, more prosaically, in the end, the chickens come home to roost. However, as Inoue suggests, the story of international justice in the twentieth century is where history parts ways with the morality tale implicit in many fictional narratives. When it comes to cynicism, reality usually beats fiction. In the image of the pilots of the Enola Gay and the command structures reaching to the Oval Office that decided on its mortal mission, the vast majority of offenders escaped trial, and even the court of history often fails to reach a final verdict.

From the vantage point of the incipient twenty-first century, international justice might appear as a high-spirited and mostly delusive project of the twentieth century. The overwhelming majority of war criminals never stood trial and, on average, they enjoyed more support from their national state authorities than the victims of their crimes ever did. If the yardstick by which to measure the success of attempts at international justice is the ratio of convicted criminals to the total number of offenders, the final score is dismal for every war and conflict that took place between 1900 and 2000. If the criterion is caring for victims, penal justice, be it national or international, is the wrong place to look for answers. Penal justice punishes the guilt of the offender; it does not compensate the damage suffered by the victim. The victim can then sue the offender under civil law, but Hisashi Inoue already warned us of the difficulty of holding an agent of the state accountable before a court of justice. Even the ad hoc international tribunals established for Rwanda and the former Yugoslavia in the 1990s did not provide for compensation to victims. The reparations programme of the International Criminal Court (ICC) is in its infancy and the large number of victims when it comes to international crimes is not the least of the challenges.[5] If the balance sheet comprises overall evaluations of the restoration of the rule of law, the promotion of peace and democracy, or the failure or success of coming to terms with a criminal past, so many other factors come into play that it is problematic to isolate penal justice as a variable. If the German and Spanish cases are anything to go by, they suggest the opposite: the less a postwar state is committed to judging past crimes, the better it manages its democratic transition.

In September 1918, the French Prime Minister Georges Clémenceau declared that 'no victory could justify an amnesty for so many crimes'.[6] The First World War ushered in the idea that impunity for war crimes (and for waging war) was not self-evident. However, the understanding of what role justice should play in rebuilding the postwar Europe was very divergent, even among the Allies. At stake was the sovereignty of nation states, typically by organizing international trials or prosecuting heads of State.[7] As this book will illustrate, despite an unprecedented political and legal arsenal written into the peace treaty, almost no war criminal ever stood trial after the First World War. In Belgium, France and Istanbul, most of the couple of hundred trials were held *in absentia*, while the Leipzig trials in 1921 ended in much-contested acquittals or lenient sentences in the eyes of the Allies. The interwar episode produced disappointment at the time and was remembered only for the failure it stood for. It was therefore ever-present in the minds of the designers of the Nuremberg trials: this time, the defendants would be present. Yet, only a few thousand Nazi war criminals stood trial after the Second World War, in addition to the twenty-one in Nuremberg, which amounts numerically to a disappointment of comparable scale. Attempts at legal innovation were cautious and curtailed by the fear to create universal standards applicable to the victors as well as the vanquished. The *raison d'état* or higher interest of the state took primacy over considerations of historical redress, in the Roosevelt and Truman Administrations no less than in the postwar German Federal Republic. In this context, relief for the victims of egregious violations of international law could only ever come from the national welfare states, in Belgium after 1918 no less than in Japan after 1945, regardless of what the international law conventions, peace treaties or the absence thereof had to say on the criminal nature of the offence they had suffered.

By 1948, the major Allies had dismantled their war crime trials and by 1956, all but a handful of Nazi criminals had been set free, even those in Soviet captivity. A 'second wave' of trials started with the Adolf Eichmann trial in Jerusalem in 1961 and, for instance, the Klaus Barbie trial in Lyon in 1987, challenging the postwar record of impunity and oblivion. The end of the Cold War opened up a new chapter of twenty-five years of long-running ad hoc tribunals for the crimes committed in the former Yugoslavia and Rwanda, which were very different from the intense but short judicial aftermaths of both world wars. The International Criminal Tribunal for Rwanda (ICTR) and the International Criminal Tribunal for the Former Yugoslavia (ICTY) have not escaped criticism either and were blamed for their slowness, high cost, limited attention paid to victims and alleged partiality (especially in the case of Rwanda). The permanent members of the United Nations Security Council, who quite surprisingly agreed on the creation of these two institutions, entrusted the ICTR and the

ICTY not only with stopping violations and prosecuting those responsible, but also with contributing to the restoration of peace (the ICTY)
and reconciliation (the ICTR). Fifty years after Nuremberg, international criminal justice had to be rethought, and for the first time since
then, the ICTR and the ICTY applied, interpreted and adapted the
offences defined directly after the Second World War. This reinvention,
which is discussed by Isabelle Delpla in Chapter 9, took place at the
same moment as the adoption by several states of laws of universal
jurisdiction. In Belgium, the 1990s and early 2000s finally saw the
inclusion of war crimes, crimes against humanity and genocide in its
Penal Code, fifty years after the Belgian judiciary struggled with the
absence thereof, as Marie-Anne Weisers shows in Chapter 6.

The project of international justice does not need renewed depreca-
tion under the form of a collective volume. The Geneva Conventions
command us to treat the sick and wounded humanely. So what can this
book contribute to our understanding of international justice? As the
title indicates, with this volume, we aim to downsize the ambition that
the project of international justice has harboured at various points
in its history to just one issue: defeating impunity. Trying to make
sure that no crime remains unpunished is a self-defeating project.
Trying to make sure that not all crimes remain unpunished is a goal
that has been attained several times during the twentieth century.
We can draw some hope from this record. Its history does not read
as the Gospel of the advent of universal justice. It is a story of many
failures and some successes, one that can only provide a useful record
for the future if it is told critically. This should also take the form
of an exercise of self-criticism by the disciplines of history, law and
social sciences, which have over the last couple of decades significantly
contributed to the inflation of expectations driven by the mantra of
transitology. *Transitology* has too often claimed to dispense universal
cures for the curses of conflict and dictatorship in inconsistent, patron-
izing and condescendingly normative ways, confounding the registers
of morality, politics, economy and penal justice.

The texts assembled in this volume point to the experimental
nature of international justice in twentieth-century Europe. Based
on original archival material, they tell an alternative tale of international justice, discussing minor successes and major failures, episodes
remembered and forgotten since 1914. There is obviously nothing
inherently 'European' in the project of international justice. Much of
twentieth-century history instead reads as the story of the systematic
injustice done by European nations to much of the rest of the world.
At a time when international justice is criticized as a neocolonial tool

of European interference in its former colonies, it might be useful and timely to focus on the hurdles that the project to bring egregious violations of humanitarian law to justice encountered in Europe itself. This volume is focused on Europe, not because European successes contain lessons to teach to the rest of planet, but because the failures, the stalemates and the systematic diversions of the course of international justice at the heart of the European experience in the twentieth century constitute an ideal fieldwork for the critical approach we advocate. By downsizing its ambitions to the minor successes in defeating absolute impunity, there is even some positive inspiration to draw from this experience. But international justice is obviously a universal language and a genuinely global project that calls for many more collective volumes paying tribute to the full diversity of geographical settings across the globe. It seems only appropriate for a volume that pleads against overstretching the ambitions for international justice to formulate modest ambitions for its own geographical span. The global dimensions of international justice deserve better than one volume pretending to cover it all.

The conventional chronology indeed starts with 'the road to Nuremberg'[8] and ends in The Hague. The history of international criminal justice is certainly much more diverse in time and space. For instance, the Istanbul trials from 1919 to 1920, the Tokyo trial and the Allied trials in the Pacific (1946–54) all provide fascinating case studies on the pursuit of justice. The exceptionally long and multinational judicial process after the genocide perpetrated against the Tutsi in Rwanda in 1994 also constitutes a case study that adds to our understanding of what it means to seek to 'defeat impunity' in the aftermath of genocide.[9] However, we are convinced that a closer look at forgotten European precedents and modest attempts that failed to make legal history allow us to tell a different story in a different timeframe. We propose to look closer rather than looking elsewhere. In the Conclusion, we will return to this point of departure, asking whether this new timeframe and these new case studies can indeed provide inspiration for the challenges that international justice faces today.

In revisiting the traditional chronology of 'Nuremberg to The Hague', this volume starts with the First World War. It is not surprising that Belgium occupies a special position in this narrative. The Belgian case indeed provides contrasting insights into a cumulative but also fragmented process. Throughout the First World War, the Allies massively referred to Belgium, a small neutral country both invaded and occupied, in their statements on justice as a war aim – and later a peace aim. Crimes committed against Belgian civilians and villages (murder, arson, deportation and looting) were understood at the time as clear and *prima facie* breaches of the rules of warfare.[10] Belgium and Germany had signed the Hague Conventions. During the course of the war, Belgian authorities prepared for postwar justice at the local, national and international levels. However, Belgium did not, of course, play alone in the emerging field of international justice. The first postwar justice efforts thus led to a hybrid model: first, trials were held before a German court under the scrutinizing eye of the Allies in Leipzig in 1921; and, second, trials *in absentia* were organized before French and Belgian military courts from 1923 to 1925. The latter were based on the offences defined in the Hague Conventions and on the Belgian Penal Code. For the first time, national courts interpreted internationally defined offences and structured their inquiries based on this Convention.[11] Unlike most post-Second World War trials that came to a close by the end of the 1940s, in the 1920s, France and Belgium reclaimed the right to judge (based on the Treaty of Versailles) five years after the war had ended and ten years after the crimes had been committed (at least for crimes committed during the invasion). This decision is as forgotten as it is surprising. What led the French and Belgians to put hundreds of German military officers on trial before their courts? Public opinion? Political strategy? A commitment to not leave crimes unpunished, as a statement of a military prosecutor to the Auditorat Général (General Military Prosecutor's Office) might suggest?:

> A conviction in absentia would, it is true, be a weak remedy to appease the public conscience, but it could, however, if necessary in the more or less near future, allow the prosecution of this crime, whose impunity would constitute an attack on the principles of justice.[12]

In recent years, records of early interwar trials have been the subject of renewed attention and led researchers to rethink these 'preludes' to the Nuremberg trial moment. This is true for the Belgian trials,[13] but also for the Armenian genocide trials.[14] The French case law (more than 1,000 trials) is still totally unexplored. After the mid-1920s, the First World War atrocities were not forgotten, but the trials *in absentia* were erased from legal history. The fact that the records were lost for over sixty years because they were seized by the Germans in 1940 and then by the Red Army in 1945 certainly explains this oblivion in part.

The symbolic and pioneering role Belgium played in the First World War was not repeated during the Second World War. However, once again, it was invaded and occupied by Germany. Thus, twice in a row, Belgium had to frame postwar responses to international crimes. Twice it participated in the international discussions too. In this sense, the Belgian case is compelling because it reveals how, with an interval of twenty-five years, justice was designed and implemented outside of the circle of the 'Big Three' (France, the United Kingdom and the United States).

The first two chapters look at the German occupation of Belgium from 1914 to 1918, a major early test case for the enforceability of international law. The brutal invasion of 1914 had triggered a wealth of commissions of investigation gathering judicial evidence, from the local level to the international level. National authorities coordinated a massive effort to document violations of the Hague Convention in every single invaded and occupied town and village. While the Commission of Inquiry was proceeding with its investigations and ordinary jurisdictions initiated prosecutions, in June 1919 a peace treaty was signed at Versailles. Article 228 of the Treaty stipulated that the Allied nations had the right to prosecute enemy war criminals before their national military tribunals. The Treaty also foresaw the prosecution of the Kaiser before an international court. It was unprecedented for a peace treaty to include such provisions. However, their botched implementation explains why Versailles is often referred to as the failed inaugural act in the history of international criminal justice.

In Chapter 1, Thomas Graditzky shows how the Hague Convention of 1907 constituted the central frame of reference for both the German occupier and the Belgian local authorities between 1914 and 1918. Germany's manifest violations of the Law of Military Occupation were constantly denounced and received ample international attention. It was therefore a central aim of the Belgian government to bring high-ranking German officials to trial on precisely this account, as the Treaty of Versailles explicitly authorized it to do. However, Article 43 of the Hague Convention outlines the contours of a balancing act between the sovereign rights of the occupied nation and the operational necessities of the occupier, rather than clearly stating what constitutes a violation, thereby preventing smooth incorporation into domestic law. This made postwar indictments difficult to achieve and open to litigation. Belgian and other allied trials were entirely dependent on the willingness of the sovereign postwar German state to extradite its nationals. Extensive diplomatic negotiations between the Allies forced the Belgian authorities to drastically reduce their part of the Allied extradition list. The German government refused to extradite its soldiers, but offered to organize trials on Allied indictments before its own High Court in Leipzig. After the first acquittal in June 1921, the Belgian authorities refused further cooperation. Three years later, Belgium launched a series of decentralized and largely haphazard trials *in absentia* in 1924 and 1925. The Belgian cases were last-chance trials and produced pioneering jurisprudence. The protracted process by which extradition lists were cut down and the initiative was ultimately left to local military judges had the effect of eliminating most of the complex cases of violations of the Law of Military Occupation to the benefit of more clear-cut cases of traditional war crimes.

In Chapter 2, Arnaud Charon focuses on one of the most egregious violations of the Law of Military Occupation by the German occupier in Belgium during the First World War: the deportation of Belgian workers to Germany and to the military frontline. Requisitioning civilians for war-related work was explicitly forbidden by Article 52 of the Hague Convention. Starting in October 1916, more than 120,000 Belgian workers were forcefully drafted for front service or to replace German workers in factories in Germany. They proved to be a recalcitrant workforce, showing a massive reluctance to work for their enemy. Miserable housing, heating and food further weakened their productivity, causing widespread illness. It is estimated that close to 6,000 workers died during or as a consequence of their deportation. In June 1919, the Belgian Parliament adopted a law organizing the compensation of deported workers for the losses suffered, largely based on the legal framework for veteran soldiers, but with considerably lower entitlements. The National Federation of Deported Workers never stopped campaigning for a more favourable legal compensation scheme. With this legislation, the nascent Belgian welfare state had anticipated the reparation payments that the Treaty of Versailles imposed upon Germany, including explicitly for the deportation of Belgian workers. Faced with the double frustration of reparation payments by the Belgian state it deemed insufficient and the absence of criminal prosecution of those responsible for the deportation within the German government and administration, the national federation decided to file a class action suit before the German-Belgian Mixed Arbitral Tribunal. This jurisdiction was created under the provisions of the Treaty of Versailles to deal with private litigation over outstanding debt resulting from private contracts concluded during the war between German and Belgian parties. The Tribunal was established in Paris and was presided over by a Swiss judge. The case opened in January 1924 and resulted in a major defeat for the claimants. The Tribunal decided that by claiming compensation from Germany, the Belgian state had substituted itself for the deportees, who could no longer file a second claim in their own name. At most, the Tribunal awarded the deportees compensation for food parcels sent from Belgium to the work camps and never delivered. Even if this had been a Pyrrhic victory at best, an important but overlooked precedent had been set. Private litigation against an occupying state had made it possible to obtain recognition for a tort, where state-to-state reparation under international treaty law or criminal trials under public law had failed. Crucially, however, the efforts of the Belgian Federation of Deported Workers underlined a truth that would only be confirmed by later conflicts of the twentieth century, namely that, mostly, victims of war can only ever count on recognition and reparation from their own national welfare states.

It was in the heart of wartime London and in the summer of 1945 that the modern definitions of international crimes – as we still know them to a large extent today – took shape. Chapters 3, 4, 5 and 6 offer four complementary perspectives on legal innovation during the Second World War. They resonate with the rivalry between 'crimes against humanity' and 'genocide' pictured in Philippe Sands' work and the eventual 'victory' of the concept of 'crimes against humanity' in the Charter of the International Military Tribunal.[15] In Chapter 3, Kerstin von Lingen analyses the intense brainstorming that took place in London, starting in 1941. Long before the punishment of Nazi crimes and criminals became a major preoccupation of the Big Three, exile lawyers from occupied Europe took the lead in intellectual debates in rather undefined fora situated at the intersection of academia and informal diplomacy, such as the International Commission for Penal Reconstruction and Development at the University of Cambridge, and the London International Assembly. Both can be considered as forerunners providing the intellectual armour to the United Nations War Crimes Commission, which was created in October 1943. Emigré jurists such as Marcel de Baer and his Czech colleagues Bohuslav Ečer and Egon Schwelb were the driving forces of legal activism and innovation, militating against the legal formalism of many of their British and later American colleagues, for whom the punishment of Nazi offenders was secondary to the defence of their domestic legal order. They were especially worried that some of the most charac-teristic crimes of Nazi rule in occupied Europe would remain blind spots, uncovered by current definitions of war crimes. The notion of 'crimes against humanity' was central in their strategy to include massive and systematic crimes against civilians into the allied war crimes programme. It is striking to notice how their pioneering part in the early planning phase of the war crimes programme did not provide them with a leading role in the war crimes trials themselves, once the major Allies took control. Their brainchild, 'crimes against humanity', was also considerably downsized in its scope. De Baer and Schwelb later pursued international careers rather than taking a leading role in the domestic courts of their countries of origin. Ečer, who did make the choice to return to Czechoslovakia and took part in the Czechoslovak delegation at the International Military Tribunal (IMT) in Nuremberg, would fall victim to the political purges after 1948, being suspected of excessive cosmopolitanism.

In Chapter 4, Wolfgang Form takes a very different look at the United Nations War Crimes Commission (UNWCC) not as a cradle of legal innovation, but as a testing ground of judicial cooperation. In October 1943, the seventeen founding members charged the organization with overseeing a global war crimes programme covering both the European and Pacific theatres of war. A couple of days later, at the Moscow Conference, it was agreed that Nazi criminals had to be sent back to the country where the alleged crimes had been committed to stand trial before national courts. These postwar plans implied intense cooperation on the gathering of judicial evidence and identification of suspects. Substantial efforts were made to standardize criminal charges, implement mechanisms to exchange information, agree on procedures and extradition issues, and organize trials. It is in this context that the discussion on the criminal categories covered by the Allied War Crimes Programme had huge technical implications: would the information gathering be limited to classical war crimes or would it also include 'crimes against humanity', the legal innovation promoted especially by exile lawyers? The UNWCC thus became the clearing house of investigations conducted by national states and Allied military from Norway to New Zealand and from China to Canada. The central tool of the information-sharing platform was the Central Registry of War Criminals and Security Suspects (CROWCASS), containing index cards of about 39,000 individuals. Until its dissolution in 1949, the UNWCC developed a multilayered system of indexes and cross-references, turning its archive into a central depository of war crimes during the Second World War on a global scale. Its value for historians is manifest, but its contribution to the creation of standards and routines of judicial cooperation in a complex international setting is of no less durable significance.

In Chapter 5, Guillaume Mouralis offers a radically new perspective on the role of US lawyers in the formulation of the category of 'crimes against humanity' in the run-up to the proceedings of the IMT in Nuremberg. Since November 1941, the US government had been very reticent to go beyond a restrictive definition of war crimes in international law. However, by the end of 1944, the outlining of a US policy on the postwar treatment of Germany became subject to rivalries of different kinds: between the Department of State and the War Department on the one hand, and between academic lawyers (experts on 'law in the books') and corporate lawyers (experts of 'law in action') on the other hand. Corporate lawyers had extensive experience of bringing complex trials to a good end and direct access to policy makers. In the 1930s antitrust trials, East Coast law firms had played a central role in enforcing governmental economic policies by charging private corporations with the crime of 'conspiracy'. They served as a model for the charges of 'conspiracy to wage aggressive war' that stood at the heart of the US judicial strategy against the Nazi elite in Nuremberg. Placing aggressive war centre stage as the main offence was difficult to square with the aim of the proponents of the new concept of 'crimes against humanity', which covered crimes committed by the Nazi state against its own nationals, including in times of peace. This crucially concerned the crimes against the Jews. Mouralis demonstrates that the relentlessness with which US representatives sought to limit the scope of the category of 'crimes against humanity' to crimes committed in wartime against enemy citizens was motivated by the unconditional defence of sovereignty. Even though explicit expressions of this rationale are rare, US lawyers were first and foremost concerned that an international endorsement of racist crime as a legal category would expose the United States to international scrutiny over its legal system of segregation and the state-endorsed impunity of racist lynchings. They were very effective in avoiding this risk. Civil rights activists in the United States from the 1940s to the 1960s were reduced to recourse to human rights law rather than international criminal law in order to justify their campaigns.

In Chapter 6, Marie-Anne Weisers takes this analysis one step further to the level of national jurisdictions. As Chapters 1 and 2 suggest, Belgium had an extensive, though essentially frustrating experience with German war crimes and the challenge to bring them to justice. In the interwar years, precious time was wasted, and Belgian law was caught every bit as much unprepared for the prosecution of war crimes in 1940 as it had been in 1914. Like all other nations occupied by Nazi Germany, it could hardly be criticized for having failed to anticipate the unprecedented crimes of this second occupation, especially the persecution, deportation and extermination of its Jewish population. The acrimonious diplomatic tensions between Belgium and Germany over war crimes trials[16] – the Leipzig trials and later the trials *in absentia* in Belgium – had produced a rather unexpected effect, whereby the Belgian authorities wanted to show the example with an unassailable jurisprudence, built on legal orthodoxy and ruling out any form of retroactive legislation. It was thus with very inadequate legal tools that Belgian judges had to try to bring to justice the members of the occupation apparatus in charge of organizing the deportation to the centres of mass death of over 25,000 Jews from Belgium. It proved excruciatingly arduous to bring serious criminal charges against the architects of genocide in Belgium, except for arbitrary arrest, for instance, which carried minimal penalties. In the end, almost none of Eichmann's men in Belgium ever stood trial. Weisers shows that this disappointing outcome was not due to a lack of motivation or inventiveness on behalf of the Belgian judiciary. The trial of Otto Siegburg in particular shows the obstinacy with which the prosecutor tried to corner the defendant and managed to get witnesses to testify in relation to a racist murder he committed while on his daily duties as a Jew hunter. The chapter also documents the legal inventiveness of the judges at the trial to qualify Siegburg's act as a 'crime against humanity'. This was a sensational legal decision, but it failed to make legal history, being overturned on appeal by a more conservative legal interpretation. Weisers shows that the record of international justice cannot be reduced to published case law. She also tells the story of local judges fighting impunity against all odds and against legal orthodoxy.

In Chapter 7, Vanessa Voisin turns our gaze eastwards after four Western contributions. The Soviet Union took part in the preparation of the Allied war crimes programme, but Allied cooperation suffered from mutual mistrust. The territory of the Soviet Union was where the vast majority of victims of Nazi crimes were killed. However, the distrust resulted in limited attention in Western European public opinion and historiography for the Nazi crimes on the Eastern Front for the duration of the Cold War. Voisin shows that the Soviet authorities never tried to hide Nazi atrocities from view, but on the contrary very early on understood the power of filmed footage of crime scenes: mass graves, destroyed villages and witness testimony. Atrocity footage was used as a tool to mobilize the Soviet population for the war effort, as proof of Nazi criminality for global opinion and as a record for posterity of the Great Patriotic War. Camera operators were incorporated in army units, and instructions to film atrocities became increasingly scripted and standardized throughout the war. The documentary value of Soviet footage of Nazi atrocities faced the challenge of redemption from its original sin, namely the blatantly falsified images of the Katyn massacre, where the Soviets tried to blame the Germans for a mass crime perpetrated by the People's Commissariat for Internal Affairs (NKVD). It is therefore essential to understand the logic behind the production, conservation and selection of Soviet atrocity footage. Documentary, aesthetic and political considerations guided the instructions. The footage, which was widely circulated through Soviet and international cinema newsreels, was supposed to trigger strong emotional identification with the victims, which also implied representing them as Soviet citizens first and foremost, and only rarely as Jews or Ukrainians. Great care was taken to authenticate the footage. However, the screening of documentary films in the Kharkov and Krasnodar trials (1943), and later at the IMT in Nuremberg (1945–46) performed an illustrative rather than forensic function. Still, crucial Soviet footage of Babi Yar, Majdanek and Auschwitz are the first and often only images available of these crucial sites of Nazi crime liberated by the Red Army. They constitute unique historical records if carefully interpreted according to the context of their production.

In Chapter 8, Rebecca Wittmann takes stock of judicial efforts to bring Nazi criminals to justice in the German Federal Republic after 1945. The central prosecution office initiated over 100,000 investigations and organized 13,000 trials, but German tribunals convicted no more than 6,500 defendants, less than 7 per cent of whom for their participation in the genocide of the Jews. This dismal record has its roots in the legal orthodoxy of the West German judiciary, ruling out any form of recourse to retroactive legislation, much like the Belgian judiciary studied in Chapter 6 by Weisers. Rigorously sticking to the Penal Code of 1870 meant that Nazi offenders were most often found guilty of breaching Nazi orders rather than of applying them. The reluctance to bring Nazi offenders to trial was in turn linked to the personal trajectories of postwar magistrates, who had often started their careers as zealous Nazi judges. The contrasting and contemporary proceedings in 1975 of the trial of Nazi guards of the Majdanek extermination camp and of the left-wing terrorists of the Rote Armee Fraktion (RAF) show the manifest double standards at work between legalist clemency for the former and judicial ruthlessness in prosecuting the latter. The German Demjanjuk trial in 2009 is another striking example of how a Ukrainian prisoner of war (POW) drafted into the Nazi auxiliary forces was held up to judicial standards never applied to German SS volunteers earlier on. If the way in which the Federal Republic of Germany dealt with its Nazi past can be considered a success, this is not in the first place due to the work of German tribunals, which guaranteed impunity for several generations of Nazi criminals.

For the reader reaching Chapter 9, undeterred by the accumulation of misfortunes of international justice over the century, some solace is in view. In this chapter, Isabelle Delpla analyses the astounding – in the light of what came before and after – success of the International Criminal Tribunal for the Former Yugoslavia. Created while the Yugoslav wars were still raging in 1993 and dissolved almost a quarter of a century later in 2017, the ICTY built up a record of establishing a judicial and historical truth that even its detractors were forced to recognize. The Tribunal combined the best of several worlds, staging documentary trials modelled on Nuremberg while benefiting from the orality of witness accounts beyond the theatrical value they held in the Eichmann trial. The recourse (unprecedented in international justice) to guilty pleas provided the Tribunal with a wealth of judicial evidence. The dissolution of the Yugoslav federation motivated several of the successor states to proactively cooperate judicially, supplying the court with their wartime intelligence and eavesdropping on their enemies, and more crucially still by mandating their local police forces to harvest witness accounts during or very shortly after the commission of the crimes. The prospect of entry negotiations into the European Union constituted a powerful incentive, which was very explicitly used as leverage to obtain information and the extradition of suspects. Extensive recourse to forensic science also contributed to an unprecedented degree of precision in the identification of the victims, despite systematic efforts by the perpetrators to destroy evidence, as occurred in the Srebrenica case. The construction of high-tech mortuaries and the development of a comprehensive DNA database required huge investments, but also benefited from the spontaneous cooperation of the families of victims and their associations. The cooperation of victim associations with the judicial authorities, both at a local level and in The Hague, proved to be exceptionally beneficial. Delpla describes the emergence of a culture of proof, whereby it became more important for the victim associations to establish unassailable figures, identifying each victim by his or her name, than to enter into a competition of victimhood by inflating the figures. The success of the ICTY therefore lies in the successful cooperation between local and international authorities, public and private actors, and probably most of all by its imposition of very high standards of evidence. That the achievement of the ICTY cannot easily be repeated has unfortunately been illustrated by the ICC, which has had to cope with difficult judicial cooperation, the remoteness and inaccessibility of investigation areas, the selectivity of prosecution choices and slowness.

In Chapter 10, Chris De Cock introduces us to one of the ways in which the prevention of crimes and violations of international law has become an integral part of the modus operandi of armed forces in the twenty-first century. The legal advisor in operations is embedded with frontline troops to provide advice in real time on the conformity of operational orders with international law. Contemporary armed forces operate on very different missions such as peacekeeping, counterterrorism, counterinsurgency and law enforcement under the authority of national governments, but more often under that of international organizations such as the United Nations or the North Atlantic Treaty Organization. Depending on the scope and mission, different operations are regulated by different bodies of international law and regulations, most prominently international human rights law and the law of armed conflict. The context and the mission of each operation determine what constitutes a legitimate target, a proportionate response, and the authorized or unauthorized arrest of armed or unarmed opponents. More than ever, contemporary armed forces operate under the scrutiny of local and global public opinions, nongovernmental organizations, national and international judges. Crucially, legal advisors in operations have to look to recent jurisprudence for guidance for what constitutes lawful or unlawful behaviour in any given situation. Chapter 10 therefore allows this volume to come full circle. Despite the considerable development of international law, at the start of the twenty-first century, armed forces depend on 'law in action' as defined by case law more than on 'law in the books' to make crucial decisions in the field and in the heat of action. It is what has been punished that draws the line between the law and a crime. Defeating impunity is therefore more than a moral imperative; it is what makes it possible to transpose rules into acts. It stands at the heart of any attempt to build a world based on law and justice rather than lawlessness and violence.

This volume offers no triumphant narrative of the unrelenting march of international justice in holding criminals to account. The ten chapters offer more information on the stumbling blocks on that road than on decisive strides forward. The story of international justice is very much an unfinished, incomplete story, finding itself at a difficult crossroads. It is also a global one, reaching far beyond Europe. The time is not for celebration, but for reflection on the pitfalls met, the errors made and, especially, the adversity and outright hostility encountered. As such, the chapters in this book offer glimmers of hope. Not all crimes have remained unpunished over a long and violent century. International law has provided a language to formulate claims – for instance, in Paris in 1924, in London and Krasnodar in 1943, in Düsseldorf in 1975, and in Srebrenica and The Hague in 2004. All that the Belgian workers obtained through civil litigation was the reimbursement of the food parcels their hungry relatives had sent and that never reached their stomachs. The Soviet trials, the IMT in Nuremberg, the Belgian military courts and the tribunals of the German Federal Republic did not live up to the hopes of exile lawyers and victims of racist violence that a court decision would label the crimes of which they had been a victim for what they were. However, the fact that they formulated this hope is probably more important than the fact that their hopes were not met. This volume helps to illustrate that the language of law and the horizon of justice it drew were international. We hope that the reader will have the experience that it somehow makes sense to navigate from occupied Belgium in 1914 to Katyn and New York in the 1940s, Biljani in 1992 or Somalia in 2008. The accumulation of attempts to defeat impunity constitutes a record of crime, but also a record of courage, determination and inventiveness to bring justice. This is a record to cherish, as this book does.

Ornella Rovetta is a postdoctoral researcher in contemporary history at the Centre de Recherche Mondes Modernes et Contemporains (Université libre de Bruxelles). Her research interests include the history of international criminal justice and of Rwanda. She has published *Un génocide au tribunal. Le Rwanda et la justice internationale* (Belin, 2019) and coauthored a radio documentary on the ICTR.

Pieter Lagrou has taught contemporary history at the Université libre de Bruxelles since 2003. He has published on the legacy of the Second World War in Europe, war crime trials and European contemporary historiography. He is currently working on the histories of popular sovereignty since 1789.

Notes

1. Inoue, *The Seven Roses of Tokyo*. We used the French translation by J. Lalloz (*Les 7 Roses de Tôkyô*. Arles: Editions Picquier, paperback edition, 2014, 441–70 and 566–71).
2. Ibid., 464–65.
3. Ibid., 570–71.
4. Lagrou, '"Historical Trials"'; Lagrou, 'Ce que le jugement ne dit pas'; Koskenniemi, *The Gentle Civilizer of Nations*.
5. *Janssen and Kool, 'Recognising Victimhood', 237–57.*
6. Quoted in Hankel, *The Leipzig Trials*, 15.
7. Lewis, *The Birth of the New Justice*, 27–49.
8. In reference to Bradley F. Smith's book: Smith, *The Road to Nuremberg*.
9. Rovetta, *Un génocide au tribunal*.
10. Horne and Kramer, *German Atrocities, 1914*.
11. As appears from the Archives of the Belgian Commission of Inquiry created a couple of days after the invasion. Many of the Commission's documents can be found in the trial records. See Vannerus and Tallier, *Inventaire des archives de la commission d'enquête*.
12. 'Une condamnation par défaut serait il est vrai un palliatif assez faible pour apaiser la conscience publique, mais qui pourrait cependant le cas échéant dans un avenir plus ou moins rapproché, permettre la répression de ce crime, dont l'impunité constituerait une atteinte aux principes de la justice.' Letter from the auditeur militaire of East Flanders to the auditeur général, 8 March 1924, in AGR (Belgian State Archives), Auditorat militaire de la Flandre orientale, Dossier Rohlenger, 601/1923, p. 3.
13. See the chapters by Thomas Graditzky and Arnaud Charon in this volume; Lauwers, 'From Belgium to The Hague via Berlin and Moscow', 216–236; Rovetta et al., 'Jusinbellgium, A Century of Pioneering Case-Law'. On interwar justice in general, see Lewis, *The Birth of the New Justice*.
14. See in particular the work of Taner Akçam on the Armenian genocide trials: Dadrian and Akçam. *Judgment at Istanbul*; Akçam, *A Shameful Act*.
15. Sands, *East West Street*.
16. Clappaert and Kohlrausch, 'Between the Lines'.

Bibliography

Akçam, Taner. *A Shameful Act: The Armenian Genocide and the Question of Turkish Responsibility*. London: Constable, 2007.

Clappaert, Eduard, and Martin Kohlrausch. 'Between the Lines: Belgian Diplomatic Politics and the Trial of German War Crimes'. *Revue Belge d'Histoire Contemporaine* XLVIII(3) (2018), 90–114.

Dadrian, Vahakn N., and Taner Akçam. *Judgment at Istanbul: The Armenian Genocide Trials*. New York: Berghahn Books, 2011.

Hankel, Gerd. *The Leipzig Trials: German War Crimes and Their Legal Consequences after World War I*. Dordrecht: Republic of Letters, 2014.

Horne, John, and Alan Kramer. *German Atrocities, 1914: A History of Denial*, New Haven: Yale University Press, 2001.

Inoue, Hisashi. *The Seven Roses of Tokyo.* English translation. London: Thames River, 2013.

Janssen, Pauline, and Renée Kool. 'Recognising Victimhood: Lessons from the International Criminal Court and Mass Claim Programmes for the Compensation Procedure Parallel to the Trial of International Crimes in the Netherlands'. *Netherlands International Law Review* 64 (2017), 237–57.

Kévorkian, Raymond. *The Armenian Genocide: A Complete History.* New York: I.B. Tauris, 2011.

Koskenniemi, Martti. *The Gentle Civilizer of Nations: The Rise and Fall of International Law 1870–1960.* New York: Cambridge University Press, 2001.

Lagrou, Pieter. '"Historical Trials": Getting the Past Right – or the Future?', in Christian Delage and Peter Goodrich (eds), *The Scene of the Mass Crime. History, Film and International Tribunals* (London: Routledge, 2013), 9–22.

———. 'Ce que le jugement ne dit pas. Les vertus de l'enquête judiciaire, entre une loi muette et des coupables sourds, 1943–2003'. *Courrier hebdomadaire du CRISP* 2469–70 (September 2020), 31–45.

Lauwers, Delphine. 'From Belgium to The Hague via Berlin and Moscow: Documenting War Crimes and the Quest for International Justice, 1919–2019'. *Archives and Manuscripts* 48(2) (2020), 216–36.

Lewis, Mark. *The Birth of the New Justice: The Internationalization of Crime and Punishment, 1919–1950.* Oxford: Oxford University Press, 2014.

Rovetta, Lagrou et al. 'Final Report: Jusinbellgium, A Century of Pioneering Case-Law. A Digital Database of Belgian Precedents of International Justice, 1914–2014'. Brussels: Belgian Science Policy Office, 2020. Retrieved 20 April 2021 from https://www.belspo.be/belspo/brain-be/projects/FinalReports/JUSINBELLGIUM_FinRep.pdf.

Rovetta, Ornella. *Un génocide au tribunal. Le Rwanda et la justice internationale.* Paris: Belin, 2019.

Sands, Philippe. *East West Street: On the Origins of 'Genocide' and 'Crimes against Humanity'.* London: Weidenfeld & Nicolson, 2016.

Smith, Bradley F. *The Road to Nuremberg.* New York: Basic Books, 1981.

Vannerus, Jules, and Pierre-Alain Tallier, *Inventaire des archives de la commission d'enquête sur les violations des règles du droit des gens, des lois et des coutumes de la guerre (1914–1926).* Brussels: State Archives of Belgium, 2001.

CHAPTER 1

THE LAW OF MILITARY OCCUPATION AND THE BELGIAN TRIALS AFTER 1918

Thomas Graditzky

Introduction

Extensively referred to during the First World War in the context of the German presence in Belgium, the law of military occupation seems to have almost entirely disappeared from the toolkit used by different stakeholders in the framework of the postwar trials pertaining to this situation. During the war, Belgian and German authorities as well as other influential actors such as the clergy regularly invoked rules enshrined in The Hague Convention IV of 1907 and more specifically in Articles 42–56 of its annexed Regulations.[1] These provisions, which regulated the exercise of authority over the territory of an enemy state, formed a unique set of codified rules of international law, which most of the warring powers had ratified, including Belgium and Germany. Together with the rules of customary international law that may have coexisted in this field but were yet to be identified, they formed the military law of occupation of the time, and we will mainly refer to them here when using the latter terminology.

This chapter will first elaborate upon the finding that a noticeable discrepancy existed between the wartime argumentation and the postwar recourse to the law of military occupation. It will then attempt to identify explanatory factors, looking in turn at the political dynamics that surrounded the events, the path followed to draw up lists of the alleged perpetrators to be tried, and finally the intrinsic characteristics of the law of military occupation.

A Quick Measure of the Discrepancy

During the First World War, references to The Hague Convention IV of 1907 were made in relation to all major issues raised in connection with the occupation of Belgium, including the administrative separation of the country, the imposition of Dutch as the exclusive language of the University of Ghent, significant requisitions and fines, deportations and the magistrates' strike.[2] The rights and duties established under the law of military occupation were central to the wartime controversies. The German authorities in Belgium, the German government in Berlin, the Belgian government in exile and notables who remained in occupied territory (such as mayors and parliamentarians) all invoked this body of rules.[3] The most frequently cited provision was Article 43 of the Regulations annexed to The Hague Convention IV (hereinafter 'The Hague Regulations'), which provides that:

> The authority of the legitimate power having in fact passed into the hands of the occupant, the latter shall take all the measures in his power to restore, and ensure, as far as possible, public order and safety, while respecting, unless absolutely prevented, the laws in force in the country.[4]

Quite logically, the German representatives brought forward the powers and duties of the occupant to ensure the 'public order and safety' that Article 43 enunciates, whereas their Belgian counterparts insisted on the limits set by the last part of this provision. Several other provisions, dealing with more specific issues that would emerge in the context of occupation (for instance, requisitions in kind and services) were also acknowledged and legal arguments held a significant place in stakeholders' discourse, pervading even the epistolary exchanges between Cardinal Mercier – the head of the Catholic Church in Belgium – and the German Governor-Generals Moritz von Bissing and Ludwig von Falkenhausen, or their subordinates.[5]

Following the war, respect for the laws of war by the belligerents remained an intensely debated matter, particularly within the framework of the postwar trials. In this regard, five different categories of procedures must be distinguished in relation to the Belgian war experience.

First, before the entry into force of the Treaty of Versailles on 10 January 1920 and in spite of the wording of the text of Article VI of the Armistice Agreement of 11 November 1918 that seemed to prohibit such measures,[6] a small number of individuals were arrested in Germany and transferred to Belgium. They underwent trial there on the basis of the ordinary penal code in relation to acts qualified as thefts, arson and murders committed during the war.[7]

Once the armistice period was over, directly arresting and transferring suspects out of the occupied territories was no longer deemed legally feasible. In February 1920, pursuant to Article 228 of the Treaty of Versailles and paragraph 3 of a protocol signed on the same day, a list of persons to be extradited for trial by Allied courts was handed over by the Allies to Germany, which refused to act on this basis. Belgium had asked for the extradition of 334 individuals, but no trial took place as a direct consequence of the extradition list.

In 1921 and 1922, the Reich Court in Leipzig, which relied on German law, conducted three trials connected with the occupation of Belgium. The first and last trials concerned thefts committed during the chaos of the final days of the war and ultimately led to the conviction of four individuals to two to five years' imprisonment based on the German Military Penal Code. The second trial – the Ramdohr case submitted by Belgium – related to the brutal interrogation of young individuals at the end of 1917 and the beginning of 1918 and led to an acquittal. No reference was made to The Hague Convention and its annexed Regulations.[8]

Disappointed by the Leipzig trials, the Allies decided to turn back to their own courts and where possible attempted to try alleged German suspects *in absentia*. However, Great Britain was barred from doing so by its own law and Italy did not take any action either.[9] France and Belgium held several hundred such trials until October 1925: approximately 1,000 in the former and about 150 in the latter.[10] Belgian trials before military courts were based on offences described in the ordinary Penal Code, including thefts, homicides and arson.[11] The vast majority of cases pertained to the invasion period of 1914 and, out of the seven Belgian war councils (first-instance military courts), only those in Namur and Brussels made reference to The Hague Regulations. Surprisingly, the only provision from the part thereof devoted to the law of military occupation – Article 46 on respect for the lives of persons and private property – was mentioned in cases that did not strictly deal with the situation of military occupation. The texts of the court decisions never included any discussion regarding the substance of the provisions of The Hague Regulations. Of the available cases,[12] it appears that none was related to the most emblematic (alleged) violations of the law of occupation, such as those associated with the administrative separation of Belgium, deportations, requisitions and fines.[13]

Lastly, a trial of the Kaiser was anticipated in Versailles. It never took place and, given the peace treaty referring to 'a supreme offence against international morality and the sanctity of treaties',[14] no indication exists that the law of military occupation would have been discussed within this framework. We shall leave the issue of the Kaiser's trial aside for the remainder of the discussion presented here.[15]

To sum up at this stage, relatively few cases related to the period of occupation and there was an almost total absence of references to international law provisions dealing with military occupation. The experience was chaotic and the results were generally unsatisfying,[16] but as far as the law of military occupation was concerned, the outcome was dismal. We shall now look at the factors that may have contributed to this disappointing state of affairs.

The Global Picture: Political Dynamics

First, the political context deserves to be quickly recalled here, as it directly affected the prosecutions (or lack thereof) and played a role alongside other factors. Armistice transfers for trial outside Germany were closely linked to military operations and capabilities. Their interruption was then essentially dictated by legal considerations. Indeed, legal experts consulted by the Belgian government concluded that with the entry into force of the peace treaties, Germany had regained jurisdiction over individuals who were within its borders and that this treaty barred Belgium and the other Allies from transferring further detainees to their own territories, save in exceptional circumstances. Alleged perpetrators were therefore to be either extradited and tried on the basis of Articles 228–30 of the Treaty of Versailles or prosecuted before a German court. Under this framework and connected to the interpretation and implementation of those provisions, political factors became salient.

Article 228 of the Treaty of Versailles, in conjunction with paragraph 3 of the protocol signed on the same day, required that the Allies draft a list of individuals to be extradited by Germany and tried by Allied national courts. The countries that were willing to include names on the list began to work separately. The Supreme Council of the Principal Allied and Associated Powers then appointed an Inter-Allied Commission to finalize the joint list. However, during the entire process, which lasted several months, the Allied Powers were under a strict time constraint: according to a protocol annexed to the peace treaty, the list had to be handed over to Germany within a month following the entry into force of this treaty. When the Inter-Allied Commission – in which Edouard Rolin-Jacquemyns represented Belgium – met for the first time in November 1919, three 'national' lists were submitted: the British one, with about 100 names, the French one, with about 600 names, and the Belgian one, with about 1,000 names.[17] Discussions proceeded as to the content and appropriate size of the global list and each national section of the list. Two objectives were clearly set: to reduce numbers and target officials responsible at the highest level.

The selection process that led to names appearing, remaining or being removed from the various lists will be further examined in the following section. However, it is worth mentioning here that Belgium looked carefully at the number of individuals that France would include on its next list. Internal discussions took place regarding whether Belgium should have (many) more names than France – given that Belgium had suffered more – or if it should come up with an identical or a slightly bigger number because it did not wish to be overexposed to German vindictiveness. The two national lists ultimately included the same number of names: 334. The joint list, with 931 names, was finally handed over to Germany on 7 February 1920.[18]

The communication of the list triggered a particularly strong reaction in Germany within the press, the government, the military and elsewhere.[19] The German government claimed that some names on the list were highly problematic, especially those of high-ranking officials, whom no German government could take the risk of extraditing without being overthrown. The government thus suggested conducting the trials in Germany at the Reich Court in Leipzig.

Faced with the risk of severe political and social unrest in Germany, the Allies (France, Great Britain, Italy and Belgium) decided at a meeting held in London on 12 and 13 February 1920 to put the German government's proposal to the test.[20] They would submit a limited number of cases to see how Germany would deal with them. They insisted that accepting this test did not mean that they were permanently putting aside the procedure under the peace treaty. Belgium had no difficulty agreeing with its allies on this, joining the new line of thought that emerged on the impossibility of expecting the extradition of 'big fish' such as Paul von Hindenburg and Theobald von Bethmann-Hollweg.[21] Although such a stand was not explicitly communicated to Germany, the wording of the note transmitted by the Allies on 17 February 1920 had been carefully drafted to leave the door open to the dropping of such names, and Belgium actively contributed to the drafting.[22]

The Leipzig Court held ten trials before the end of 1921. However, to varying degrees, the results frustrated the Allied Powers, which were facing different options by which to proceed. Indeed, they could put an end to the whole process, revert to and insist on the extradition request, or conduct trials *in absentia*.[23]

Another Inter-Allied Commission, made up of legal experts, was then established by the Supreme Council to analyse the results and make proposals for the future. This commission concluded at the beginning of 1922 that with limited exceptions, the Leipzig trials were a failure, that the Allies should not send further names and that they should revert to the provisions of the peace treaty. In the spring and summer of 1922, the Allies discussed the Commission's proposal.

The British government resisted any reference to the extradition list in future communication with Germany. France strongly pushed for the option of holding *in absentia* trials; in the meantime, it had conducted a few without waiting for the joint decision of the Allies on the proposal submitted by the commission of lawyers. Belgium was convinced that there was a need to revert to a national prosecution of German suspects by Allied jurisdictions, possibly *in absentia*. However, some voices within the Ministry of Foreign Affairs were sceptical in relation to this option. In any event, the Belgian government was convinced that there should be a common Allied policy.[24]

On 22 August 1922, a letter was finally sent to the German government stating that the Allied Powers would stop any form of cooperation and that they reserved their right to hold trials, even *in absentia*.[25] Such trials took place in Belgium and France, as mentioned earlier, and were of course not to Germany's taste. They ceased in 1925 as part of the new 'Locarno spirit'. Moreover, the concerned Allied governments had become convinced that they served no useful purpose.[26]

Throughout the process, Belgium had always carefully observed and often mirrored France. It had simultaneously tried not to displease the British government and had taken due account of the tense social and political situation in Germany.[27]

The impact of political dynamics on the cases selected for prosecution and the way in which they were handled could at first sight be deemed potentially negligible. The *in absentia* trials (before they were stopped) were indeed theoretically able to substitute for all of the trials that had been envisaged, including prior to the reductions of the various lists. However, I do suggest that the political dynamics affected the imbalance regarding the reference to the law of occupation in two distinct ways.

First, when considering the visibility of this body of law on the Belgian lists, it appears that the antagonistic effect of the initial pressure to focus on the individuals considered to be primarily responsible, followed by the dropping of the names of high-ranking officials from the lists, meant that very little remained in these documents as to the law of military occupation, except for cases of violence to persons. These individuals were those identified as being primarily responsible for the most emblematic violations of the law of military occupation.

Second, and turning to the trials themselves, prosecution became limited to *in absentia* trials disconnected from the various lists, and a careful, centralised and mostly coherent selection process was replaced by a decentralised and barely supervised selection process. Emblematic violations of the law of military occupation had mostly been committed at the central rather than at the local level by high-ranking officials who were no longer to be prosecuted.

The Selection of Names and Cases

We will now examine the selection process of names to be included in the successive extradition lists and the cases to be prosecuted either by the Reich Court in Leipzig or *in absentia* in Belgium. Whether violations of the law of military occupation reached the court obviously depended first and foremost on this very selection process. Comparisons between successive 'extradition lists' and within the lists and cases actually handled in court show that discussions on inclusion or exclusion were almost relentless. The percentage of trials ultimately handled that include persons on the lists reveals a discrepancy. Certainly, only about 20 per cent of the trials held in Leipzig or *in absentia* in Belgium related to individuals whose names were on the February 1920 list of 334 names, and about 40 per cent of such trials corresponded to individuals listed on the initial Belgian extradition list, which included about 1,000 entries (November 1919). This demonstrates the importance of reviewing the entire process. By doing so, it is possible to see that many of the other decisions made and arguments advanced along the road, both alongside and in combination with political considerations, can facilitate an understanding of why the law of military occupation came to be substantially disregarded.

The very first list of alleged perpetrators drafted by Belgium was a list submitted to the Commission on the Responsibility of the Authors of the War and on Enforcement of Penalties, which it used to draft a report in March 1919.[28] Composed rapidly, with limited information available,[29] it was primarily the product of the Ministry of Foreign Affairs. At this time, it was sufficient to report as alleged perpetrators 'German authorities' without further specifics.[30] Crimes committed during the period of occupation were fairly represented therein, with one of the two recorded categories of infraction pertaining to this period. The violations reported in this category focused on administrative and economic measures (covering contributions, fines, etc.) and measures of political oppression (including arrests, executions or requisitions committed in this framework, and attacks on institutions and the unity of the country).

Later in the same year came the first Belgian extradition list, i.e. the first list shared by the Belgian government with the names of individuals suspected of having committed violations of the Laws and Customs of War that the country wished to see extradited for prosecution. Named the *liste fondamentale* (fundamental list), this more detailed list was prepared by the Ministry of Justice over a more extended period and from a broader array of elements, including information provided by various prosecutor offices, Members of Parliament, mayors and so forth.[31] The approximately 1,000-name-long list was compiled by Fernand Passelecq, who had headed the Belgian Documentary Office (Bureau documentaire belge) during the war and had joined the Ministry of Justice specifically to perform this task. On 14 October 1919, he submitted to the minister a report in which he explained several of the challenges he had faced. Some of these are of particular interest here.

Confronted with a vast number of allegations, Passelecq first identified the importance of limiting the number of names. He therefore opted against including certain offences, especially those where only material damage was caused. He also insisted on the need to be careful and to exclude references to violations based on facts of a dubious criminal nature and where the suspect might invoke the practice of the laws of war as a mitigating circumstance. Passelecq thus suggested omitting the following: excessive war contributions or requisitions, collective fines, the taking of hostages, and interference with the course of justice. He further explained:

> All the facts included in the examples above certainly constitute, in the light of the Regulations annexed to the Fourth Hague Convention, either

breaches of the laws and customs of war as defined in those Regulations, or at least very serious abuses of the invader and the occupier to the detriment of the Belgian population; but, as individual offences under ordinary law, it is difficult to formulate them in terms of charges, and often their criminal nature depends on a more or less arbitrary assessment of the circumstances.[32]

However, Passelecq did not go as far as to leave aside two violations of The Hague Regulations that had profoundly shocked the Belgian population: the administrative separation of the country and the proclamation of the political autonomy of Flanders. He proposed to keep these violations on the list and to target the chief German representatives involved. Nevertheless, von Bissing, who as Governor-General had signed the decree on the administrative separation of Belgium, had died on 18 April 1917.

This *liste fondamentale* then needed to be compressed according to the principles agreed upon within the Inter-Allied Commission tasked with the preparation of the joint list to be transmitted to Germany according to Article 228 of the Treaty of Versailles. The agreement reached was that the names of the following individuals should be deleted from the country lists: individuals suspected of attacks against property only; those whose responsibility might have been difficult to demonstrate; and those who seemed to have acted broadly within received orders. Although Belgium underlined the difficulty of applying logical criteria in this further compression of its list, it was willing to work on this basis.

The results on the Belgian side were threefold. First, attacks on property were only included if the individual was also suspected of another offence. Moreover, within this category, excessive requisitions or fines were only mentioned if deportation or atrocities committed at the beginning of the war in 1914 were also alleged to have been committed by the same individual.

Second, a halving of the number of names under the heading 'Attacks on Belgian Sovereignty' ('Atteinte à la souveraineté belge') occurred.[33] The two single references to the administrative separation of the country and the proclamation of the autonomy of Flanders that appeared on the *liste fondamentale* disappeared. The three remaining cases of 'Attacks on Belgian Sovereignty' were all linked to deportations: Theobald von Bethmann-Hollweg, Ludwig von Falkenhausen and Friedrich Ecker were the names that remained.

Lastly, applying the principles agreed upon within the framework of the Inter-Allied Commission led to a further reduction of the portion of the list that pertained to the military occupation of Belgium.[34]

Later in 1920, following the Allied decision to test the Leipzig Court with a few selected cases, a short list needed to be drawn up.[35] The new Inter-Allied Commission, with Rolin-Jacquemyns and Passelecq representing Belgium, ultimately selected forty-five names. The principle behind this selection was to include cases where it was not questionable that violations of the Laws and Customs of War had been committed and where accusations would not seem to be politically motivated or legally controversial.

Belgium proposed keeping three situations on the short list, totalling fifteen names.[36] One was a 'typical case' related to atrocities committed during the invasion phase (Andenne),[37] one was a case of atrocities committed against young individuals during the occupation likely to arouse strong emotions (Grammont),[38] and one was a case of ill-treatment against prisoners (the Sedan camp).

Given that some offences – in particular, attacks against property – had already been excluded and that the exclusion of 'big names' had been accepted, it was unsurprising that the 'typical case' selected regarding the occupation period pertained to violence against individuals. As for deportations, in a meeting held on 21 February 1920, Rolin-Jacquemyns had indicated that as a consequence of the exclusion of Bethmann-Hollweg and Hindenburg, all their subordinates suspected of being involved had to be removed as well.[39] Around 30 per cent of the individuals whose names or functions appeared on the 'extradition list' were allegedly involved in deportations, of whom only 15 per cent were reported to have committed other crimes as well.[40] A substantial proportion of this list therefore became inoperative regarding the law of military occupation.[41]

With the decision to hold *in absentia* trials after the Leipzig proceedings came new limitations, and further steps were taken in the deconstruction process. The Ministry of Justice, which first asked the ordinary courts to handle the cases, changed its position and, with due consideration given to the content of Article 228 of the Treaty of Versailles, turned to the military courts in 1924. The names on the various lists did not bind military prosecutors, but they had to restrict themselves to acts that had been committed in Belgium, which were contrary to the Laws and Customs of War, were punishable under Belgian criminal law and whose alleged perpetrators could be identified with certainty.[42]

The initiative shifted to the local level, with limited monitoring at the ministerial level. The decisions available to the author revealed that although a variety of suspects with diverse ranks and functions were tried, a limited range of categories of offences were in focus. One can note on the lists of individuals who were prosecuted a fairly small number of generals and other officers of various ranks, as well as soldiers, police officers, judges and so on.

In short, throughout the process of selecting names and cases, the portion of the lists devoted to the occupation period kept decreasing. Furthermore, more emblematic elements – in particular, attacks on sovereignty, requisitions and fines, which were already largely absent from the initial lists – tended to disappear altogether. In the end, even the cases of deportations did not lead to any results, such as acts committed abroad or other alleged violations of the laws of military occupation.[43]

Some arguments presented in this section devoted to the selection of names and cases have hinted at other factors of a legal nature that may help explain the underrepresentation of the law of military occupation in the postwar prosecution phase. We shall now turn to these before concluding.

Characteristics of the Law

Constraints stemming from the broader framework of international law, from the state of incorporation of the laws of war into the national legal system or from the very nature of the law of military occupation, may have influenced the poor result regarding the visibility of this latter body of law. Each of these three factors will be examined in turn.

A first constraint, already illustrated above, derived from the Rhineland agreement that entered into force on the same day as the Treaty of Versailles. Under this new regime, arrests in the occupied Rhineland territories were no longer permitted.[44]

Signed on the same day as the Treaty of Versailles, the protocol to provide for greater precision on its implementation added a further constraint. As already mentioned above, it set a one-month deadline for the submission to Germany of the list of individuals the Allies wanted to see extradited, exercising considerable pressure and reducing the level of care given to the drafting of the corresponding list.

As for the Treaty of Versailles itself, this also included a few elements that imposed constraints on the process. It referred first to prosecution by the military courts of the Allied Powers. However, this constraint did not have a substantial impact in the case of Belgium. Indeed, its military courts were able to prosecute and use the ordinary Penal Code to find appropriate definitions for offences. Half a year before the Ramdohr trial in Leipzig, Belgium had started a legislative process aiming to adapt its military criminal procedure and providing the possibility for its military courts to hold trials *in absentia*.[45]

However, the Treaty of Versailles also required that the facts behind the prosecutions taking place constitute criminal offences under national law and violations of the Laws and Customs of War. This introduced elements linked to the nature and substance of the law, as Passelecq rightly noted in his report. Any motive for excuse or justification that would exist under the Laws and Customs of War would prevent a request for extradition, even if the alleged conduct constituted a crime under Belgian law.[46] But the reverse limitation was also significant as it required a sufficient level of adaptation of national criminal law.

Certainly, conducting trials at the national level within the framework of the peace treaties required adequate legislation at the national level too. Moreover, the Belgian courts had to face the fact that Belgian criminal legislation did not include tailor-made provisions to prosecute violations of the Laws and Customs of War. They were also ill-equipped concerning prosecutions of foreign offenders of crimes that might have been found in the Military Criminal Code.[47] Both factors contributed to the constriction of the prosecution to acts such as murder, arson and theft, which were contained in the ordinary Penal Code with possible application to foreign citizens.

A legitimate question is therefore whether Belgium failed to act as required under international law regarding the national incorporation of the laws of war, including in particular the law of military occupation. To answer this, it is essential to consider a discrepancy that existed between the Geneva Convention of 1906 regarding the treatment of the wounded and the sick and the 1907 Hague Regulations Respecting the Laws and Customs of War on Land: the former required the adaptation of a State Party's military criminal law,[48] whereas the latter only required the issuance of instructions to their armed land forces.[49] There was therefore no obligation to incorporate criminal sanctions into national legislation about the provisions contained in The Hague Regulations.[50] Some states went further than others in this regard. For instance, one difference could be observed between France and Great Britain on one side, which had conceptualized the implementation of The Hague Regulations as a form of criminalization, and Germany on the other side, which deemed it more of a disciplinary issue.[51]

The imbalance between the availability of a few relevant ordinary crimes for wartime misconduct and the absence of provisions specifically devoted to violations of the Laws and Customs of War turned out to be critical when it came to the situation of military occupation.

Passelecq realized this, but also referred to an element that, had the level of national incorporation into criminal law been higher, would have nevertheless provided an additional obstacle: the nature of the law of occupation.[52]

An essential part of the law of military occupation pertains to the way in which the occupying power might exercise sovereign rights. It sets limits to its power to change the legislative framework, adopt policies and perform administrative acts. The lines delimiting its powers are not always easy to identify, as the notions such as necessity and proportionality are difficult to define. Challenging the legislative measures or policies of an occupying power in court based on the law of military occupation, where possible at all, is not an easy task, as petitioners before the Israeli High Court can testify today.[53]

The nature of the law of occupation also influences the feasibility of the incorporation of its rules into the national legal system. As Belgium underlined when the first version of The Hague Regulations was discussed, it is barely conceivable for a parliament to discuss and adopt provisions that would anticipate a military defeat.[54] One way out is, of course, to look at this body of law from the opposing perspective and for the legislative body to anticipate a military occupation of territories by a country's force, or to consider unspecified situations. If both options are technically feasible – with the caveat mentioned above – they are not necessarily easy paths to follow either.

Conclusion

The nature of the law of occupation is probably one of the most critical elements that can facilitate understanding of the discrepancy between the frequency and intensity with which this law was used during the First World War and its discretion when it came to the criminal prosecution experience thereafter. The provisions that were actively debated during the war were often those related to the exercise of sovereign rights. If they proved useful references to argue, grounding resistance and convincing neutrals during the war, they were unable to offer a sufficient basis for criminal prosecution afterwards. The nature of their content had rendered it difficult, if not impossible, to incorporate them into the national legal system and made it unlikely that existing criminal offences, notions and concepts could be interpreted in ways that would make it possible to cover violations of the law of occupation.

All other factors also contributed to this disappointing outcome. The absence of visibility of deportations – a matter that during the war was the cause of a massive outcry and intense legal debate – was, for instance, primarily due to a new resolution not to target high-ranking officials.[55]

Thomas Graditzky is a lawyer specialized in international humanitarian law and more specifically the law of military occupation, areas in which he has published several articles and contributions. He has worked several years for the International Committee of the Red Cross, including in contexts of military occupation. He was a researcher at the Centre for International Law of the Université libre de Bruxelles and currently works for the Belgian Federal Agency for the Reception of Asylum Seekers.

Notes

1. For the official records of the diplomatic conference and the text of the convention, see Ministère des affaires étrangères, *Deuxième Conférence Internationale de la Paix*. For Convention IV, see vol. I, 626. An English translation of the original French text of the Convention is available on the website of the International Committee of the Red Cross (ICRC): https://ihl-databases.icrc.org/applic/ihl/ihl.nsf/Treaty.xsp?documentId=4D47F92DF3966A7EC12563CD002D6788&action=openDocument (retrieved 21 April 2021).
2. On the occupation of Belgium during the First World War, see in particular de Schaepdrijver, *De Groote Oorlog*, 111–84, 229–70.
3. Graditzky, 'Les expériences belges d'occupation autour de la Grande Guerre', 153–64.
4. ICRC. Convention (IV) Respecting the Laws and Customs of War on Land and its annex: Regulations Concerning the Laws and Customs of War on Land, The Hague, 18 October 1907. Retrieved 21 April 2021 from https://ihl-databases.icrc.org/applic/ihl/ihl.nsf/Article.xsp?action=openDocument&documentId=3741EA-B8E36E9274C12563CD00516894.
5. Graditzky, 'Les expériences belges d'occupation autour de la Grande Guerre', 153–64.
6. Hankel, *The Leipzig Trials*, 351.
7. Fourteen individuals were transferred from Germany to Belgium before 10 January 1920 and tried for such acts committed during the occupation of Belgium and northern France. They were tried by ordinary jurisdictions, such as courts of assizes in the case of murder; see Lagrou, 'Eine Frage der moralischen Überlegenheit?', 340. A 1920 list seems to suggest that over 100 individuals had been sent to, tried and convicted in France or Belgium; see Hankel, *The Leipzig Trials*, 351.
8. The first of these Belgian cases was in fact the very first case the Leipzig Court heard based on the German 1919 War Crimes Law (Law on the Prosecution of War

Crimes and Offences, 18 December 1919). The third happened to be the last that the Court dealt with in a public hearing. The names of the defendants in both trials were on none of the lists. Convictions related to theft and pillage were based on the German Military Penal Code; see Hankel, *The Leipzig Trials*, 48–49, 73, 148.

9. Hankel, *The Leipzig Trials*, 357.

10. According to Hankel, 340 trials *in absentia* took place in France and 153 in Belgium; ibid., 360. Current research on such trials (for instance, within the framework of the Jusinbellgium project) suggests that the numbers were probably even higher. Clappaert and Kohlrausch mention the number of over 1,200 convicted Germans in France; Clappaert and Kohlrausch, 'Between the Lines', 108.

11. Occasionally, the military court in Liège also refers to Articles 1, 3 and 5 of the Military Criminal Code, defining military penalties. This was, for instance, the case in the *Pfalz* decision of 30 June 1925. The decisions are available in the Archives of the Belgian Ministry of Foreign Affairs (ABMFA), Diplomatic Archives, Cl. B 324, XII–XVII (hereinafter cited as: ABMFA, Cl. B 324).

12. It was possible for the author to access ninety-two of these.

13. On deportations, see Arnaud Charon, Chapter 2 in this volume.

14. *Treaty of Peace between the Allied and Associated Powers and Germany,* 97.

15. The idea discussed in 1919 to set up a permanent international court to try alleged perpetrators of violations of the Laws and Customs of War and of the laws of humanity, abandoned before the signing of the Treaty of Versailles, is also left aside here. Clappaert and Kohlrausch, 'Between the Lines', 94–95.

16. Lagrou, 'Eine Frage der moralischen Überlegenheit?', 329, 331.

17. As was common at the time, the terminology 'names' is used here as well, although lists include names or functions to designate individuals. Furthermore, the number of 'names' (or 'entries') does not reflect with any precision the number of individuals concerned. Where functions are listed, the exact number of people targeted under one entry is sometimes left open. It is also likely that two (or more) 'names' correspond to the same individual (appearing, for instance, in the nominative part of a list and in the part listing functions). The same individual may also be listed in relation to different categories of misconduct when lists are organized according to such categories, as was the case for the first Belgian list.

18. The list can be found in the Belgian archives: ABMFA, Cl. B 324, XVIII, Liste des personnes désignées par les Puissances Alliées pour être livrées par l'Allemagne en exécution des articles 228 à 230 du Traité de Versailles, sent to the German Chancellor on 7 February 1920.

19. This had to some extent been anticipated by the Allied Powers, and E. Rolin-Jacquemyns, who pressed his government at the end of 1919 to significantly reduce its list, mentioned his concerns as a freshly nominated Belgian member of the Inter-Allied Rhineland High Commission. See the correspondence in ABMFA, Cl. B 324, I.

20. Discussions were intense and Italy played a special role in encouraging France (which was keen not to exhibit weakness) and Great Britain (which demonstrated a more pragmatic attitude) to agree on a common position. See Hankel, *The Leipzig Trials*, 32–33.

21. See, for instance, a note prepared for the Belgian Prime Minister on 9 February 1920: ABMFA, Cl. B 324, II.

22. See, for instance, the British Secretary's notes of the meeting held in London. At the beginning of February 1920, Germany attempted to put pressure on Belgium by threatening it with a unilateral denunciation of a bilateral financial agreement as a reaction to the fact that Belgium persisted in requesting the extradition of suspected German war criminals. Documents are available in ABMFA, Cl. B 324, II.

23. Hankel, *The Leipzig Trials*, 356.
24. ABMFA, Cl. B 324, VII and VIII, Correspondence and Notes, 1922.
25. Hankel, *The Leipzig Trials*, 357.
26. Ibid., 362. The Locarno Treaties were signed on 16 October 1925. The Belgian Council of Ministers, which had already in June 1925 considered ending the trials, unanimously decided to do so on 20 October 1925. The French government, consulted by Belgium before Locarno, mentioned that it could not foresee a complete abandonment of the process, but that it had already reduced judicial activity in this regard. It opted for a complete stop a few months after Belgium resolved to do so. Correspondence and notes are available in ABMFA, Cl. B 324, IX.
27. Nominated at the end of 1919 as Belgian High Commissioner in the Rhineland, E. Rolin-Jacquemyns was especially aware of the situation in Germany. The position in which Belgium found itself, caught between two increasingly contentious Allied Powers – France and Great Britain – was far from limited to this specific issue.
28. 'Commission on the Responsibility of the Authors of the War and on Enforcement of Penalities', 95–154. At this point in time, E. Rolin-Jacquemyns and F. Passelecq were already among the main actors involved, the former as Belgian representative in the Commission and the latter as director of the Bureau Documentaire Belge (Belgian Documentation Office (Belgian Ministry of Foreign Affairs)) and actual drafter of the Belgian list.
29. F. Passelecq warned his colleagues at the Ministry of Foreign Affairs that given the time pressure, he had to draft the list without first accessing the content of the 500 boxes full of documentation that were scattered across the offices in complete disorder. ABMFA, Cl. B 324, I, Notes of 23 and 30 January 1919.
30. However, it may already be noticed that in the Commission report, some categories of offences or violations linked to military occupation failed to mention the Belgian experience.
31. ABMFA, Cl. B 324, XVIII, Ministry of Justice, Personnes désignées par la Belgique pour être livrées par l'Allemagne en exécution des articles 228 à 230 du Traité de Versailles et du Protocole du 28 juin 1919. Liste fondamentale.
32. Original quotation: 'Tous les faits rentrant dans les exemples ci-dessus constituent assurément, au regard du Règlement annexé à la IVe Convention de La Haye, soit des infractions aux lois et coutumes de la guerre telles que ce Règlement les définit, soit au moins des abus très graves de l'envahisseur et de l'occupant au détriment de la population belge ; mais, en tant que délits individuels de droit commun, la prévention en est difficile à libeller, et souvent leur caractère délictueux dépend d'une appréciation plus ou moins arbitraire des circonstances.' ABMFA, Cl. B 324, XVIII, Liste des Allemands à réclamer à l'Allemagne en exécution des articles 228 à 230 du Traité de Versailles du 28 juin 1919. Rapport général de F. Passelecq à Monsieur le Ministre de la Justice (14 October 1919); Rapport complémentaire (22 October 1919), 1919, 8.
33. Of the six names, only three remained on the following list.
34. However, quantifying this reduction is difficult, given the classification challenges associated with the terminology used and the very limited description of facts appearing under 'nature de l'infraction' (nature of the offence) on the list with 334 names (the Belgian part of the list was submitted to Germany on 7 February 1920). The 'liste fondamentale' of 1919 was structured in a way that makes classification easier, but its numbers are more difficult to extract because the non-nominal designations included in the list may indicate one or several persons holding a specific charge during the war.
35. Hankel, *The Leipzig Trials*, 37 ff.

36. This was the greatest number. France had eleven names on the list, Great Britain seven, Italy five, Romania three, Poland three and Serbia one.
37. However, not the 'main' ones (Dinant and Leuven) in order not to indicate that Belgium could then forget about the others. ABMFA, Cl. B 324, II, Letter from F. Passelecq to the Minister for Foreign Affairs, 23 February 1920.
38. Two individuals – Ramdohr and Zahn – were suspected in this case, but the latter fled and managed to escape German justice. See Hankel, *The Leipzig Trials*, 79–80.
39. ABMFA, Cl. B 324, IV, Commission on the Responsibility of the Authors of the War and on Enforcement of Penalties, Minutes of the meeting of the subcommittee responsible for the drafting of the lists held on 21 February 1920.
40. The victims of labour deportation therefore turned to reclamation claims before the German-Belgian Mixed Arbitral Tribunal, as analysed by Charon in Chapter 2 in this volume.
41. As for the treatment of cases by the Leipzig Court in general, it was observed that the Court viewed them essentially from the perspective of 'common crimes' committed on the occasion of war (pillage being a specific example), ascribing importance to military discipline but being resistant to the idea that 'international law set limits on warfare and that overstepping those limits could carry with it the risk of criminal sanction'; Hankel, *The Leipzig Trials*, 80. This also had an impact on the fact that important aspects of the law of occupation were given no attention by the court.
42. ABMFA, Cl. B 324, XII, Letter from the Belgian Minister of Justice to the Auditeur Général [Chief Military Prosecutor], 29 March 1924.
43. Although some results were presented, the second-biggest category of offences on the extradition list of 334 names (violence to people in the framework of the occupation) also led to very little in the end.
44. Lagrou, 'Eine Frage der moralischen Überlegenheit?', 330. Article 3 of the Rhineland agreement states that German courts shall exercise civil and criminal jurisdiction subject to only two exceptions. Foreign military law and jurisdiction is relevant in relation to: (1) Allied Powers' armed forces, their accompanying personnel and persons employed by them or at their service; 2) any person who commits an offence against the persons or property of such forces. Agreement between the United States of America, Belgium, the British Empire and France', 404–9.
45. A bill was introduced in Parliament on 14 December 1920. It became the Law of 25 June 1921 on default proceedings before military courts. Parliamentary documents are available on the website of the Belgian House of Representatives: https://www.lachambre.be/kvvcr/showpage.cfm?section=flwb&language=fr&cfm=/site/wwwcfm/flwb/flwbngenesis.cfm?dossierID=0020-1920-1921&legislat=genesis%5C26&inst=K (retrieved 21 April 2021).
46. Liste des Allemands à réclamer, 1919, 8.
47. Although the military court in Liège refers in its decisions to articles from the Military Criminal Code of 1890, nothing in this code regulated the prosecution of foreign nationals. Lagrou, 'Eine Frage der moralischen Überlegenheit?', 330.
48. *Convention for the Amelioration of the Condition of the Wounded and Sick in Armies in the Field.* Geneva, 6 July 1906, Article 28. Available on the website of the ICRC: https://ihl-databases.icrc.org/applic/ihl/ihl.nsf/Article.xsp?action=openDocument&documentId=23C79F89FD0DE1B4C12563CD005163BB (retrieved 21 April 2021).
49. 'The Contracting Powers shall issue instructions to their armed land forces which shall be in conformity with the Regulations respecting the laws and customs of war on land, annexed to the present Convention.' Hague Convention IV of 1907, Article 1, https://ihl-databases.icrc.org/applic/ihl/ihl.

nsf/Article.xsp?action=openDocument&documentId=4DA62D0D49A7A5C-
4C12563CD00516566 (retrieved 21 April 2021). Nevertheless, one exception exists: Article 56(2) of the Regulations annexed to the Hague Convention, which
states that seizure and destruction of private property (in times of military occupation) are to be prohibited and made the object of proceedings.

50. In terms of sanctions, Article 3, which had been added in 1907 to the text of the
previous Convention based on a German proposal, only provides for interstate compensation in cases of violation of the Convention (see note 49 above for the only
exception (seizure and destruction of private property)).

51. Hankel, *The Leipzig Trials*, 121–22.

52. Liste des Allemands à réclamer, 1919, 8–9. See also the annex to the report, which
constitutes an attempt to identify in the Belgian legislation the equivalent to the
different types of offences listed by the Commission on Responsibility. Here, difficulties appear to have been experienced in relation to 'usurpation de droits sou-
verains de l'État pendant l'occupation' (usurpation of sovereignty during military
occupation) and 'imposition de contributions et requisitions illégitimes et exorbi-
tantes' (exaction of illegitimate or of exorbitant contributions and requisitions).

53. However, it must be noted that such proceedings do not relate to the criminal field.

54. Ministère des affaires etrangères. *Conférence Internationale de la Paix*, part III, 89.

55. Common criminal offences to adequately cover deportations and prosecute
high-ranking officials may have been difficult to find in Belgian law. However, F.
Passelecq noted in the annex to his first report of October 1919 provisions of the
Belgian Criminal Code relating to unlawful and arbitrary arrest and detention, in-
fringement of the rights guaranteed by the Constitution and kidnapping of minors;
Liste des Allemands à réclamer, 1919, 22.

Bibliography

Published Sources

'Agreement between the United States of America, Belgium, the British Empire and
France, of the One Part, and Germany of the Other Part, with Regard to Military
Occupation of the Territories of the Rhine'. *American Journal of International Law*
13(4) (1919), 404–9.

Clappaert, Eduard, and Martin Kohlrausch. 'Between the Lines: Belgian Diplomatic
Politics and the Trial of German War Crimes, 1919–1926'. *Journal of Belgian
History* 48(3) (2018), 90–114.

'Commission on the Responsibility of the Authors of the War and on Enforcement of
Penalities: Report Presented to the Preliminary Peace Conference'. *American
Journal of International Law* 14(1/2) (1920), 95–154.

De Schaepdrijver, Sophie. *De Groote Oorlog: Het Koninkrijk België in de Eerste
Wereldoorlog*. Antwerp: Houtekiet, 2013.

Graditzky, Thomas. 'Les expériences belges d'occupation autour de la Grande Guerre :
quelle mobilisation du Règlement de La Haye ?', in James Connolly, Emmanuel
Debruyne, Élise Julien and Matthias Meirlaen (eds), *En territoire ennemi 1914–
1949 : Expériences d'occupation, transferts, héritages* (Villeneuve d'Ascq: Presses
Universitaires du Septentrion, 2018), 153–64.

Hankel, Gerd. *The Leipzig Trials: German War Crimes and Their Legal Consequences
after World War I*. Dordrecht: Republic of Letters, 2014.

Lagrou, Pieter. 'Eine Frage der moralischen Überlegenheit? Die Ahndung deutscher Kriegsverbrechen in Belgien', in Norbert Frei (ed.), *Transnationale Vergangenheitspolitik: Der Umgang mit deutschen Kriegsverbrechen in Europa nach dem Zweiten Weltkrieg* (Göttingen: Wallstein, 2006), 326–50.

Ministère des affaires etrangères. *Conférence Internationale de la Paix, La Haye 18 mai–29 juillet 1899*. The Hague: Imprimerie Nationale, 1907 (new edition).

———. *Deuxième Conférence Internationale de la Paix: La Haye, 15 juin–18 octobre 1907: Actes et Documents*. The Hague: Imprimerie Nationale, 3 vols, 1907.

Treaty of Peace between the Allied and Associated Powers and Germany, Signed at Versailles on 28 June 1919. London: H.M. Stationery Office, 1920.

Archival Sources

Archives of the Belgian Ministry of Foreign Affairs (ABMFA), Diplomatic Archives, Fonds Guerre 1914–1918, Cl. B 324, I, II, IV, VII–IX, XVII–XVIII.

CHAPTER 2

THE CLAIMS OF BELGIAN DEPORTED WORKERS AT THE PARIS MIXED ARBITRAL TRIBUNAL IN 1924

Arnaud Charon

Introduction

The deportation of Belgian civilian workers began a little over a century ago. However, this brutal policy of the German occupation on the Western Front has received relatively little attention. After first attempting to find volunteers, the occupier decided in 1916 to deport tens of thousands of men aged eighteen to fifty-five to work in German industries or in the military area in northern France. The German measures are infamous, mostly thanks to Jens Thiel's research.[1] However, little is known about the impact of labour deportations on Belgian society and on the deportees themselves, as well as their quest for justice and recognition after the conflict.[2] Despite their controversy, labour deportations during the First World War would be overshadowed by the much bigger draft during the Second World War and would be largely consigned to oblivion.

This chapter first examines a specific aspect of this struggle: the collective action undertaken by the deportees against Germany before the German-Belgian Mixed Arbitral Tribunal (GB MAT) in 1924 to obtain compensation directly from the former occupier. However, before explaining this trial, we must consider the historical background and understand the reparation scheme put in place by the Belgian state and trace the evolution of the laws supporting civilian victims of war. We will then investigate the competences that were granted to the mixed arbitral tribunals by the Treaty of Versailles, before finally examining the trial and its consequences.

Historical Context

When the Western Front stabilized in November 1914, the occupier settled and organized life in the occupied territories. It requisitioned the raw materials and tools required to run industries and shipped them to Germany. As a result, factories closed one after the other, causing massive unemployment. At the beginning of 1915, approximately 640,000 people (about one-third of the active population) were jobless. Even though this figure fell slightly in 1916 and 1917, it remained considerable.[3]

Meanwhile, little military progress and significant casualties meant that Germany lacked manpower. Men like Carl Duisberg (chemical industry Bayer) encouraged the government to use this 'great pool of men that Belgium is' (*'Öffnen Sie das Große Menschenbassin Belgien!'*).[4] By the end of 1914, the Germans launched the Deutsches Industrie-Büro, located in the industrial cities of Belgium, to recruit workers for contracts of four to eight months in Germany. The propaganda promised numerous advantages to the volunteers:

> Workers! We offer you employment at wages unknown in Belgium to this day and far more generous than those paid out here before the war. You will receive sufficient food at minimal prices. This salary will allow you to come to the aid of your families. Those who enroll receive on the spot a bonus of fifty francs. Family allowances, in different monthly installments, serving to fend off the current shortages. In one word: work, the opportunity to emancipate yourselves from the shame of the poor relief, a good wage, abundant food, family allowances all over the country. Each and every man who wishes to work in Germany and wants to spare his family the horrors of the coming harsh times, can call on us.[5]

This type of propaganda did not meet with the expected level of success and so in 1916 the War Ministry of Prussia (Preußisches

Kriegsministerium), German industrial managers and the Supreme Army Command (Oberste Heeresleitung), taken over by Paul von Hindenburg and Erich Ludendorff, increased their pressure on the civilian authorities. They adopted the Rathenau plan, named after the main instigator Walther Rathenau, President of the Allgemeine Elektricität Gesellschaft. This plan was intended to weaken Belgian industries, especially those competing against their German equivalents. Moreover, hiring of jobless workers by local authorities, authorized until then by the Germans, was forbidden. The actions of the Comité National de Secours et d'Alimentation (National Relief and Food Committee) to help jobless civilians were limited in order to encourage as many people as possible to leave for Germany. Despite these measures, only 20,000 Belgians had taken a job in enemy country by 1916, far from the hundreds of thousands of workers expected by the occupier. Faced with this failure, and despite the lack of enthusiasm on the side of the Governer-General in Brussels and even Kaiser Wilhelm II, the civilian authorities permitted mass deportations, a clear violation of The Hague Convention.

The Hague Convention IV of 1907 defining the Laws and Customs of War on Land allowed a state, by virtue of Article 6, to use prisoners of war as workers.[6] However, Article 52 prohibited civilians from working, with the exception of precise work on the territory of the municipalities themselves:

> Requisitions in kind and services shall not be demanded from municipalities or inhabitants except for the needs of the army of occupation. They shall be in proportion to the resources of the country, and of such a nature as not to involve the inhabitants in the obligation of taking part in military operations against their own country. Such requisitions and services shall only be demanded on the authority of the commander in the locality occupied. Contributions in kind shall as far is possible be paid for in cash; if not, a receipt shall be given and the payment of the amount due shall be made as soon as possible.[7]

Deportations began on 3 October 1916 in the *Etappengebiet* (rear area), the requisitioned area close to the frontline, and reached the territories ruled by the General Government on 25 October. Official numbers show that 120,655 people were deported between 1916 and 1918, including 58,500 in just three months from the General Government territories.[8] Once in Germany, deportees were sent to concentration camps, called repartition camps or 'housing for industry workers', to avoid legal terms used by The Hague Convention. These places were usually annexes to prisoner-of-war camps and were hastily constructed. They were supposed to host Belgian civilians for a few days only, while waiting for them to sign their contracts. The German plan stated that:

> Every person in the distribution point should be convinced during their stay to sign a work contract ... Through strict discipline and by recruiting them for necessary internal tasks at the distribution point, preconditions must be created that Belgians would welcome any well-paid labour outside of the distribution point as desirable and an improvement of their current situation.[9]

In reality, most Belgians refused to sign a contract and were forced to stay inside the camp or were transferred to punitive camps. The Germans used coercive measures to compel the deportees to sign their contracts. Indeed, they were forced to work inside or outside the camps and faced freezing temperatures, hard work, lack of food or warm clothes, as well as mistreatment.

Deportees were also supposed to be paid decent wages, which, according to propaganda, would allow their families to lead an easy life. In reality, few deportees were paid at all, and those who received several marks a day were forced to pay for their food or housing. *In fine*, most only had 30 pfennigs a day or simply nothing. Families of deportees were allowed to send food packages to help their husbands, brothers or fathers. Many of those packages were never distributed or were delayed to such an extent that the food became spoiled.[10]

At the beginning of 1917, deportations and coercion were deemed a failure. The German authorities decided to stop them by an imperial decree of 14 March 1917, but only for the territories of the General Government. A total of 20,000–25,000 deportees who were still in camps were allowed to go home in May 1917. However, this decree did not concern the *Etappengebiet*, where deportations continued until the end of the war and affected 62,155 Belgians. This area included the two provinces of Flanders, parts of Hainaut, Luxembourg and northern France.[11]

Deportees from the *Etappengebiet* were gathered in Zivil Arbeiter Bataillonnen (ZAB), battalions of civilian workers organized in military formations, with four companies of 500 workers each. Between October 1916 and the beginning of 1918, 34 ZABs were created and assigned to various tasks: the construction of defence lines, railroad work, the building of underground bunkers, digging trenches, pouring concrete to install heavy artillery, unloading ammunition and so forth. Deportees also worked in quarries, chopping wood or refurbishing roads. These tasks directly assisted the German war effort and were therefore banned by The Hague Convention, both for military men and civilians (Articles 6 and 52).[12] Living conditions were the same as in Germany or even worse: miserable housing and a lack of warm clothes (especially during the rigorous winter of 1916–17), food, hygiene and medical treatment. Life in the ZAB was exacerbated by violence and the frontline's proximity.

Detention and work conditions were so extreme that most deportees, both those sent to Germany and those sent to northern France, returned home weak, sick and often incapable of going back to work, sometimes permanently. According to official numbers, 2,614 people died in captivity.[13] Many more died after their return. It is impossible to ascertain an exact number, but thanks to Donald Buyze's analysis of war monuments and graves, it can be estimated that approximately 6,000 deportees died as a result of deportation by Germany.[14]

The Compensation Laws

On 10 June 1919, the Belgian House of Representatives unanimously voted for a law granting compensation to the civil victims of war, including deportees, for the physical injuries caused by the war. Indeed, Members of Parliament agreed that the 'compensations to the civil victims are the most imperative and the most urgent'.[15] The number of victims urged the representatives of the nation to establish new forms of entitlement in Belgium, considering that the war itself had been of an unprecedented nature: the Germans transgressed the fundamental principle according to which war was a matter between states. They claimed that Germany had waged a war against civilians. This new right did not organize assistance, but granted real indemnity, as previously states were not deemed to be responsible. Moreover, the law considered and evaluated both civilian and military victims for the new pension scheme and invalidity rates. Members of Parliament argued that soldiers and civilians faced similar sacrifices and deserved equal compensation. All Belgians were therefore equally the victims of German crimes.[16]

Deportees were allowed to claim compensation for physical prejudice and the breach of rights during the occupation. But the law went further for this category of victims. Indeed, Article 6 concerned deportees and granted them an additional form of compensation for unpaid salaries:

A sum of 150 francs may be granted to the deportees who were submitted to forced labour during more than three months without a fair remuneration.[17]

The conditions attached to obtaining this compensation were clear. Only deportees were eligible. People who were forced to work (for example, civilian prisoners) without being deported were not eligible. Moreover, this law only granted compensation to those who had suffered physical injury. Being deported was not enough to be awarded reparations, except where a person met the conditions of Article 6, in which case 150 francs were given as a one-off payment.[18]

This law allowed deportees to bring their case to the War Damages Courts and Tribunals, temporary administrative courts that had been created before the end of the conflict.[19] These institutions became flooded with requests as soon as the law was voted in on 10 June 1919. Indeed, around 250,000 files have been preserved for civilian war victims of the First World War.[20] These courts, led by jurists and other experts, examined evidence before reaching a verdict on the war experiences of deportees. Temporary and permanent invalids were awarded pensions, medical fees in cases of physical injuries were repaid, and a sum of 150 francs was given where deportees had undertaken forced labour for more than three months without being paid.

Members of Parliament voted for this law as a first step and claimed that it would soon be extended. As stated earlier, the law-makers wanted to treat all war victims, whether military or civilian, equally. However, the law for military pensions was voted for a few months after the law of June 1919 and equality was never established. Military pensions were decided by the administration and were subject to revision, while pensions to civilian victims were given as a final judgment.[21]

Protests were heard everywhere, especially given that civilian victims believed that their pensions were too low. Deportees were unhappy and deemed the law unfair. The government, which had followed the crisis and who also intended to extend the law, created a Commission centrale des déportés, réquisitionnés et prisonniers civils on 15 December 1919. This commission investigated the case of Belgian deportees in order to complement the law of 10 June 1919. It comprised twenty-four members, twelve of whom were ex-deportees or civilian prisoners, to demonstrate the government's goodwill. It examined how ex-deportees and their families lived, their structure and the financial burden they faced (rent, contribution, etc.). The investigators sent a very precise form investigating the civilian war experience.[22] These forms provide a rich source of information. In addition to data about the identity of the person in question and the composition of his or her household, the forms present information about the deportation itself (length, different camps in Germany, France or Belgium, the measures that led to the deportation, the type of work carried out, whether or not a work contract was signed, whether or not a wage was paid, etc.). They also provide information on the material and physical damage the person suffered and his or her state of health upon his or her return. However, it should be underlined that such documentation was created for the particular objective of obtaining compensation. Moreover, they demonstrate the influence of the deportees' associations. The stereotyped answers found in the forms of the municipalities of Tubize and Braine-le-Château provide examples of this influence. Unfortunately, only 30,000 forms were archived and the lack of primary sources regarding the Commission itself makes it impossible to understand how this inquiry impacted the law.[23]

The law was finally changed on 25 July 1921. Sums granted for invalidity were increased and Article 6 was revised. Indeed, deportees had criticized the old law for being too restrictive. People deported for less than three months were automatically excluded, even if they had been sent to forced labour. This reflected a desire to put the civilian and military victims on an equal footing; the latter needed to be in active service for at least three months to obtain compensation. The lump sum of 150 francs was also intended to compensate unpaid wages, calculated on the basis of the three-month threshold. [24] Likewise, equality between those deported for three months and those for more than a year was perceived poorly. The new article allocated 'A sum of 50 francs per month of deportation to the deportees who were submitted to forced labour without a fair remuneration or who always refused to do so'.[25]

This amendment meant that deportees were compensated according to the duration of their stay, the minimum of three months being removed. The question of granting 150 francs to those who had refused to work was also raised. The revised law granted this category of deportees the sum, but only when they had 'always refused to do so [to work]'. This meant that deportees who had initially refused to work but had been coerced into doing so in Germany were not awarded the money. War indemnity courts had been generous with this category of deportees, stating that even if they had ultimately gone to work, they had been morally constrained. The revised law no longer allowed courts to use this interpretation. Moreover, Jules Poncelet asked the House of Representatives about those who had been deported without being asked to work by the Germans, but this matter was left unresolved. They were not given the opportunity to refuse to work and were not exposed to forced labour; therefore, they were not concerned by this article.[26] This new modification did not satisfy deportees. They asked for more, but the Belgian state was unwilling to concede. Instead, the state opted for an approximation and established a flat-rate system, renouncing full reparations.[27]

Reparations had been decided in the Treaty of Versailles. According to the provisions of Annex I of Part VIII ('Reparations') of the Treaty, Belgium was entitled to claim money from Germany for civilian war victims. Indeed, Annex I provided ten categories of damage, of which the second and eighth points were particularly interesting:

> Compensation may be claimed from Germany under Article 232 above in respect of the total damage under the following categories ... 2°: Damage caused by Germany or her allies to civilian victims of acts of cruelty, violence or maltreatment (including injuries to life or health as a consequence of imprisonment, deportation, internment or evacuation, of exposure at sea or of being forced to labour), wherever arising, and to the surviving dependents of such victims ... 8°: Damage caused to civilians by being forced by Germany or its allies to labour without just remuneration.[28]

In order to determine how much Germany had to pay the Allied nations, a Commission of Reparations was established. Using Annex I and its ten points, the Belgian government claimed about three billion gold francs for the reparations dedicated to the population, for a total of 32 billion francs for all of the damage caused by Germany in Belgium. A total of 500 million francs was sent to invalids and the families of those who had died. Finally, 144 million francs were dedicated to forced workers, to be used strictly as compensation as stated in Article 6 of the law of 1919 (modified in 1921).[29] The compensation sum was determined by assuming that the deportees would have earned (as a fair remuneration) six francs a day for 150 days, the average length of time spent in forced labour (five months), for an average deportation of seven months, multiplied by the number of deportees, which was estimated at the time as being 160,000 men. The sum was fixed and listed by the Commission of Reparations, as recorded in *Mémoire sur les dommages de guerre subis par la Belgique*.[30]

The Mixed Arbitral Tribunal

The Mixed Arbitral Tribunal (MAT) was a jurisdiction created by Article 304 of the Treaty of Versailles between the Allied nations on the one side and Germany on the other. A tribunal for Belgium and Germany was composed, like the other MATs, by a triumvirate of jurists, with a president from a neutral country acceptable to the two nations formerly at war, a Belgian jurist and a German jurist. The President of the German-Belgian (GB) MAT in 1924 was the Swiss Paul Moriaud, Professor at the Faculty of Law in Geneva; the German arbitrator was Richard Hoene, Advisor to the Court of Appeal in Frankfurt; and the Belgian arbitrator was Albéric Rolin, General Secretary of the Institute of International Law and Professor at the Faculty of Law in Ghent. In addition to this triumvirate, two agents were appointed, one from each government as well as a representative of the Office of Verification and Compensation. They were intended to play the part of the public prosecutor's department to the MAT.

Offices of Verification and Compensation were created by Part X (economic clauses) of the Treaty of Versailles. They were aimed at paying debts while avoiding settlement in front of enemy courts,[31] which the Allies deemed to be partial.[32] Moreover, debts were guaranteed by governments in case of the insolvency of debtors. Four types of debts were targeted in Article 296 of the Treaty of Versailles: those that were payable before the war; those that became payable during the war based on a prewar contract; interest due that had been accrued before and during the conflict; and capital sums that became payable before and during the war. Moreover, the offices had special competences regarding damaged possessions, the liquidation of sequestrated property, and concerning industrial, literary or artistic properties.[33]

The MAT was competent to settle conflicts and disagreements between creditors and debtors or between offices. However, our focus lies with the MAT jurisdiction regarding goods, rights and citizens' interests, as stated by Article 297e of the Treaty of Versailles:

> The nationals of Allied and Associated Powers shall be entitled to compensation in respect of damage or injury inflicted upon their property, rights or interests, including any company or association in which they are interested, in German territory as it existed on August 1, 1914, by the application either of the exceptional war measures or measures of transfer mentioned in paragraphs 1 and 3 of the Annex hereto. The claims made in this respect by such nationals shall be investigated, and the total of the compensation shall be determined by the Mixed Arbitral Tribunal provided for in Section VI or by an Arbitrator appointed by that Tribunal.[34]

The GB MAT had been in session since the beginning of 1921 and in just over a year had examined 1,000 cases. Even if this court was supposed to be fair, Georges Sartini van den Kerckhove, the Avocat Général près la Cour d'Appel (Attorney-General) of Brussels and agent of the Belgian government for the GB MAT, criticized its complexity and sluggishness, discouraging some of the plaintiffs. He claimed that the goal of this jurisdiction was not met, because to give justice to the interest independently of the sums involved would have required a 'fast, simple and precise instrument ... to restore violated rights with punctuality, destroying in the process injustice with the almighty strength of unlimited justice'.[35]

The procedure took place both in writing and orally, this being a specificity of that particular court. Claims were sent in written form and the defendant had to respond within two to three months, with the possibility of reply and rejoinder. The case was then debated in a public trial in the case of the GB MAT in Paris, where the secretariat was established, or in another city designated by the MAT. Decisions of the MAT were final and binding.[36]

The National Federation of Deportees and the Idea behind a Trial

At the end of the war, deportees founded local associations, soon to be supervised by the National Federation of Deportees of Belgium (NFD). This federation was created after a meeting of local associations on 6 April 1919. Its headquarters were located at the Cornet brewery in Brussels. Soon, a bilingual periodical was created and first issued in September 1919. Members of the Federation had to be Belgian and been forced to work or deported to concentration camps of civilian workers in Germany, France or Belgium. People who had been deported for refusing to work after having been sentenced to prison were also accepted by the Federation.

Commemorating deportation was the first goal of the Federation, but it also sought to defend the interests of its members. The *Bulletin des Déportés (Deportees' Bulletin)* was to inform deportees of the NFD's actions and give all necessary elements to these victims to defend themselves (the existence of War Damages Courts, etc.). It is therefore unsurprising to find in the first issue of the newspaper the text of the law of 10 June 1919 on reparations for war victims, a text that would be analysed in the following editions of the journal.[37]

Finally, the Federation attempted to track those who had been responsible for the deportations in the first place. Articles 228–30 of the Treaty of Versailles gave Belgium the power to prosecute those responsible for actions violating the laws of war in front of military courts. A list of Germans was established by Fernand Passelecq, a lawyer working for the Appeal Court of Brussels. Passelecq had been interested in the deportations ever since they began. He was head of the propaganda office attached to the Belgian government in exile and after the war was a member of the Commission d'enquête sur la violation des règles du droit des gens (Commission of Investigation), which in 1919 was tasked with investigating the German occupation. In addition to the Commission's findings, he had written other publications on the topic.[38] He was therefore a natural choice for Emile Vandervelde, the Minister of Justice, to draft a list of criminals to be extradited by Germany. This list examined each camp or ZAB. All leaders were listed, in addition to between 136 and 142 other people who individually committed specific war crimes.[39] In total, Belgium wanted to bring about 900 people before the court, for all the crimes committed by Germany.[40]

Although the Treaty of Versailles had allowed criminals to be judged, it did not in fact ensure that trials would be held.[41] No international court was competent for war crimes and none was created. Extradition was preferred, accounting for the creation of a list, but the Germans did everything they could to prevent this from happening. Instead, they offered to judge those accused of crimes. After months of negotiations, the Allies finally accepted the German idea in 1920. These trials, held before the Supreme Court in Leipzig, were quickly seen as a scandal by the Allies. The Belgians and the French judged those incriminated *in absentia* before their military courts, but the sentences remained without any effect, unless the defendants could be arrested when crossing the border into Belgium or France.[42]

Given the lack of primary sources, it is impossible to determine the role played by the NFD in the creation of these lists. The lists were developed using testimonies collected by the Commission of Investigation. Did the NFD or local associations encourage their members to testify? This question cannot be answered. The periodicals of the association did not print such appeals even if they published numerous stories of deportation.

In 1921, the deportees were still not satisfied with the current laws and resolved to ask for complete reparations. To do so, the NFD hired a young lawyer named Jacques Pirenne, the son of the well-known historian Henri Pirenne, to study the possibility of a trial against Germany. The NFD probably used the new law creating the statute of ASBL[43] (nonprofit organization) to amend its charter in 1921. It issued a statement saying that the Federation was there not only to help deportees in need, but also to defend the interests of deportees by 'bringing forth a legal action on behalf of its members before the German-Belgian mixed arbitral tribunal'.[44] However, this was just a draft because when the charter of the NFD was published in 1925, any mention of a trial had been removed as it had already taken place.[45]

Eugène-Paul Lévêque, Secretary-General and founding member of the NFD, precipitately sought advice from Eugène Hanssens, a jurist and attorney at the Court of Cassation, who was not in favour of legal action before the MAT. He admitted that deportees did not obtain the complete reparations they were entitled to according to the general principles of law, but believed that this was not the issue. He recalled that the Treaty of Versailles had addressed questions concerning positive law. These provisions foresaw reparations to the Belgian state for certain matters, including deportation and work carried out without fair remuneration. He concluded that 'it is undoubtedly unfortunate that the government shows itself so parsimonious in the allocation of work allowances in these conditions. But claiming an additional indemnity would mean asking Germany to pay twice'.[46] For him, the only solution was to change the Belgian law.

Jacques Pirenne blamed the Secretary-General for hurrying through the case and believed that Hanssens did not have at his disposal all the information he required in order to evaluate the feasibility of legal action.[47] However, Pirenne was of the opinion that the MAT was the appropriate jurisdiction to seek justice. The demands of the deported were quite clear: full reparations for bodily harm, compensation for the deportation itself (the deported already faced the burden of low finances with expenses for clothing, shoes and provisions), compensation for food packages they did not receive, and the recovery of unpaid wages. These were reparation claims for necessities and goods in addition to compensation for bodily harm, as foreseen under Belgian law. The deported tried in vain to assert these rights before the Belgian War Damages Courts, since the law stated that these damages must have occurred in Belgian territory. However, the crimes were suffered abroad in France or Germany. Consequently, the claims were systematically dismissed. This is the reason why Jacques Pirenne deemed the MAT the competent jurisdiction by virtue of Part X of the Treaty of Versailles.[48] In this case, Germany had to be considered as a private legal entity; private persons sued Germany. It was simply not a trial of state against state, or of one corporate body under public law against another.

The Trial and Argumentation

Being convinced that his legal action was justified, Jacques Pirenne brought the case before the GB MAT. Some 80,000 deportees subscribed to his action to sue Germany through the NFD, and about 50,000 complaints were filed. These files are today held at the National Archives of Belgium and contain the complaints themselves, the confirmations of deportation and a list of witnesses able to prove the veracity of the deportations. As the MAT only judged claims made by individuals, Jacques Pirenne decided to submit ten representative claims. Indeed, processing all of the existing files would have taken decades, and before being able to process all the remaining claims, the conclusions of the tribunal needed to be known. However, Jacques Pirenne believed that these ten proceedings must not be considered as ten isolated cases, but as a whole, because they were part of a general drain of people in the autumn of 1916.[49] Before the tribunal, in his introductory statement, Jacques Pirenne considered that 'this judicial proceeding is not intended to stir up poorly healed wounds of hatred. It is a legal case. The NFD … wants to have a public legal debate about the deportations, in order to reach a judgement that can be incorporated in public international law (*ius gentium*) in the future, in the interest of all people, in particular of working class people'.[50]

Finally, following numerous stonewalling tactics about the replacement of the German judge[51] and after two years of investigations, the proceedings were held from 7 to 10 January 1924 in Paris at the former Austrian embassy. The content of the trial is known only through the press; it appears that no archives of the MAT were kept. Had Jacques Pirenne not bequeathed his archives of the trial to the National Archives of Belgium in 1925,[52] it would have been difficult to comprehend the judicial arguments put forward and even less so the findings and consequences of the trial.[53] The leaders of the NFD and the ten deportees whose cases were being judged were present at the trial. Nevertheless, it seems that few people attended the trial, except for the press. The pleadings were made successively in the course of the trial days. At the end of the trial, the representative of the Belgian government was outraged by the lack of regrets expressed by Germany. It appears that this conclusion was reaffirmed by Moriaud, the President of the Tribunal, just before the deliberations.[54]

It would be too lengthy a task to delve further into the content and details of the trial and to elaborate on the pleadings and other elements advanced. However, we can point out that the written proceedings from 1922 to 1923 state how the deportees were actually treated, compared to how they were theoretically treated as claimed by the defendant (who asserted that the living conditions were good enough, that wages were paid and sufficiently high, etc.). The archives of Jacques Pirenne contain the annexes to the pleadings, which are compilations of documents, testimonies and excerpts from the Report of the Commission of Investigation regarding the violation of the Laws and Customs of War, bearing on subjects such as the camps, food rations, work on the ZAB, wages and so forth. His pleadings, both written and oral, are documented and substantiated by factual arguments that refute those proffered by the defendant. Let us examine the arguments presented by the Belgian lawyer.

As we have seen, Germany already had to pay compensation for deportation, as foreseen by Annex I of Part VIII of the Treaty of Versailles. Indeed, by deporting Belgian workers, Germany acted as a corporate body under public law and violated Article 52 of The Hague Convention, independently of the kind of work undertaken by the deportees. According to the jurist Jules Basdevant, the whole German economy was geared towards war and, given the content of Article 52, this labour opposed the interests of the Belgian nation and was therefore prohibited by the Convention.[55] It was not a requisition as authorized by Article 52: Germany had to provide compensation for violating the Laws and Customs of War. Germany accepted this fact, and the defendant withdrew his demand while claiming the contrary to be true in his oral pleading.[56] For Germany, deportation was no less than a means to counter unemployment in order to ensure, as Article 43 of the Convention allowed, public order and public life.[57]

Thus, labour was indeed provided and the deportees were considered by Germany as free civilian workers (*Freie Zivilarbeiter*). Pirenne deemed that there was de facto a work contract, even implicitly as no documents had been signed, except for cases in which people finally gave in to signing a contract after having been exposed to violence and constraint. According to Pirenne, this state of fact did not fall under public law, but rather under private law and, more specifically in this case, the law of contracts.[58] Consequently, and according to Article 304b of the Treaty of Versailles, this matter could be brought before the MAT:

> In addition, all questions, whatsoever their nature, relating to contracts concluded before the coming into force of the present Treaty between nationals of the Allied and Associated Powers and German nationals shall be decided by the MAT.[59]

Germany stated that the compensation demanded in this case fell under the competence of the Commission of Reparations and not the MAT, and that it had already been paid. Nevertheless, Belgium recognized that the sum obtained by virtue of the law of 1919 was fixed compensation and that according to Article 1, individuals could demand total reparations before an international jurisdiction. Therefore, Pirenne asserted that the MAT was competent in this matter of private law. He argued that in matters of the law of contracts, it is the law of the place where the contract is to be executed that governs relations between the two contracting parties, and the German law in this matter is very clear: reparations must be paid in case of physical damages and wages must be paid. Germany could not oppose this because it could not ignore Article 242 of the Treaty of Versailles, which drew a clear distinction between the reparations foreseen in Part VIII and the reparations to individuals foreseen in Part X and its Articles 304b and 297e.[60]

The deportees attacked Germany on the basis of these articles. For Pirenne, it was clear that the sums already granted by the Belgian state must be understood as an advance payment of the total compensation and should be subtracted from the total sum to be paid to the victims. The damage for which compensation would be claimed was of several kinds. Indeed, deportees claimed 300 francs for loss or wear of clothes, 150 francs a month of deportation for subsistence costs, including the value of the food packages sent by their families, compensation for temporary or definitive work incapacity, and 10 francs a day of deportation for wages due, from which the wages already received in Germany had to be subtracted. This corresponded to the wage promised to deportees if they signed a work contract via the Deutsches Industrie Büro.[61]

The Conclusions of the Triumvirate

With regard to unpaid wages, the MAT stated that the capacity of a worker to offer his or her labour was not a property as such in positive law and that, consequently, Article 297e could not be applied, a position defended by Pirenne.[62] Indeed, goods, rights and interests were elements of the property and were supposed to be distinct from the person. Furthermore, the tribunal asserted that deportation was no less than a measure directed against a person. As a consequence, the tribunal was not competent to judge these damages.

Accordingly, the tribunal declared itself incompetent with regard to Article 304b. Pirenne asserted that the fact that deportees worked under constraint for Germany implied the existence of a work contract, as we have seen. On the other hand, the tribunal asserted that work contracts imposed by strength were subject matters of Annex I of Part VIII, which foresaw no distinction between work carried out with or without contract. Part VIII gave birth to the Commission for Reparations, which had to determine the amount of damage to be given, that is, Germany's total compensation obligations. This was the manner in which the Belgian state, claiming a total of 144 million francs for the deportees, understood this part of the Treaty by fixing the just wage at six francs a day. Furthermore, this sum was integrated into the total of Germany's reparation obligations, as foreseen by Article 233, thereby amounting to 132 billion francs. If the tribunal had allowed compensation according to Article 304b, it would have created thousands of obligations from which Germany had been freed according to Article 233. According to Annex I of Part VIII, it was not surprising to see the Belgian state taking the place of the Belgian citizens, because the work contracts derived from the violence carried out in violation of The Hague Convention. Finally, based on the jurisprudence and particularly the case of Roger Milaire, who volunteered and to whom the provisions of Annex I of Part VIII consequently did not apply, the Tribunal declared that (in opposition to the allegations of Pirenne) a clear limit could be drawn between forced labour and contractual labour, an argument that the Belgian War Damages Courts actually admitted by refusing compensation to voluntary workers. In the Tribunal's point of view, forced labour did not imply a work contract. Therefore, the Tribunal decided that the issue of work wages as posed according to Article 304b had been settled by the Commission for Reparations and that the Tribunal was not competent in the matter.

The argumentation about the issue of work incapacity accorded with this point of view: compensations were planned in the form of payments from Germany through the Commission for Reparations. Moreover, if work contracts had indeed existed, compensation would have been governed by German law, rendering the MAT incompetent in this matter. The same was true for the loss or wear of clothes: such prejudice did not in fact result from a German instruction stating which clothes the deportees had to take with them, but from the harsh working conditions. For the Tribunal, compensation to the Belgian state included a wage calculated by taking into account the wear of clothes. Consequently, the issue fell under the authority of the

Commission for Reparations, with the Tribunal not being competent in this matter.

The only issue for which the MAT was competent pertained to subsistence costs, including the value of the food packages and money orders sent by families. The compensation for nondelivery was subject to the rules of the transportation contract between the sender and the German Army, which was in charge of the transportation of these packages. The Tribunal thus demanded compensation for such damage by the German state.

Consequences

The trial represented a defeat for the deportees. Although the Tribunal acknowledged their right to reparations for nonreceived food packages, it rejected their other claims and deemed that their prejudices had already been compensated by the Belgian state. Paradoxically, as the Belgian state wanted to compensate civil victims through its own laws by claiming compensation from Germany, it substituted itself for the deportees, thereby preventing them from claiming full compensation themselves, as the Tribunal stated. Of course, this was not the goal of the Belgian state, because Article 1 of the law about reparations for civil victims authorized private individuals to undergo legal action for damage in addition to the reparations already foreseen. However, suing for full payment of salaries and other damage claims became impossible.

The verdict granted the deportees the right to compensation for nonreceived food packages. Both parties realized as early as the summer of 1924 that an arrangement allowing them to extinguish judicial action would prove more practicable than handling each of the 50,000 claims individually, which could have taken decades, for example, simply to gather all necessary evidence for the loss of food packages for each case. A transaction would have rendered it possible, on the basis of a number of complete case files, to attain an idea about the scope of financial compensation claimed by legal action.[63] The disgruntled deportees only saw one advantage in this transaction, namely to receive a given amount of money immediately. Negotiations commenced and Pirenne estimated the compensation sum, based on documentation gathered regarding the food packages,[64] as 75 million francs that could be claimed from Germany. However, the deportees demanded guarantees from the Belgian state about the payment of the compensation and asked the government to pay the sum in advance. Nevertheless, the government only guaranteed a maximum of 40 million francs. Eventually, the deportees and the German government agreed on 21 million francs, to be distributed among the deportees represented by Pirenne, boiling down to 500 francs per deported person. By accepting this convention, the deportees explicitly renounced making any further claims from the German government for the deportations they suffered.[65] It must be underlined at this stage that tens of thousands of other deportees, who were not represented in this legal action, did not receive any compensation whatsoever through this agreement.

The whole case left a bitter taste in the mouths of the deportees, as all their actions failed, be it the search for perpetrators, the legal action before the MAT or the claims for better Belgian laws about compensations. They wondered where the 144 million francs that were claimed by the Belgian state for unpaid salaries had gone. Indeed, the law of 1921 foresaw compensation of 50 francs per month of deportation. However, the Belgian state considered that they should have received six francs a day for an average of 150 days, amounting to more than 50 francs a month. Thus, why did the Belgian state not impart the same amount in compensation to the deportees that it claimed from Germany? Anger rose among the victims and eventually burst out openly in 1925. In the course of the negotiations for the agreement between the deportees and Germany, the deportees also reached (as we have seen) a settlement with the Belgian state that guaranteed the payment of the compensation obtained and in which they renounced any further action against the state. On 12 February 1925, Pirenne explained: 'What I feared has now started to become true. The deportees have gotten into politics in order to obtain compensations they do not seem to be able to achieve through legal challenge.'[66] In April, the Secretary-General of the NFD published a brochure about the millions claimed from Germany by Belgium entitled *Les 144 millions réclamés par la Belgique à l'Allemagne pour les déportés belges* (The 144 Million Claimed by Belgium from Germany for Belgian Deportees), for which Jacques Pirenne denied any responsibility.[67]

The 144 million francs case continued to constitute a matter of discussion, the issue regularly being raised in Parliament. For example, in 1929, a legislative proposal was put before the representatives to increase the compensation to 10 francs a day, instead of 50 francs a month as stipulated by the law of 1921, but the proposal was rejected. It would be too much to explain the details of all the discussions that took place with regard to the 144 million francs. Let us only mention that the subject was raised again in the 1950s and 1960s, but the deportees never received what they claimed.

Conclusions

As we have seen, the legal action brought against Germany by the deportees in order to obtain full reparation was a complete failure. All possible judicial means were exploited and were unsuccessful, instigating the deportees to turn to politics so that their voices would be heard.

Nevertheless, the trial was not unnecessary and had a substantial impact to the extent that a Polish delegation visited Jacques Pirenne to seek his advice in view of a trial for Polish deportees before the German-Polish MAT. Pirenne recognized that there was no hope for the Polish deportees to obtain compensation for unpaid wages, but noted that they might be entitled to compensation for the packages that were not received (Article 304b) and for the wear to their clothes (Article 297e). He nevertheless encouraged the Polish deportees to reintroduce a claim for the wages, given that Poland might not have claimed money via the Commission for Reparations, unlike the Belgian state, which obtained 144 million francs.[68]

Furthermore, the deportation and forced labour crimes committed against the civilian population during the occupation revealed the shortcomings of international law on the matter, as it only vaguely addressed the issue. These deficiencies led the International Congress of Deportees, at its gathering in Lessines on 7 November 1926, to introduce a request before the League of Nations in order to make an amendment to The Hague Convention that would formally proscribe deportations of workers in times of war, protect the freedom of labour and, in the case of forced labour, stipulate that a work contract is mandatory, including all of its related legal effects, and to appoint an international tribunal to supervise the application of future international regulations.[69]

This case study has also shown that despite the promises they held, the peace treaties between the belligerent parties were unsuccessful in guaranteeing reparations for damage suffered owing to their complexity.[70] Indeed, the Treaty of Versailles recognized the right to reparations for deportees, but these people were unable to obtain compensation due to another part of the same treaty as well as the unilateral action of Belgium.

Finally, we must share the conclusions of Matthew Stibbe and Daniel Marc Segesser. The impunity of the Germans responsible for the deportations and the shortcomings of the Treaty of Versailles left the issue of violence against civilians during the First World War unaddressed, despite waves of protest from many people affected and involved, including lawyers. This impunity had in some sense legitimized crimes against civilians, which were now fixed in public opinion as part of a new culture of warfare and therefore did not prevent the crimes being repeated during the Second World War.[71] The Versailles 'diktat' did not enable former enemy governments to reach common ground and to reconcile. Germany had claimed to render justice by itself and not through Allied courts. However, the few trials that did take place did not yield any meaningful conclusions, as what mattered most was to clear the accused from the charges that were brought against them.[72] After the Second World War and during the Nuremberg trials, among others, the Allies would not make the same mistake again. The Belgian deportees of the First World War did not succeed in asserting their rights and would eventually be eclipsed at the end of this fight for justice by the Second World War.

Arnaud Charon is a historian and archivist at the State Archives of Belgium (Archives générales du Royaume). He specialized in the history of the deportations of the Belgian population during the First World War as part of a doctoral thesis within the project 'The Great War from Below', supported by the Belgian Science Policy Office (Belspo). He also specializes in the history of the Belgian police services and police information in the twentieth century.

Notes

I would like to thank Bernard Wilkin, Alexander Hezel and Pieter Lagrou for the translation of this chapter.

1. Thiel, *'Menschenbassin Belgiën'*.
2. These aspects are currently being analysed in doctoral research under the supervision of Professor Dr Serge Jaumain (Université libre de Bruxelles).
3. De Schaepdrijver, *La Belgique et la Première Guerre mondiale*, 106–7, 219. See also Ministry of the Interior, *Annuaire statistique de la Belgique*, 89.
4. Thiel, *'Menschenbassin Belgiën'*, 68–72, 111.
5. National Archives of Belgium (NAB), Archives of the Bureau documentaire Belge, no. 184, Propaganda Tract from the Deutsches Industrie-Büro, c. 1915–16.
6. Basdevant, *Les déportations du Nord de la France et de la Belgique*, 41–42; Rolin, *Les Allemands en Belgique, 1914–1918*, 35–36.
7. Hague Convention IV of 1907, art. 52. Retrieved 22 April 2021 from https://ihl-databases.icrc.org/applic/ihl/ihl.nsf/Article.xsp?action=openDocument&documentId=A0B26A7782CD608FC12563CD00516918.
8. NAB, Archives of the Commission d'enquête sur la violation des règles du droit des gens, des lois et des coutumes de guerre, no. 740–742, Statistics of Deportation in Belgium; Thiel, *'Menschenbassin Belgiën'*, 118–20; Delplancq, 'Une chasse aux "oisifs"', 525–27.

9. Thiel, "'Slave Raids" during the First World War?', 7.
10. Ibid., 8.
11. Passelecq, *Déportation et travail forcé*, 368.
12. Basdevant, *Les déportations du Nord de la France et de la Belgique*, 42–43.
13. Commission d'enquête sur les violations des règles du droit des gens, des lois et des coutumes de la guerre, *Rapports et documents d'enquête*, 24–25; Delplancq, 'Une chasse aux "oisifs"', 532–33.
14. Donald Buyze was a local historian attached to the In Flanders Fields Museum for the project 'The Names List'.
15. Van Bladel, *Commentaire des lois belges de réparation des dommages de guerre*, 7.
16. Ibid., 7–9; Depoortere, *La question des réparations allemandes*, 20.
17. Loi du 10 juin 1919 sur les réparations à accorder aux victimes civiles de la guerre, *Moniteur belge*, 22 June 1919, 2785.
18. Van Bladel, *Commentaire des lois belges de réparation des dommages de guerre*, 120–22, 126–27.
19. Arrêté-Loi du 23 octobre 1918 proclamant le principe du droit à la réparation, par la Nation, des dommages résultant des faits de la guerre, *Moniteur belge*, 24–26 October 1918, 865.
20. These files have been preserved by the Directorate-General for War Victims of the Federal Public Service of Social Security until 2017. They are now kept by the National Archives of Belgium. They contain the different judgements but also provide testimonies, medical reports, etc.
21. Smolders, *Loi du 25 juillet 1921*, 5–7.
22. Arrêté Royal instituant la Commission centrale des déportés, Réquisitionnés et Prisonniers civils, *Moniteur belge*, 20 December 1919, 7306–7307.
23. Amara, Simoens and Windels, *Inventaire des Archives de la Commission centrale des Déportés*, 8.
24. Belgian House of Representatives, Parliamentary Proceedings, Ordinary Session 1918–19, 10 April 1919, 778.
25. Loi du 25 juillet 1921 portant révision de la loi du 10 juin 1919 sur les réparations à accorder aux victimes civiles de la guerre, *Moniteur belge*, 28 August 1921, 6954.
26. Smolders, *Loi du 25 juillet 1921*, 21–24.
27. Van Bladel, *Commentaire des lois belges de réparation des dommages de guerre*, 128–30.
28. *Treaty of Peace between the Allied and Associated Powers and Germany*, Annex 1 to Part VIII.
29. Depoortere, *La question des réparations allemandes*, 339.
30. Ministry of Finances, *Mémoire sur les dommages de guerre subis par la Belgique*, 41.
31. Raquez, de Wée and Houtart, *L'office de Vérification et de Compensation*, 9–10.
32. Sartini van den Kerckhove, *Les Tribunaux Arbitraux Mixtes*, 6.
33. Raquez, de Wée and Houtart, *L'office de Vérification et de Compensation*, 12–23; Sartini van den Kerckhove, *Les Tribunaux Arbitraux Mixtes*, 9.
34. *Treaty of Peace between the Allied and Associated Powers and Germany*, Art. 297e.
35. Sartini van den Kerckhove, *Les Tribunaux Arbitraux Mixtes*, 7, 30–31.
36. Ibid., 7–8; Tribunal Arbitral Mixte Germano-Belge, *Règlement de procédure*, 1–3.
37. 'Statute of the NFD', *Bulletin des Déportés*, 7 September 1919, 1.
38. Tallier and Vannerus, *Inventaire des archives de la commission d'enquête*, 17–20.
39. Horne and Kramer, *1914. Les atrocités allemandes*, 649; Ministry of Justice, *Personnes désignées par la Belgique pour être livrées*, 101–117; Thiel, *'Menschenbassin Belgiën'*, 296.

40. Ministry of Justice, *Personnes désignées par la Belgique pour être livrées*; Passelecq, *Liste des Allemands à réclamer*, 30.
41. See Thomas Graditzky, Chapter 1 in this volume for more on this.
42. Horne and Kramer, *1914. Les atrocités allemandes*, 48, 493–513. For further information, see also Thiel, '*Menschenbassin Belgiën*', 296–304.
43. Loi du 27 juin 1921 accordant la personnalité civiles aux Associations sans buts lucratifs et aux établissements d'utilité publique, *Moniteur belge*, 1 July 1921, 5409–16.
44. NAB, Archives of *Het conglomeraatsarchief van de Raad van Vlaanderen, het Propagandabureau, Nationaal Verweer, de nationalen Bond voor de Belgische Eenheid, Jacques Pirenne en Henri Pirenne (1908–1939)*, no. 5592, Statute of the NFD, c. 1921. Hereinafter 'Archives of Jacques Pirenne'.
45. Acte 667: Fédération Nationale des Déportés de Belgique à Bruxelles, 'Statuts', *Moniteur belge*, Annex, 1925, 646.
46. NAB, Archives of Jacques Pirenne, no. 5591, letter from Hanssens to Levêque, 4 August 1921.
47. NAB, Archives of Jacques Pirenne, no. 5591, letter from Pirenne to Lévêque, 8 August 1921.
48. NAB, Archives of Jacques Pirenne, no. 5591, 'Réparation des pertes matérielles subies par les déportés', 1921.
49. NAB, Archives of Jacques Pirenne, no. 5607, *Exorde*, c. 1924.
50. Ibid.
51. Who would be Richard Hoene during the trial: NAB, Archives of Jacques Pirenne, no. 5593, Correspondence with the MAT, 1922–24.
52. NAB, Archives of Jacques Pirenne, no. 5602, File containing letters to the National Archives of Belgium, 1925.
53. Records related to this trial are also, according to Thiel, held in the Archives of the Ministry of Justice. See Thiel, '*Menschenbassin Belgiën*', 308–11.
54. NAB, Archives of Jacques Pirenne, no. 5595. Article of *Le petit Parisien*, 11 January 1924.
55. Basdevant, *Les déportations du Nord de la France et de la Belgique*, 40–43.
56. Pirenne, 'Le procès des déportés contre le Reich allemand', 107–8.
57. Basdevant, *Les déportations du Nord de la France et de la Belgique*, 58; Segesser, 'The Punishment of War Crimes', 145.
58. Pirenne, 'Le procès des déportés contre le Reich allemand', 108–9; NAB, Archives of Jacques Pirenne, no. 5607, oral argument, hearing notes, 1924; NAB, Archives of Jacques Pirenne, no. 5609, writing procedure, 1922–23.
59. *Treaty of Peace between the Allied and Associated Powers and Germany*, art. 304b.
60. Sartini van den Kerckhove, *Les Tribunaux Arbitraux Mixtes*, 22.
61. Pirenne, 'Le procès des déportés contre le Reich allemand', 108–9; NAB, Archives of Jacques Pirenne, no. 5607, oral argument, hearing notes, 1924; NAB, Archives of Jacques Pirenne, no. 5609, writing procedure, 1922–23.
62. On the basis of the judgments given by the GB MAT on 3 June 1924: NAB, Archives of Jacques Pirenne, no. 5594.
63. NAB, Archives of Jacques Pirenne, no. 5593, Letter from Pirenne to Sartini, 22 January 1925.
64. This can be consulted under no. 5600 of Pirenne's archives.
65. NAB, Archives of Jacques Pirenne, no. 5601, GB MAT approved settlement agreement of 8 July 1925.
66. NAB, Archives of Jacques Pirenne, no. 5593, Letter from Jacques Pirenne of 12 February 1925.

67. NAB, Archives of Jacques Pirenne, no. 5593, Letter from Sartini to Pirenne of 11 May 1925 and Answer from Pirenne to Sartini of 13 May 1925.
68. NAB, Archives of Jacques Pirenne, no. 5594, Letter from Pirenne to the President of the International Commission of War Damages caused to the Polish workers by the Germans, 29 May 1925.
69. NAB, Archives of Jacques Pirenne, no. 5594, Motion adopted during the Congress of Deportees, 7 November 1926.
70. NAB, Archives of Jacques Pirenne, no. 5594, Report of the Congress of Deportees, 7 November 1926.
71. Stibbe, 'Civilian Internment and Civilian Internees in Europe, 1914–1920', 73.
72. Segesser, 'The Punishment of War Crimes', 150.

Bibliography

Published Sources

Amara, Michael, B. Simoens and C. Windels. *Inventaire des Archives de la Commission centrale des Déportés, Réquisitionnés et Prisonniers civils*. Brussels: National Archives of Belgium, 2014.

Basdevant, Jules. *Les déportations du Nord de la France et de la Belgique en vue du travail forcé et le Droit International*. Paris: Librairie du Recueil Sirey, 1917.

Commission d'enquête sur les violations des règles du droit des gens, des lois et des coutumes de la guerre. *Rapports et documents d'enquête. Tome II : Rapports sur les déportations des ouvriers belges et sur les traitements infligés aux prisonniers de guerre et aux prisonniers civils belges*. Brussels: Albert Dewit, 1923.

De Schaepdrijver, Sophie. *La Belgique et la Première Guerre mondiale*. Brussels: Peter Lang, 2004.

Delplancq, Thierry. 'Une chasse aux "oisifs". Les déportations de civils à Bruxelles en 1917', in Frank Daelemans et al. (eds), *Bruxelles et la vie urbaine. Archives – art – histoire. Recueil d'articles dédiés à la mémoire d'Arlette Smolar-Meynart (1938–2000)*. Special issue of *Archives et Bibliothèques de Belgique* 64 (2011).

Depoortere, Rolande. *La question des réparations allemandes dans la politique étrangère de la Belgique après la Première Guerre mondiale (1919–1925)*. Brussels: Académie Royale de Belgique, 1997.

Horne, John, and Alan Kramer. *German Atrocities 1914: A History of Denial*. New Haven: Yale University Press, 2001 (French edition: *1914. Les atrocités allemandes: La vérité sur les crimes de guerre en France et en Belgique* (trans. H.-M. Benoît). Paris: Tallandier, 2011).

Ministry of Finances. *Mémoire sur les dommages de guerre subis par la Belgique*. Brussels: Dewarichet, 1921.

Ministry of the Interior. *Annuaire statistique de la Belgique et du Congo Belge*, vol. XLVI, 1915–19. Brussels: Lesigne, 1922.

Ministry of Justice. *Personnes désignées par la Belgique pour être livrées par l'Allemagne en exécution des articles 228 à 230 du Traité de Versailles et du Protocole du 28 juin 1919. Liste fondamentale*. Brussels: Larcier, 1919.

Moniteur belge, 1918, 1919, 1921, 1925.

Passelecq, Fernand. *Liste des Allemands à réclamer en exécution des articles 228 à 230 du Traité de Versailles du 28 juin 1919. Rapport général de F. Passelecq à Monsieur le Ministre de la Justice (14 octobre 1919)*. Brussels: Larcier, 1919.

——. *Déportation et travail forcé des ouvriers et de la population civile de la Belgique occupée*. Paris: Presses universitaires de France/New Haven: Yale University Press, 1927.

Pirenne, Jacques. 'Le procès des déportés contre le Reich allemand'. *Revue de droit international et de législation comparée* 1–2 (1924), 102–16.

Raquez, Leon, Maurice de Wée and Albert Houtart. *L'office de Vérification et de Compensation et le Tribunal Arbitral Mixte*. Brussels: Larcier, 1920.

Rolin, Albéric. *Les Allemands en Belgique : 1914–1918. Conclusions de l'enquête officielle*. Liège: Georges Thone, 1925.

Sartini van den Kerckhove, Georges. *Les Tribunaux Arbitraux Mixtes. Discours prononcé par M. l'Avocat Général Sartini van den Kerckhove prononcé à l'Audience Solennelle de rentrée du 2 octobre 1922*. Brussels: Larcier, 1922.

Segesser, Daniel Marc. 'The Punishment of War Crimes Committed against Prisoners of War, Deportees and Refugees during and after the First World War', in Matthew Stibbe (ed.), Captivity, *Forced Labour and Forced Migration in Europe during the First World War* (Abingdon: Routledge, 2009), 134–56.

Smolders, Théodore. *Loi du 25 juillet 1921 portant révision de la loi du 10 juin 1919 sur les réparations à accorder aux victimes civiles de la guerre*. Brussels: Larcier, 1921.

Stibbe, Matthew. 'Civilian Internment and Civilian Internees in Europe, 1914–20', in Matthew Stibbe (ed.), *Captivity, Forced Labour and Forced Migration in Europe during the First World War* (Abingdon: Routledge, 2009), 49–81.

Tallier, Pierre-Alain and Jules Vannerus. *Inventaire des archives de la commission d'enquête sur la violation des règles du droit des gens, des lois et des coutumes de la guerre (1914–1926)*. Brussels: National Archives of Belgium, 2001.

Thiel, Jens. *'Menschenbassin Belgien'. Anwerbung, Deportation und Zwangsarbeit im Ersten Weltkrieg*. Essen: Klartext Verlag, 2007.

——. '"Slave Raids" during First World War? Deportation Forced Labour in Occupied Belgium'. *Historikerdialoge*, Louvain-La-Neuve, 24 March 2014.

Treaty of Peace between the Allied and Associated Powers and Germany, Signed at Versailles on 28 June 1919. London: H.M. Stationery Office, 1920.

Tribunal Arbitral Mixte Germano-Belge. *Règlement de procédure*. Brussels: Larcier, 1921.

Van Bladel, Georges. *Commentaires des lois belges de reparation des dommages de guerre. Loi du 10 juin 1919 sur les réparations à accorder aux victimes civiles de la Guerre*. Brussels: Lebègue & Cie, 1919.

Archival Sources

NAB, Archives of the Bureau documentaire Belge, no. 184.

NAB, Archives of the Commission d'enquête sur la violation des règles du droit des gens, des lois et des coutumes de guerre, nos. 740–42.

NAB, Archives of Jacques Pirenne (Archives of Het conglomeraatsarchief van de Raad van Vlaanderen, het Propagandabureau, Nationaal Verweer, de nationalen Bond voor de Belgische Eenheid, Jacques Pirenne en Henri Pirenne (1908–39)), nos. 5591–95, 5600–2, 5607, 5609.

CHAPTER 3

COINING POSTWAR JUSTICE FROM THE MARGINS

EXILE LAWYERS IN LONDON, 1941–45

Kerstin von Lingen

Introduction

Since its establishment in 1943, the United Nations War Crimes Commission (UNWCC) has concerned itself with legal questions relating to war crimes, to which its numerous minutes testify.[1] However, the existing literature often overlooks the extent to which the smaller Allied nations contributed to the coining of postwar justice. 'Small' does not refer here to geographical size, but rather to access to diplomatic and political power; as Madeleine Herren has argued, smaller states such as Switzerland engaged with transnational organizations like the League of Nations (or later the UNWCC) as a 'backdoor to power' tool to make their voices heard in the international arena.[2]

In the early 1940s in London, before the major Allies finally took up the subject, legal circles consisting of exiled lawyers had already started to debate how to legally address crimes committed in the ongoing war. These legal experts formed an epistemic community[3] in

London and were agents of a new supranational community. Most were already prominent lawyers in their own countries before being forced into exile by Nazi occupation.[4] In this regard, the work of the UNWCC can be seen as the institutional result of very lively theoretical discussions, which had been ongoing for some time and involved different groups of experts, lobbyists, exiled politicians and legal scholars.[5]

Retrospectively, the primary outcome of all this work was the definition of war crimes, the concept of crimes against humanity and the foundation of the International Court of Justice. It was the task of the international community to agree whether what was hitherto labelled a war crime could be prosecuted if it had occurred before an official de facto state of war, whether this definition also applied to crimes committed against national minorities or religious groups and whether an external juridical body could exert justice. In London, the debate on these critical questions in the early 1940s mirrored both the limitations of these exiled governments' members and their degrees of willingness and personal commitment following their own experiences of occupation or persecution.

London as the place of exile became a 'hub' for the legal community and its attempts to develop international law.[6] Aside from conducting meetings in different circles while living in London, it was also the common language of English that accelerated the debate by overcoming typical paths of academic exchange through conferences, publications and correspondence. In this chapter, I argue that the notion of exile and the 'London hub' were thus decisive for the advancement of legal concepts. Two forerunners to the UNWCC had contributed to postwar justice: the International Commission for Penal Reconstruction and Development, emanating from the Faculty of Law at the University of Cambridge (and thus named the Cambridge Commission), and the London International Assembly (LIA). In many regards, their tasks overlapped with the subsequent UNWCC, which is not surprising given that many members were present in all three bodies. One of their central concerns was to agree on the notion that a community of nations, often called the 'united nations',[7] was *entitled* to 'intervene juridically against crimes committed against *any* civilian population, before and during the war, and whether it was irrelevant whether or not such crimes were committed in violation of the domestic law of the country where perpetrated'.[8] The punishment of war crimes was later put into practice for the first time at the International Military Tribunal (IMT) at Nuremberg in 1945, a huge step compared to the failure to prosecute war criminals internationally after the First World War. Therefore, an analysis of the UNWCC and these forerunners' contributions in London are crucial to understanding the legal framework of Allied war crimes policy and its implementation.

Fortunately, the documentation of the meetings and printed pamphlets from the Cambridge Commission and LIA have survived in several archives and libraries. Analysis of the meetings' participants and the authors of their lengthy memorandums shows a sample of European lawyers who held progressive ideas concerning the development of international law. In particular, the Czech and Polish government-in-exile representatives, whose proposals were echoed by members from Belgium and the Netherlands, hoped that by establishing fierce legal guidelines, the Nazis could be deterred from committing further crimes.[9] This chapter focuses on the exiled community's debates during the Second World War that originated not at a political level, but from the desks of legal experts. It seeks to analyse the framing of a global war crimes policy from two perspectives: (1) how they discussed and later developed key legal terms such as 'crimes against humanity' and advocated an international tribunal; and (2) who was active in the debate and how networks were formed.

It was the London Conference (26 June–8 August 1945) that catalysed the newly developed legal tools into a political concept and set the Charter for the Nuremberg Tribunal to judge the Nazi elite. The first achievement of the London Charter was to install an international tribunal, which was one of the demands of the exiled lawyers. However, the London Conference also produced other far-reaching implications, as its charter, valid for the IMT of Nuremberg and later additionally serving as a blueprint for the charter of the IMT at Tokyo that introduced the concepts of aggressive warfare and crimes against humanity alongside the notion of conventional war crimes. In this regard, I argue that the UNWCC and its predecessors developed an internationally accepted standard in dealing with mass atrocities.

In the following, I will first provide an overview of the biographical background of some key protagonists before analysing selected debates of the three commissions. Finally, I conclude on the nature of the 'legal crossroads' identified during the Second World War.

Biographical Approach: Individual Experiences and New Legal Concepts

A biographical approach can help us understand why exiled lawyers in particular deemed their engagement in the UNWCC an opportunity to implement new legal concepts, while fostering no illusions about the powerlessness of their political situation in exile. Legal experts formed a particular group, as Siegelberg observes:

> Émigré jurists in Britain and the United States who had turned against international law as a substitute for power politics kept up a fierce campaign to publicize the limitations of the legalist approach to international relations.[10]

Distinguishing between these individuals' official and unofficial statuses is challenging, as the lines blur according to which perspective is taken and which actor is being considered:[11] the lawyers acted on behalf of their national governments in exile (and saw themselves as representatives thereof), but acted under the guise of scholarly activity, involving colleagues from law faculties in Britain who clearly saw their engagement in academic debates as what we would today term 'civil society interest'. However, the circles in which these lawyers acted were backed by politicians and lobbyists (also taking part in the meetings) who fought for recognition of their cause amongst British and US government officials,[12] thereby giving the work of these two committees an at least semi-official character. The forerunners of the UNWCC were crucial to the war crimes debate, but were powerless to implement the new concepts. Though they enjoyed the approval of the Allied powers, only the later UNWCC became a genuinely international commission dealing with war crimes punishment.

By analysing their contributions, it becomes clear that although they had to move within the perimeters set by their respective governments in exile and work towards their expectations, these representatives acted in the first place as legal scholars deeply marked by their personal experiences of forced exile to find a valuable solution to bring the criminals to trial. However, British as well as US officials who had not experienced the brutality of Nazi war crimes on their own populations did not give the topic much priority and regarded debates about a possible future handling of war crimes as a political means of assuring the exiled governments that something would be done after the conflict.[13]

The context of exile in Great Britain during the early 1940s was economically difficult, but offered the unexpected possibility of personal exchange through the situation of exile. The British government had offered the Polish as well as the Czech exiled governments a house at their disposal at Russell Square, which became the venue for most meetings. Moreover, legal circles endorsed each other with practical help, for example, regarding office materials and translation.

It should be acknowledged that most legal scholars were fluent in several languages, but that in particular those from Central Eastern Europe, the old Habsburg Empire, struggled with English. Research on Western exile governments is both more common and further developed than research concerning Central and Eastern European exile governments,[14] for their task obviously ended shortly after the communist takeover after 1945, when they could not return to their homelands. This chapter tries to synthesise both perspectives, which were not yet as deeply divided as they would become during the Cold War era, and analyses the entanglement between exile politics, academic scrutiny and engagement in what was at the time a politically powerless civil society by focusing on three personalities. Some of the most active advocates of international criminal law in London were the Belgian representative Marcel de Baer and the Czech representatives Bohuslav Ecer (1893–1954)[15] and Egon Schwelb (1899–1979), the latter of whom was later nicknamed 'Mr Human Rights' and became very active within the UN. They can be perceived as transnational legal actors who were particularly interested in formalizing how war crimes committed in Europe during the Second World War and beyond should be handled.

Marcel de Baer was born in 1890 in Antwerp. He studied law and became a judge in the Belgian colonial administration in Leopoldville.[16] In 1929, he was appointed Chief Justice of the Oriental Province of Congo, and in 1939, he served as Justice in the Court of Appeal at Brussels. After the Nazis invaded Belgium in the summer of 1940, he fled to Portugal and finally reached England. In 1942, he was nominated Chief Justice of the Belgian government in exile and served as President to the LIA. After 1943, he was also a member of the UNWCC. After the war, in 1946, he attended the trial of Karl Hermann Frank, the Nazi governor of Bohemia and Moravia, as an observer, to support the work of Czech prosecutor Bohuslav Ecer, who had become his friend. De Baer enjoyed a postwar career, as in 1947, he was elected Chairman of the Review Board and in 1950, he became the Belgian Resident UN representative to Iran.

Bohuslav Ecer was born in 1893, studied law in Vienna and Prague,[17] and after earning his doctoral degree in 1920 served as Deputy Mayor in Brno from 1935 to 1939. Ecer was a political figure as a socialist delegate, but also a gifted scholar interested in international law. He was fluent in German, English, French, Russian and several other languages from the Habsburg Empire, and was thus able to access a large variety of academic literature. In 1938, shortly before parts of Czechoslovakia were annexed by Adolf Hitler as approved by France and Britain in the 'Munich Agreement', Ecer travelled to Great Britain to alert political leaders and the general public of his country's fate.[18] After German forces occupied Czechoslovakia in March 1939, he was imprisoned and, after his release, fled with his family via Yugoslavia to France, where he helped found a bureau of the Czech government in exile in Paris.[19] As early as the winter of 1939–40, he started drafting a paper on a possible peace conference and the penal accountability of Nazi war criminals for crimes committed in Czechoslovakia.[20]

Following the Nazi occupation of France in June 1940, Ecer flew to Nice, where he enrolled as a student at the evacuated Institut des Hautes Etudes Méditerranéennes Internationales (French Institute of International Law) and earned a degree in international law in August 1942. He subsequently immigrated to London, where, upon his arrival, the exiled Czech President Edvard Benes offered him a position within the exiled government, which he declined in order to become an advisor to the designated Czech Minister of Justice, Jaroslav Stransky. Ecer's task at London was to develop a theory on how to deal with war crimes, a position that enabled him to take part in the London International Assembly's meetings, where he was among the members who submitted the most proposals.

My last example is Egon Schwelb, also from Czechoslovakia. Born in 1899, he studied law in Prague after the First World War and worked as a lawyer. He was a prominent Social Democratic attorney who handled numerous civil liberties cases and who represented, among other clients, anti-Nazi German refugees who had fled to Prague after Hitler and the Nazis came to power in Germany in 1933. On 15 March 1939, German troops entered Prague and the following day, Schwelb was taken into custody and held at a Geheime Staatspolizei (Gestapo) prison (as a socialist of Jewish descent, he was in particular danger), being released after some weeks only following British intervention in May 1939.[21] After obtaining British visas and an exit permit, Schwelb and his family travelled by train from Prague through Nazi Germany to the Netherlands and arrived in Britain on 13 August 1939. Other members of his family who did not manage to leave Czechoslovakia before the German occupation ultimately perished in the Holocaust. In 1940, in London, President Benes named Schwelb a member of the Legal Council (Pravni Rada) of the government in exile, a position he held until the end of the war.[22]

The postwar career of the two Czech delegates echoed the tragic fate of eminent lawyers trapped in transition between exile and communism. Ecer was entrusted in July 1945 with preparing the Czech delegation at the IMT at Nuremberg and fostered good relationships with the Soviet prosecution team, a fact that may have mirrored his disappointment regarding some of the political stances of the Western powers concerning war crimes. After the conclusion of the IMT trial, he wrote an academic monograph on the Nuremberg trials and memoirs on the exile period, both of which were published in 1946. He was at the peak of his international recognition after the Nuremberg IMT, when he was offered a position as one of the fifteen judges at the International Court of Justice at The Hague, which he held until 1948. However, after the communist takeover in Czechoslovakia in 1948, he was stripped of all his positions, ordered back to Prague and retired to a private life in Brno, teaching at the city's university until it was closed down in 1950. After taking over some cases in court in defence of his persecuted socialist friends, he came into conflict with the secret police. After several shorter imprisonments, he died in March 1954 from a heart attack, only hours before the police came to arrest him again for 'anti-state activities and high treason'.

Schwelb enjoyed a better fate: he never returned to Prague and after the communist takeover in 1948, he decided to become a naturalized British citizen. After serving in the UNWCC from 1943 to 1947, he was then appointed Deputy Director of the Human Rights Division of the UN in 1947. He had a very distinguished career and worked tirelessly in drafting resolutions and leading debates on human rights questions, such as for the Genocide Convention that came into effect in 1949. Once his service for the UN had come to an end, he returned to university life, teaching at Yale University. It was there that he published his book *Human Rights and the International Community* in 1963.[23] One of his lifelong concerns remained to find a way to develop legal tools to enforce human rights and protect them against state criminality, as numerous articles and pamphlets testify. In 1979, shortly after his death, he posthumously received the Dag Hammarskjold Award for his contributions to peace and human rights.

The London Hub and Its Commissions

The bodies where the exiled lawyers were active can be seen as powerful hubs of legal innovation. Already before the St James Conference on 14 November 1941, the representatives of nine European countries met at a conference in Cambridge on 'Rules and Procedures to Govern the Case of Crimes against International Public Order'. This body became known as the Cambridge Commission. This conference aimed to restore a criminal justice system, to be adopted in armistice treaties after the conflict in Europe had ended, and to arrange for continued collaboration in its legal development after the war.[24] Belgium, Czechoslovakia, France, Greece, Luxembourg, the Netherlands, Norway, Poland and Yugoslavia sent delegates. The conference was hosted by the Faculty of International Law from the University of Cambridge under Chair Professor H. Winfield (Department of Criminal Science), with Professor Hersch Lauterpacht as Whelwell Chair for International Law and Professor A.L. Goodhart from the University of Oxford as observers, the latter also delivering the keynote in the conference. Sir Arnold McNair, the Vice-Chancellor of the University of Liverpool, was made the Commission's chairman.

The Commission primarily saw itself as a body of legal scholars and judges, and therefore chose the form of an academic conference at the University of Cambridge to discuss its ideas.[25] Its political implications soon became clear, as several members, including Czech President Benes, held ministerial positions in the exiled governments they represented. Apart from academics, there was a considerable percentage of high functionaries, amongst them several former ministers of justice (for example, Jean Burnay from France, Jaroslav Stransky from Czechoslovakia, Terjé Wood from Norway, Milan Gavrilovitch from Yugoslavia and Victor Bodson from Luxembourg), judges such as de Baer from Belgium and Johannes Maarten de Moor from the Netherlands, and well-known university professors holding prominent positions in their exiled governmental administrations, such as Professor René Cassin from France and Professor Stefan Glaser from Poland.[26] In its official presentation leaflet, the Conference emphasized that it included 'representatives whose membership is approved by the appropriate Ministry of their country'.[27] However, some scholars who were not sent by their governments also took a very active part, including the British law expert Professor Lauterpacht, Professor Goodhart, who spoke on behalf of US legal theory, and exiled legal scholars from Germany as observers.[28]

The Cambridge Commission conducted enquiries into the legal obstacles to judging Nazi atrocities as well as the question of whether an international or national court should call for justice.[29] In April 1942, a questionnaire was circulated amongst its members under the heading of 'Committee upon Rules and Procedures Relating to the Present War'. The information gathered was particularly noteworthy because it documented the kinds of crimes reported, the groups of victims affected and the legal tools already available.[30] Answers to the questionnaire were received from Belgium, Czechoslovakia, France, Greece, Luxembourg, the Netherlands, Norway, Poland and

Yugoslavia. Not only was the questionnaire a valuable resource for subsequent UNWCC debates,[31] but it also served an important function by identifying the alternative legal codes upon which different states based their criminal jurisdiction. The questionnaire focused on four issues: (a) the locus of the crime (territorial principle); (b) the nationality of the criminal; (c) injury to the state; and (d) injury to a national of the state. The results were quite promising: the majority of states were already able to prosecute all of the alleged crimes under their present jurisdiction. Only in the last question, concerning crimes committed abroad by nationals or foreigners against nationals of the state exercising jurisdiction, were the majority of nations unable to prosecute. Given the nature of the racial war of Nazi Germany, the extent of its occupation politics and its heinous system of slave labour, which involved dispatching nationals from all European countries to distant camps throughout Europe,[32] the final category posed the main issue that should be dealt with in court after the war.

Consequently, the Commission established three subcommittees on 15 July 1942. De Baer chaired two of these and wrote two memoranda: one on whether 'National Law and Jurisdiction' was sufficient (together with notes from Minister Burnay, Professor Glaser and Professor Lauterpacht) and another on the 'Meaning and Scope of War Crimes'. Comments on de Baer's note concerning the definition of war crimes were received by Glaser and Lauterpacht, who both held that a larger definition including crimes against nationals outside of an armed conflict was indispensable.[33] The third subcommission, led by Dutch Judge de Moor, discussed 'Defence of Superior Orders' with Goodhart and Lauterpacht responding, to which the other Commission members replied in writing. Ultimately, Vaclac Benes, the nephew of Czech President Benes, discussed in a note the question of extradition, especially when asked of neutral states. As a kind of summary to the work of the Commission, Lauterpacht issued a 52-page memorandum on the 'Punishment of War Crimes', which bundled his arguments together and discussed possible options to circumvent existing legal problems.[34] In this memorandum, Lauterpacht argued in favour of an international criminal court if impartiality within the framework of municipal law could not be guaranteed. This would involve, in his view, not only the 'expansion of military tribunals by inclusion of lay judges of high standing' and the 'participation of neutral assessors and judges', but also the 'participation of enemy assessors' and the creation of 'quasi-international courts of Appeal'.[35] Lauterpacht had also issued a scheme for an international rule of law on a prior occasion, which must be seen as complementary to his work for the Cambridge

Commission; therein, he reproduced his liberal, cosmopolitan credo in ten principles.[36]

The potential establishment of a permanent international body of justice was another topic of debate, and the members collected arguments in favour of and against such a notion. The failure of war crimes trials following the First World War, which were held before the Supreme Court in Leipzig and directed against the German military,[37] rendered an international court of justice appealing, as previous efforts to define war crimes or to set up a permanent international court of justice for war crimes had proved unsuccessful.[38] Establishing such a court would, the Commission argued, prevent the need for normative discussions during future conflicts. Nevertheless, the creation of such an institution would need to be accompanied by a new codification of law, so applying this new penal law to war criminals of a contemporary conflict could be criticized as unjust, as *ex post facto* law.[39]

Arnold McNair, the Chairman of the Commission, consequently opposed the idea, arguing that there were at least four arguments against it: setting up a new court would be a time-consuming process; the question of involvement of allies and victors in such a tribunal was unsettled and neutral states could not be expected to step in; its *ex post facto* code of law would be fodder for criticism; and punishment and realization would present practical difficulties.[40] In the meantime, and in view of the *longue durée* of setting up such a court, an ad hoc tribunal agreed upon by the UN would enable the international community to put Hitler and his henchmen to justice, as Judge de Baer argued in his note.[41] A decision could not be reached and the debates – which were not laid down, but only summarized in the report – revealed two strongly opposed groups. In principle, the question of establishing a permanent body of justice was passed on to another commission that was soon to emerge.[42]

The second pioneering body to precede the UNWCC – the LIA – was founded in the autumn of 1941 on the initiative of the British Peace Movement under Lord Robert Cecil.[43] It is an interesting twist that one of the most successful organizations on legal innovations was formed by a peace organization, operating since the League of Nations period (we would call it a nongovernmental organization today) with a clear interest in creating public awareness of the problem.[44] As an advisory body, the LIA included prominent members like Czech President Benes, Professor Cassin, the Polish Minister for External Affairs August Zaleski, former Czech President Jan Masaryk, Judge de Moor and peace activist Cecil,[45] as well as experts like the newly arrived émigrée Ecer. It had the task of adopting a line on how to

deal politically with the Axis occupation policy and the crimes it
had committed in the meantime.[46] However, the number of members
had increased and, in contrast to the more Eurocentric Cambridge
Commission, the LIA targeted non-European members such as China,
India and Brazil, as well as involving delegates from the big Allies,
hinting at its global scope and the clear political implications of its
legal endeavour. In this regard, the LIA can be seen as a blueprint
for the future UNWCC and represented a transnational body that
understood war crimes as a threat to global justice. Its preface stated
that it would:

> Serve the common cause of all those nations that are resisting aggression
> by providing greater opportunities for the People of Great Britain and each
> of the Allied and Associated Nations to understand more fully each other's
> history ... and to consider the principles of post-war policy and the appli-
> cation of these principles to the problems of national and international
> affairs.[47]

Members, most of whom were legal scholars, were sent from Belgium,
Brazil, China, Czechoslovakia, France, Great Britain, Greece, India,
Luxembourg, the Netherlands, Norway, Poland, the United States and
Yugoslavia. In breaking the nationalist member principle, expertise
was also welcomed from former German or Austrian judges of Jewish
descent, who had migrated to London.[48]

The LIA formally started work in February 1942. In addition to
debating legal issues, it primarily aimed to exert pressure on the
British Foreign Office and raise public interest in its cause. Its
Chairman, the Belgian judge de Baer, put several critical issues at
the centre of the debate concerning the problem of the codification of
international criminal law and trial procedures.[49] This debate widened
academic understanding of what constitutes a war crime. Until 1939,
legal theory maintained that war crimes should be dealt with in military courts or in civilian courts applying the laws of war – a line the
British Foreign Office still adhered to during the 1940s – and could
only involve cases committed within a state's territory or against its
nationals.[50] However, the unprecedented Nazi war of aggression and
occupation of half of Europe formed the basis for growing concern
amongst the governments now forced into exile in London. The situation called for the establishment of new norms and guidelines to hold
trials after the end of the conflict.[51] For this reason, defining the term
'war crimes' proved crucial. War crimes, as observed by de Baer in
1942, could include offences against national laws and were therefore
punishable by national courts. Nevertheless, de Baer also observed

that in a wider sense, war crimes could be seen as 'offences against the *ius gentium*, or against international agreements (such as The Hague and Geneva Conventions) or unwritten internationally recognized ethical rules, and for some of these offences, no sanctions had hitherto been designed'; thus, war crimes were an universal offence.[52] The second definition highlighted the need to formulate a new legal category to fit these new offences.

Forming the UNWCC

When considering the Nazi crimes of occupation, especially in Eastern Europe, the Benelux states and Norway, the LIA made several proposals to the British government, suggesting an international criminal court.[53] The idea was to establish a legal body to bring to justice crimes in respect to which no national court had jurisdiction, or did not want to exert its jurisdiction, or when crimes had been committed in several countries or against nationals of different countries. It was also de Baer who in December 1943 was sent as an envoy to New York to campaign for the necessity of an international court to punish Axis criminality.[54]

During this time, de Baer also began to develop ties with another actor in the war crimes trial policy debate, the World Jewish Congress (WJC).[55] Judging from the findings of Lewis[56] and Weinke,[57] the WJC's agenda emphasized the uniqueness of the Holocaust,[58] which in turn engendered conflict with the agenda of the exile lawyers who focused on general legal tools and were not interested in addressing special cases, as they saw it. When de Baer met informally with the WJC in London in March 1944, the WJC's Secretary Easterman stated: 'The Nazi conspiracy against the Jews as Jews was a crime of a special and unique character.'[59] De Baer objected that Jewish victims were in his view no special case and emphasized the universalist approach: 'Other groups have been the victims of criminal Nazi plots.' In a letter to Belgian's WJC representative Léon Kubowitzky, de Baer was even more explicit: 'Whatever the case may be, I personally feel that it is our duty towards morality and justice to see that all these crimes are punished.'[60] Consequently, de Baer's meetings enabled no further collaboration between the UNWCC and WJC at an official level.

As a result, when the UNWCC started its work in early 1944, several proposals from renowned lawyers dealing with an Allied war crimes policy on legal grounds, the jurisdiction of the courts and their possible foundation as well as the collection of evidence were already at hand, and were later presented to the British Foreign Office and the State Department for approval.[61]

As an organization, the UNWCC comprised three committees, of which the Legal Committee in London was committed to developing contemporary international law. Committee I, the Facts and Evidence Committee chaired by de Baer, was intended to establish whether the evidence submitted was legally sufficient to open a case. The Committee on Means and Methods of Enforcement (Committee II) would recommend the methods and machinery to adopt, while the Legal Committee (Committee III), chaired by the Czech representative Ecer and his secretary Schwelb, carried out an advisory function within the UNWCC. The Legal Committee spearheaded the debate, as 'it was active in the clarification of legal issues, the gradual elimination of uncertainties in the spheres of the laws of war and the promotion of rules, many of which were to become part of contemporary penal law'.[62] The exiled lawyers' prominent positions in all three commissions reflected how interested and active they were in their work.

Upon reviewing the meetings of the predecessor commissions as well as the early UNWCC documentation, it becomes clear that the absence of the Soviet Union from the meetings as well as the apparent friction between Joseph Stalin and the British government on questions of war crimes policy were key concerns for the scholars involved. Czech and Polish delegates were in constant exchange with Soviet scholars, and their political representatives (Czech President Benes being the most prominent example) never hid the fact that the smaller Central and Eastern European states were in search of justice and support for the war crimes issue and were willing to accept help from Stalin if Washington and London proved too hesitant.[63] This attitude was surely bolstered by the fact that Lauterpacht as well as scholars like Ecer and Schwelb could read Russian and were quite attracted by new legal theories such as 'aggression' and 'complicity'.

Sellars underlines that in Western scholarship, it has often been overlooked that Soviet law scholars were among the first to advocate criminal proceedings against the Nazi elite.[64] As Hirsch notes, Aron Trainin's theoretical work on the prosecution of war criminals included the early stages of the concept of conspiracy, later attributed to the US prosecution at Nuremberg.[65] His book was translated into English and distributed shortly before the meeting of the foreign ministers of Great Britain, the United States and the Soviet Union in Moscow in October 1943, as if Stalin wanted to test his position on his Western counterparts.[66] In 1945, Trainin was among the members of London's Soviet delegation who formulated the principles of the Charter for the

International Military Tribunal, held in Nuremberg, and advocated the principles of war against peace and conspiracy, which would guide the future prosecution of war crimes.[67] However, given that Stalin was hesitant to give the Soviet delegation at Nuremberg sufficient freedom to continue developing international law principles in collaboration with law scholars from other Allied powers, Soviet law developed in a different direction.

Nevertheless, the Soviet legal doctrine also influenced exile debates in London. Following the Moscow Conference of October 1943, where the foreign ministers of the three big Allies had agreed on a swift and joint punishment of war criminals, the Soviet Union held a trial in Kharkov.[68] Ecer was among the scholars who were attentive to the Soviet message emanating from the Kharkov trial[69] that justice for war crimes was at the top of the agenda of Soviet policy.[70] In his booklet 'Lessons of the Kharkow Trial', Ecer praised the proceedings conducted against three German officers and one local collaborator as a model for future war crimes trials, advocating the practice of judging crimes where they occurred (*lex loci*).[71] However, in later LIA and UNWCC debates, the *lex loci* was abandoned and the concept of an ad hoc tribunal was advocated as a means of addressing similar crimes occurring in different regions.

The UNWCC was officially founded in London on 20 October 1943 and began functioning in early 1944. Unsurprisingly, given the continuity of its members, the UNWCC – as its predecessors had already shown – went beyond its mandate of simply collecting information and pushed for a real war crimes policy.[72] The UNWCC defined its objectives in three main spheres: investigating facts and evidence regarding war crimes, enforcing the punishment of war criminals, and promoting legal opinions related to war crimes and the penal liability of perpetrators.[73] However, constant tension arose from this roadmap, as both the British Foreign Office and the US State Department had instead foreseen that the UNWCC would serve principally as a clearing office to collect evidence, but felt that it should not intervene in the actual planning of postwar justice until the big Allies had adopted a line themselves.

Advocating an International Court

The issue of setting up an international criminal court was one of the key features of the UNWCC's debates, following the trend of earlier controversies within the LIA. On 29 August 1944, the LIA

Chairman and Belgian representative de Baer launched a proposal to the UNWCC advocating the establishment of an international criminal court, an idea that had already been proposed in the Cambridge Commission and LIA meetings.[74] A Convention for the Establishment of a 'United Nations War Crimes Court' was drafted in September 1944. For the sake of expediency, the punishment of Axis criminality was later dealt with in ad hoc tribunals, but the eventual goal of setting up a permanent court lived on.

Ecer's aim was for the UNWCC to hold greater responsibility and he envisioned it as the forerunner to an international organization that would set up courts to act as an instrument of international justice. Thus, in May 1944, he launched a proposal in which he advocated a new term that in his opinion would realize universalist strands laid down in the Martens Clause of 1907: 'crimes against humanity', designed to cover offences against civilians.[75] In his paper, he deemed it unacceptable that those who had broken the law so many times should go unpunished simply because established national codes were not sufficient to deal with them.[76] He maintained the position that the expansive nature of the Second World War had created a new situation, with war crimes incomparable to earlier conflicts and to which new legal responses must be formulated. He claimed that the Nazis 'had stepped outside international intercourse and exempted themselves from the protection afforded belligerents by humanitarian law'.[77] He surely relied on Trainin's theories when he wrote 'Preparation and launching of the present war must be punished as a crime against peace' and 'if there are gaps in the law, it is our duty to fill them'.[78]

The motivation of exile lawyers to comply with the task of judging war criminals, which had failed after 1919, was evident.[79] Ecer recalled in his memoirs his deep personal commitment:

> The atmosphere was tense, as in my opinion we discussed the whole rationale of the war in light of international law, that must necessarily lead to the victory of justice over the dark forces of evil and bring its perpetrators to the justice they deserve.[80]

It seems that Ecer's initiative focused heavily on the Holocaust crimes, which until then had been dealt with among the bulk of Nazi occupation crimes, an act that minimized their uniqueness. He was therefore seen as a friend of the Jewish cause.[81] However, in his writings, he refers more to political oppression and occupational crimes. Therefore, it is doubtful that he intended to put the Holocaust centre-stage at that time and instead referred more to his own experience, one of persecution of political opponents.

Ecer's proposal was rejected following an intervention by McNair, but he maintained his minority opinion, questioning whether the foundation and enactment of the present war represented crimes that fell within the competence of the UNWCC to judge. The only way to enforce his new ideas was thus to create networks and circumvent the official channels of the UNWCC. Ecer, who already had strong ties with the Polish delegate Glaser, the Dutch de Moor, the Yugoslav Zivcovic and the Belgian de Baer, now turned to the Australian delegate, Lord Wright, who officially backed his position. In the following meeting, he spoke up for Ecer:

> It seems to me to put on a firm basis whatever might have been derived from what I should call the common law, and it is consonant with the moral sense of the world at large. It seems to me that it would be a retrogression to accept the view which is set forward in this report [by McNair]. It would shock people; it would destroy credit in the world and it would be condemned as a reversion to obsolete ideas, which possibly 17 years ago [when the Pact of Paris was created] had a certain vogue. It has not really come face with acts which might be committed if this easy view of responsibility were accepted. I wish to support the notion which has been proposed by Dr. Ecer.[82]

After Wright had spoken, the Chinese delegate Wunsz King also supported Ecer's claims (a fact Ecer noted in his memoirs with satisfaction)[83] and then Yugoslavia, New Zealand, Poland, Belgium and the Netherlands joined in as well, and the proposal was finally accepted.

The notion of crimes against humanity emanated from the legal debates of the LIA and the UNWCC. The concept attempted to address such diverse cases as the persecution of political opponents such as the Social Democrats within Germany, the persecution of German Jews and the crimes committed against Czech nationals during the so-called Sudetenland Crisis in 1938. It was nonetheless universalist, as it also targeted crimes committed upon Chinese nationals by Japanese troops in Manchuria in 1931; all were crimes committed by a state against its nationals, on its territory, prior to an official state of war.

However, even when the UNWCC started to endorse the concept, the British Foreign Office continued to reject suggestions to coin a new law, as they saw it. UNWCC Chairman Sir Cecil Hurst was stuck between the Foreign Office, the War Office and the UNWCC, and gave to the exile lawyers the frustrating impression that he was pursuing British policy above all else. De Baer complained in a private conversation in December 1944 to Lord Wright (the minutes of which have been retained in the Australian papers):

De Baer said that it was just another example of the way one had to fight to
get Hurst to do anything. It seems to him that there were very obstructive
forces behind Hurst as chairman; I asked him to amplify this and he said
that he believed the Foreign Office did not want to make it too hard on the
Germans. I said did they desire that Germany should not be too weak so
that she might still remain a barrier for the west against Russia. He said
that he thought that was the idea but did not believe in the soundness of
the idea ... He then said that in addition to the obstructive forces behind
Hurst he had been very obstructive right from the beginning and quoted
examples right back in the first months of 1941 when I was not attending
Commission meetings.[84]

The exiled Central European lawyers, including the Czechs, Poles and
Yugoslavs, thus openly debated whether siding with a Soviet commission would be the better option:

The Russians, with their organised machinery, would attract the eastern
European countries now represented on the Commission in London to the
Extraordinary Commission functioning at Moscow. De Baer said he had
thought this over and quite believed that would be the case. He had heard
Ecer and Zivkovic express sentiments that they would prefer to remain on
the Commission in London, but if things went on as at present they would
certainly turn to the strong Russian Commission.[85]

De Baer and Ecer were especially frustrated as there had never been
an official reply from Hurst to a letter Ecer had presented in October
1944 following his visit to the Soviet embassy. This letter included
a concrete offer of collaboration with the Soviet commission for the
exiled lawyers.[86] Lord Wright touched on this issue in his conversation
with de Baer, noting:

He then showed me a very interesting letter which Ecer had written to the
members of Committee I in October saying that after a conference with
the Russians he was instructed to say that they desired to get in touch
with the Commission with a view to the collaboration of the Extraordinary
Commission with the International Commission. I asked why this letter had
not been sent to all members and he said that Hurst had decided against it.
I pointed out that Ecer's letter expressly stated that the Russians wished
all members to be informed of their present attitude.[87]

The British offices realized the degree of his frustration far too late.
In January 1945, after Hurst had stepped down and Lord Wright had
replaced him, the new British representative within the UNWCC,
Lord Finlay, regretted that this road had not been taken: 'It is certainly
a disadvantage not having Russia represented, but I fail to see what

we can do about it.'[88] Undersecretary Norman Makin replied that the Foreign Office was working towards a solution, but thought that using Ecer as a transmitter was not showing 'serious' Soviet intentions.[89]

When Lord Wright succeeded Hurst as Chairman of the UNWCC, the press expressed hope for a change in UN war crimes policy. *The Times* acknowledged that the UNWCC's task was 'to carry out their duties to justice, not revenge', and the *Daily Telegraph* quoted Wright as saying: 'The failure to bring criminals to justice after the last war will not be repeated this time.'[90] Lord Wright's appointment as Chairman had a positive effect on all initiatives. The concept of 'crimes against humanity' was endorsed and recommended by the UNWCC, and later found its way into the London Charter.

When on 8 August 1945 the London Conference ended with the adoption of the Charter for the International Military Tribunal to be held at Nuremberg, the document caused a small sensation. Among the three charges listed was a new term: the Nazi leaders would face punishment not only for war crimes but also for crimes against peace and humanity. As we have seen, this term was coined within London exile circles. The international community thus responded to one of the most horrific novelties of the twentieth century: the politically organized persecution and slaughter of people under one's control.[91] Other definitions, such as that of 'crimes against peace' and war crimes, substantially followed the recommendations of the UNWCC. Although it has not yet been possible to prove how the American judge Robert Jackson came to use the term 'crimes against humanity',[92] it is plausible that Lauterpacht might be the missing link,[93] as he convened with Jackson before the London Conference and might have summed up the ongoing debates he had had with his colleagues, amongst them Ecer.

Schwelb's role in the UNWCC was that of a very influential Secretary of the Legal Committee, and after the war was over, he became an official chronicler of the work undertaken. After the Nuremberg trial, he laid down his legal conclusions from the debates he had witnessed, actively advocating the idea of crimes against humanity. Schwelb, in his article on crimes against humanity, underlined that the terms 'war crimes' and 'crimes against humanity' might frequently overlap.[94] He was reluctant to accept that a crime's connection with a war was a decisive factor for the Nuremberg court to respond to it. He concluded:

> The Crime Against Humanity, as defined in the London Charter, is not, therefore, the cornerstone of a system of international criminal law equally applicable in times of war and of peace, protecting the human rights of

the inhabitants of all countries of all civilian population against anybody, including their own states and governments', but 'a kind of by-product of the war, applicable only in times of war' and designed 'to cover cases not covered by norms of the traditional laws and customs of war'.[95]

The Nuremberg Charter, which implemented the term 'crimes against humanity' for the first time, would, in Schwelb's understanding, serve to 'make sure that inhumane acts violating the principles of the laws of all civilised nations committed in connection with war should not go unpunished'.[96] Schwelb set an agenda for following UN resolutions when he concluded that legal norm-setting was insufficient if political implementation was missing, as he observed in 1946: 'The task of making the protection of human rights general, permanent and effective still lies ahead.'[97]

Conclusion

When assessing the commitment of predecessors to the UNWCC and representatives of smaller Allied states towards the cause of international criminal justice, some general conclusions can be drawn. I argue that it was precisely the mixture between legal thinking and postwar planning that rendered the work of the UNWCC so valuable and enabled future concepts, such as crimes against humanity, to find firm ground in legal debates.

The commitment of smaller Allied states to frame international criminal law as being about war crimes was crucial. Some of its members stood out from this community of experts. Generally, the sense of being part of an international network was strong from the beginning. This stance mirrored the political situation of the time: we must not forget that the debates stemmed from an experience of political powerlessness, and that these exiled politicians and experts keenly perceived the low position of their agendas and authority to punish war criminals held among their British hosts. This community of lawyers quickly sensed that the only way to achieve political action by the 'Big Three' would be to convince them with facts and expertise, while carefully including academic expertise from their host countries. The exile situation within the London hub, with its simulation of a transnational environment and possibilities of exchange, was therefore vital to understanding the impact of their work.

The fact that war crimes policy crystallized out of the basis of European points of view and political concerns following the Nazi occupation and, to a lesser extent, the experience of the genocide against the Jews (today known as the Holocaust) becomes clear upon analysis of archival documents from that time. Only later, when the UNWCC had taken up its institutional work and meetings among its member states, were more common was the Eurocentric perspective opened up and Asian views and legal concerns regarding the Pacific War were given sufficient weight. This fact is particularly interesting as there had also been earlier meetings where Asian voices were raised, but were sidelined for political reasons – for example, the Chinese demands at the St James Conference of January 1942.

This finding is applicable to the reception of academic literature from the Soviet Union, which was also in search of a globally accepted definition of war crimes.[98] It should not be forgotten that while the war raged on, the Soviet Union was still seen as an essential ally of the European states fighting actively for their liberation, and sometimes even represented the more tempting partner when it came to war crimes policy.

The atmosphere in London's legal circles during the first half of the 1940s created the framework for an ideal breeding ground for an internationally relevant and acceptable war crimes policy, and networks were crucial in bringing about their ultimate success. Thus, the exiled lawyers gathering in London during the 1940s formed an epistemic community, involving some of the most renowned lawyers of the time, and established one of the first truly transnational networks. The concept of crimes against humanity was the main outcome of these legal debates and later served as a blueprint for the London Charter, as well as enriching international criminal law. In the long run, these exiled lawyers' experiences and the theorization of such in lengthy memorandums helped to generate a new concept in victim-centred politics: the protection of human rights.

Kerstin von Lingen is a professor at the Institute for Contemporary History at the University of Vienna. From 2013 to 2017, she led the research group 'Transcultural Justice: Legal Flows and the Emergence of International Justice within the East Asian War Crimes Trials, 1946–1954' at Heidelberg University. Her publications include two monographs in English, *Kesselring's Last Battle: War Crimes Trials and Cold War Politics, 1945–1960* (University of Kansas Press, 2009) and *Allen Dulles, the OSS and Nazi War Criminals: The Dynamics of Selective Prosecution* (Cambridge University Press, 2013).

Notes

1. For additional reflection on the topics in this chapter, see also von Lingen, 'Legal Flows'; von Lingen, *'Crimes against Humanity': Eine Ideengeschichte*, 1–19.
2. Herren, *Hintertüren zur Macht*.
3. In his chapter in this book, Guillaume Mouralis evokes the tensions within the supranational community.
4. Von Lingen, *'Crimes against Humanity': Eine Ideengeschichte*, 23.
5. For an overview of the UNWCC, see Plesch, *America, Hitler and the UN*; Kochavi, 'Britain and the Establishment of the United Nations War Crimes Commission', 323–49. For an historical account, see Schwelb, 'The United Nations War Crimes Commission', 363–64; and *History of the United Nations War Crimes Commission* (hereinafter *UNWCC History*).
6. Von Lingen, *'Crimes against Humanity': Eine Ideengeschichte*, 193–316.
7. The term 'United Nations' was the formal name for 'the Allies' following the 'Declaration by United Nations' of 1 January 1942. See Plesch, *America, Hitler and the UN*.
8. Schwelb, 'Crimes against Humanity', 179.
9. See archival documents in TNA, LCO 2/2973, Papers of the International Commission for Penal Reconstruction and Development.
10. Siegelberg, 'Unofficial Men, Efficient Civil Servants', 304.
11. Nevertheless, this does not contradict the findings of Plesch and Sattler, who affirm that the UNWCC was a result of public and private debates between the Allies on how to respond to Axis atrocities. See Plesch and Sattler, 'Changing the Paradigm of International Criminal Law', 210.
12. For an overview on British policy towards the Eastern European exile governments, see Brandes, *Großbritannien und seine Osteuropäischen Alliierten*; Heumos, *Die Emigration aus der Tschechoslowakei nach Westeuropa und dem nahen Osten*, especially 28–54.
13. Kochavi, *Prelude to Nuremberg*, 15; Kochavi, 'Britain and the Establishment of the United Nations War Crimes Commission', 323; Sellars, *'Crimes against Peace' and International Law*, 47.
14. For an overview, see Brown, *Dealing with Democrats*.
15. The correct spelling is Ečer. However, Ecer himself used an anglicized version and signed with 'Ecer' while in London. On at least one occasion, he even used the spelling 'Etcher'.
16. All biographical information following information from de Baer's granddaughter, Jacqueline Loughton-Scott, September 2015.
17. All biographical information on Ecer follow Stehlik, 'Bohuslav Ecer and the Prosecution of War Crimes', 53–63; as well as the biographical website on Ecer, written by his family. Retrieved 25 April 2021 from http://www.valka.cz/clanek_12304.html.
18. Stehlik, 'Bohuslav Ecer and the Prosecution of War Crimes', 61.
19. Siegelberg, 'Egon Schwelb and the Human Rights', 148.
20. Ecer's memoirs are titled Ečer, *Jak jsem je stíha l* [*How I Prosecuted*].
21. This is underlined by the short biography on Egon Schwelb by Rainer Huhle, Nürnberger Menschenrechtszentrum, unfortunately without a reference: retrieved 25 April 2021 from https://www.menschenrechte.org/de/2009/06/16/egon-schwelb.
22. Schwelb and Benes had their differences from the start, which likely arose from their professional background; see Brandes, *Großbritannien und seine Osteuropäischen Alliierten*, 110. In August 1940, Schwelb, in his legal expertise, denounced Edvard

Benes' claim to the political continuity of his office as president, and his subsequent legitimation to speak for all people of Czechoslovakia, including the Sudeten Germans (who belonged to Czechoslovakia before the Munich Agreement). Schwelb underlined that in normative legal terms, Benes' theory was convincing, but that politically speaking, he was not in charge of the Sudeten Germans who had become German citizens. This was an important issue concerning the war crimes policy, and the Foreign Office shared Schwelb's view that Benes was not entitled to deal with the matter of war criminals for the whole territory. In turn, this conclusion implied that a representative of exiled German citizens in London (such as Sudeten German Social Democrat Wenzel Jaksch) should also be heard, an issue that was postponed until the end of the war and later dropped for political reasons.

23. Schwelb, *Human Rights and the International Community*.
24. Nederlands Instituut voor Oorlogsdocumentatie (NIOD), Amsterdam, collection De Moor, archief 234 mr.dr. J. M. de Moor, inv. no. 36, leaflet on the foundation of the International Commission for Penal Reconstruction and Development. I thank Lisette Schouten, Heidelberg, for guiding me to this.
25. Segesser, 'On the Road to Total Retribution?', 371.
26. TNA, LCO 2/2973, International Commission for Penal Reconstruction and Development. Report of Committee concerned with Crimes against International Public Order. Letter of McNair to the Lord Chancellor, Viscount Simon, 10 August 1943.
27. NIOD, De Moor collection, inv. no. 36, leaflet on the foundation of the International Commission for Penal Reconstruction and Development.
28. See their memorandum in LCO 2/2973, Papers of the International Commission for Penal Reconstruction and Development.
29. For a summary, see *UNWCC History*, 94–99.
30. TNA, LCO 2/2973, Papers of the International Commission for Penal Reconstruction and Development, Report of Committee concerned with Crimes against International Public Order.
31. *UNWCC History*, 94–104.
32. For an overview on the latest research, see Heusler, Spoerer and Trischler, *Rüstung, Kriegswirtschaft und Zwangsarbeit im 'Dritten Reich'*; von Lingen and Gestwa, *Zwangsarbeit als Kriegsressource in Europa und Asien*.
33. TNA, LCO 2/2973, Papers of the International Commission for Penal Reconstruction and Development, Report, answers to note from De Baer of 24 August 1942.
34. TNA, LCO 2/2973, Papers of the International Commission for Penal Reconstruction and Development, Memorandum by Prof. Hersh Lauterpacht (1942).
35. Ibid., Memorandum, 25–26.
36. Koskenniemi, *The Gentle Civilizer of Nations*, 390. Koskenniemi refers here to an unpublished paper from Lauterpacht's private Collected Papers, vol. 3, 462–503.
37. Horne and Kramer, *German Atrocities, 1914*, 227–61; Willis, *Prologue to Nuremberg*, 8–12; Hankel, *Die Leipziger Prozesse*; Wiggenhorn, *Verliererjustiz*.
38. Sellars, *'Crimes against Peace' and International Law*, 1–46, 75–77; Segesser, 'On the Road to Total Retribution?', 359; Segesser, '"Unlawful Warfare is Uncivilised"', 210; Müller, 'Oktroyierte Verliererjustiz nach dem Ersten Weltkrieg', 202–222.
39. Report on the Question of International Criminal Jurisdiction by Ricardo J. Alfaro, Special Rapporteur, Extract from the Yearbook of the International Law Commission 1950, vol. II, 2–18, at 5.
40. TNA, LCO 2/2973, Papers of the International Commission for Penal Reconstruction and Development, report of the Chairman.
41. TNA, LCO 2/2973, Papers of the International Commission for Penal Reconstruction and Development; proposal of M. de Baer, May 1942.

42. TNA, LCO 2/2973, Papers of the International Commission for Penal Reconstruction and Development, Report of Committee concerned with Crimes against International Public Order. Report 1, p. 8.
43. On the LIA, some printed sources have survived; see *UNWCC History*, 99; British Library, London International Assembly, Reports on Punishment of War Crimes (this report is a printed version of the files in TS 26/873, therefore the original files are cited here).
44. Von Lingen, *'Crimes against Humanity': Eine Ideengeschichte*, 246.
45. TNA, TS 26/873, London International Assembly, Reports on Punishment of War Crimes; Sellars, *'Crimes against Peace' and International Law*, 53.
46. Report on International Criminal Jurisdiction, p. 5.
47. TNA, TS 26/873, London International Assembly, Reports on Punishment of War Crimes.
48. Ibid.
49. Ibid.; proposal of M. de Baer 'Suggestions for the Scope of Work for the Commission, Provisional Plan of Work', April 1942.
50. Kochavi, 'Britain and the Establishment of the United Nations War Crimes Commission', 325.
51. Kochavi, *Prelude to Nuremberg*, 3; Sellars, *'Crimes against Peace' and International Law*, 60.
52. TNA, TS 26/873, London International Assembly, reports on Punishment of War Crimes; proposal of M. de Baer 'Suggestions for the Scope of Work for the Commission, Provisional Plan of Work', April 1942.
53. Schabas, 'The United Nations War Crimes Commission's Proposal', 73.
54. Sellars, *'Crimes against Peace' and International Law*, 53.
55. See Weisers, 'Juger les crimes contre les Juifs'; Weisers, *La justice belge, les bourreaux allemands et la Shoah*.
56. Lewis, *The Birth of the New Justice*.
57. Weinke, *Gewalt, Geschichte, Gerechtigkeit*.
58. Lewis, 'The World Jewish Congress and the Institute of Jewish Affairs at Nuremberg', 181–210.
59. NARA, RG 238, Documents concerning Crimes of Germans against Germans in Germany, 27 March 1944. Extensive analysis of this document can be found in Kochavi, *Prelude to Nuremberg* and Weisers, 'Juger les crimes contre les Juifs'.
60. Cited after Weisers, 'Juger les crimes contre les Juifs', 82, who quotes a letter from de Baer to Kubowitzki, 25 March 1944.
61. Sellars, *'Crimes against Peace' and International Law*, 58–83.
62. *UNWCC History*, 169.
63. Smetana, 'British and U.S. Perceptions of Edvard Benes and His Foreign Policy', 141.
64. Sellars, *'Crimes against Peace' and International Law*, 48.
65. Hirsch, 'The Soviets at Nuremberg', 701–30.
66. Sellars, *'Crimes against Peace' and International Law*, 49.
67. Hirsch, 'The Soviets at Nuremberg', 701.
68. On Soviet trial policy, see an overview by Penter, 'Local Collaborators on Trial', 341–64.
69. The Kharkov trial is further discussed in Vanessa Voisin's chapter in this volume.
70. Sellars, *'Crimes against Peace' and International Law*, 53.
71. Ečer, 'The Lessons of the Kharkov Trial'; see also Stehlik, 'Bohuslav Ecer and the Prosecution of War Crimes', 55.
72. Sellars, *'Crimes against Peace' and International Law*, 58; Plesch, *America, Hitler and the UN*, *passim*; Kochavi, *Prelude to Nuremberg*, *passim*.

73. *UNWCC History*, 169.

74. NAA, A2937, 280, United Nations War Crimes Commission, Committee II, Establishment of an International Criminal Court, proposal by Marcel de Baer, 29 August 1944.

75. Von Lingen, 'Fulfilling the Martens Clause', 187–208.

76. Ečer, Additional Note, 12 May 1944, UNWCC III/4, S. 2, PURL. Retrieved 25 April 2021 from https://www.legal-tools.org/doc/6335bd.

77. Sellars, *'Crimes against Peace' and International Law*, 61.

78. TNA, FO 371/39005, UNWCC, Minutes of 36th Meeting, 17 October 1944; see also Sellars, *'Crimes against Peace' and International Law*, 63.

79. The failure of the Leipzig trials is further developed in Thomas Graditzky's chapter in this volume.

80. Ecer in his memoirs *Jak jsem je stíhal [How I Prosecuted Them]* (Prague, 1946), quote translated and cited by Stehlik, 'Bohuslav Ecer and the Prosecution of War Crimes', 56.

81. Apparently, Herbert Pell made this comment in a message to his government when Ecer threatened to resign from the UNWCC in September 1944; see Lanicek, *Czechs, Slovaks and the Jews*, 99 (referring to NARA, RG 59, H. Pell (UNWCC) to Secretary of State, 27 September 1944).

82. NAA, A 2937/273, Draft Lord Wright (October 1944). five pages, here p. 5.

83. Ecer, B., *Vývoj a základem mezinárodního trestního práva [Development of International Criminal Law]*, Prague, 1948, p. 122.

84. NAA, A 2937/273, Note of meeting with General de Baer, by Wright, 1 December 1944, p. 2.

85. NAA, A 2937/273, Note of meeting with General de Baer, by Wright, 1 December 1944, p. 2.

86. NAA Canberra A2937/274, Proposal by Dr Ecer, 'The USSR and the problem of war crime, the conception, punishment and prevention of war crimes according to the Soviet doctrine of international and criminal law'. Text of a lecture delivered under the auspices of the society for cultural relations with the USSR on 14 December 1944, pp. 176–91.

87. NAA, A 2937/273, Note of meeting with General de Baer, by Wright, 1 December 1944, pp. 2–3.

88. TNA, FO 371/51011, Minutes from Lord Finlay to Sir W. Makin, 'Russia and the United Nations War Crimes Commission', 31 January 1945.

89. TNA, FO 371/51011, Draft letter, Malkin to Finlay, 31 January 1945: 'For your own information we are working on a plan, which we propose to take in the EAC – for sound measure of the cooperation with the soviet Govt.'

90. TNA, FO 371/51011. Press clippings, 2 February 1945.

91. Luban, 'A Theory of Crimes against Humanity', 86.

92. A theory is presented in von Lingen, 'Fulfilling the Martens Clause', 187–208.

93. In *Gentle civilizer*, Koskenniemi draws on Lauterpacht's decisive role within the British prosecution, where he drafted the opening and closing speech; see the chapter 'Lauterpacht: The Victorian Tradition in International Law', 388–89. This version is bolstered by Sands, *East West Street*, 109–11.

94. Schwelb, 'Crimes against Humanity', 189.

95. Ibid., 206.

96. Ibid.

97. Ibid., 226.

98. See Polunina, 'The Human Face of Soviet Justice'.

Bibliography

Published Sources

Brandes, Detlef. *Großbritannien und seine Osteuropäischen Alliierten. Die Regierungen Polens, der Tschechoslowakei und Jugoslawiens im Londoner Exil vom Kriegsausbruch bis zur Konferenz von Teheran*. Munich: Oldenbourg, 1988.

Brown, Martin D. *Dealing with Democrats: The British Foreign Office and the Czechoslovak Emigrés in Great Britain, 1939–1945*. Frankfurt: Lang, 2006.

Ečer, Bohuslav. *The Lessons of the Kharkov Trial*. London, 1944.

——. *Jak jsem je stíhal: reportážní pásmo Edvarda Cenka [How I Prosecuted]*. Prague: Naše vojsko, 1946.

——. *Vývoj a základem mezinárodního trestního práva [Development of International Criminal Law]*, Prague, 1948.

Hankel, Gerd. *Die Leipziger Prozesse. Deutsche Kriegsverbrechen und ihre strafrechtliche Verfolgung nach dem Ersten Weltkrieg*. Hamburg: Hamburger Edition, 2003.

Herren, Madeleine. *Hintertüren zur Macht. Internationalismus und modernisierungsorientierte Außenpolitik in Belgien, der Schweiz und den USA 1865–1914*. Munich: Oldenbourg, 2000.

Heumos, Peter. *Die Emigration aus der Tschechoslowakei nach Westeuropa und dem nahen Osten, 1938–1945*. Munich: Oldenbourg, 1989.

Heusler, A., M. Spoerer and H. Trischler (eds). *Rüstung, Kriegswirtschaft und Zwangsarbeit im 'Dritten Reich'*. Munich: Oldenbourg, 2010.

Hirsch, Francine. 'The Soviets at Nuremberg: International Law, Propaganda, and the Making of the Postwar Order'. *American Historical Review*.113(3) (2008), 701–30.

History of the United Nations War Crimes Commission and the Development of the Laws of War, Edited by the United Nations War Crimes Commission. London: HMSO, 1948.

Horne, John, and Alan Kramer. *German Atrocities, 1914: A History of Denial,* New Haven: Yale University Press, 2001.

Kochavi, Arieh J. 'Britain and the Establishment of the United Nations War Crimes Commission'. *English Historical Review* 107(423) (1992), 323–49.

——. *Prelude to Nuremberg: Allied War Crimes Policy and the Question of Punishment*. Chapel Hill: University of North Carolina Press, 1998.

Koskenniemi, Martti. *The Gentle Civilizer of Nations: The Rise and Fall of International Law 1870–1960*. New York: Cambridge University Press, 2001.

Lanicek, Jan. *Czechs, Slovaks and the Jews, 1938–1948: Beyond Idealization and Condemnation*. New York: Palgrave Macmillan, 2013.

Lewis, Mark. 'The World Jewish Congress and the Institute of Jewish Affairs at Nuremberg: Ideas, Strategies, Political Goals, 1942–1946'. *Yad Vashem Studies* 36 (2008), 181–210.

——. *The Birth of the New Justice: The Internationalization of Crime and Punishment, 1919–1950*. New York: Oxford University Press, 2014.

Lingen, Kerstin von. 'Fulfilling the Martens Clause: Debating "Crimes against Humanity", 1899–1945', in Fabian Klose and Mirjam Thulin (eds), *Humanity: A History of European Concepts in Practice from the 16ᵗʰ Century to the Present* (Göttingen: Vandenhoeck & Ruprecht, 2016), 187–208.

——. *'Crimes against Humanity': Eine Ideengeschichte der Zivilisierung von Kriegsgewalt 1864–1945*. Paderborn: Schoeningh, 2018.

―――. 'Legal Flows: Contributions of Exiled Lawyers to the Concept of Crimes against Humanity during the Second World War'. *Modern Intellectual History* 3 (2018), 1–19.

Lingen, Kerstin von, and Klaus Gestwa (eds). *Zwangsarbeit als Kriegsressource in Europa und Asien*. Paderborn: Schoeningh, 2014.

Luban, David. 'A Theory of Crimes against Humanity'. *Yale Journal of International Law* 29 (2004), 85–167.

Müller, Kai. 'Oktroyierte Verliererjustiz nach dem Ersten Weltkrieg'. *Archiv des Völkerrechts* 39(2) (2001), 202–22.

Penter, Tanja. 'Local Collaborators on Trial: Soviet War Crimes Trials under Stalin (1943–1953)'. *Cahiers du Monde russe* 49(2–3) (2008), 341–64.

Plesch, Dan. *America, Hitler and the UN: How the Allies Won World War II and Forged a Peace*. London: I.B. Tauris, 2011.

Plesch Dan, and Shanti Sattler. 'Changing the Paradigm of International Criminal Law: Considering the Work of the United Nations War Crimes Commission of 1943–1948'. *International Community Law Review* 15(2) (2012), 203–23.

Polunina, Valentyna, 'The Human Face of Soviet Justice: Aron Trainin and the Origins of the Soviet Doctrine of International Criminal Law', in David M. Crowe (ed.), *Stalin's Soviet Justice: 'Show' Trials, War Crimes Trials, and Nuremberg* (London: Bloomsbury, 2019), 127–44.

Sands, Philippe, *East West Street: On the Origins of 'Genocide' and 'Crimes against Humanity'*. London: Knopf, 2016.

Schabas, William. 'The United Nations War Crimes Commission's Proposal for an International Criminal Court'. *Criminal Law Forum* 25 (2014), 171–89.

Schwelb, Egon. 'Crimes against Humanity'. *British Yearbook of International Law* 23 (1946), 178–226.

―――. 'The United Nations War Crimes Commission'. *British Yearbook of International Law* 23 (1946), 363–64.

―――. *Human Rights and the International Community: The Roots and Growth of the Universal Declaration of Human Rights, 1948–1963*. New York: Quadrangle Books, 1963.

Segesser, Daniel Marc. 'On the Road to Total Retribution? The International Debate on the Punishment of War Crimes, 1872–1945', in Robert Chickering, Stig Förster and Bernd Greiner (eds), *A World at Total War: Global Conflict and the Politics of Destruction, 1937–1945* (Cambridge: Cambridge University Press, 2005), 355–74.

―――. '"Unlawful Warfare is Uncivilised": The International Debate on the Punishment of War Crimes, 1872–1918'. *European Review of History / Revue européenne d'histoire* 14(2) (2007), 215–34.

Sellars, Kirsten. *'Crimes against Peace' and International Law*. Cambridge: Cambridge University Press, 2013.

Siegelberg, Mira. 'Unofficial Men, Efficient Civil Servants: Raphael Lemkin in the History of International Law', *Journal of Genocide Research* 15(3) (2013), 297–316.

―――. 'Egon Schwelb and the Human Rights *Via Media*', in James Loeffler and Moria Paz (eds), *The Law of Strangers: Jewish Lawyers and International Law in the Twentieth Century* (Cambridge: Cambridge University Press, 2019), 143–66.

Smetana, Vin. 'British and U.S. Perceptions of Edvard Benes and His Foreign Policy in the Last Ten Years of His Life', in Ota Konrad and René Küpper (eds), *Edvard Beneš: Vorbild und Feindbild. Politische, historiographische und mediale Deutungen* (Göttingen: Vandenhoeck & Ruprecht, 2013), 127–52.

Stehlik, Eduard. 'Bohuslav Ecer and the Prosecution of War Crimes'. *European Conscience and Communism* (Proceedings of the International Conference of 2–3 June 2008, Prague, 2008), 53–63.

Weinke, Annette. *Gewalt, Geschichte, Gerechtigkeit. Transnationale Debatten über deutscheStaatsverbrechen im 20. Jahrhundert*. Göttingen: Wallstein Verlag, 2016.

Weisers, Marie-Anne. 'Juger les crimes contre les Juifs. Des Allemands devant les tribunaux belges, 1941–1951', Ph.D. dissertation. Brussels: Université libre de Bruxelles, 2014.

———. *La justice belge, les bourreaux allemands et la Shoah*. Brussels: Editions de l'Université libre de Bruxelles, 2020.

Wiggenhorn, Harald. *Verliererjustiz. Die Leipziger Kriegsverbrecherprozesse nach dem Ersten Weltkrieg*. Baden-Baden: Nomos, 2005.

Willis, James F. *Prologue to Nuremberg: The Politics and Diplomacy of Punishing War Criminals of the First World War*, Westport, CT: Greenwood Press, 1982.

Archival Sources

British Library, London International Assembly, Reports on Punishment of War Crimes.

NAA (National Archives of Australia): A 2937/273; A2937/280; Canberra A2937/274.

NARA (US National Archives and Records Administration): RG 238.

NIOD, Collection De Moor, Archief 234 mr.dr. J.M. de Moor, inv.no. 36.

TNA (The National Archives, United Kingdom): FO 371/51011; LCO 2/2973; TS 26/873.

UNWCC, III/4(a), S.2. PURL: https://www.legal-tools.org/doc/6335bd.

CHAPTER 4

THE TREASURE TROVE OF THE UNITED NATIONS WAR CRIMES COMMISSION ARCHIVES, 1943–49

Wolfgang Form

Introduction

At the Moscow Conference (31 October 1943), it was agreed that the German officers, officials and members of the Nazi Party who were responsible for or had played an important part in the atrocities, massacres and executions in German-occupied countries would be sent back to the countries where their war crimes had been committed. The rationale was that they could be brought before the courts and punished according to the laws of the liberated countries and the free governments that would be erected therein.

Following the failed attempts to prosecute war crimes committed during the First World War, especially the Leipzig trials that were widely considered a farce, this was a long-awaited decision. The fear of another failure ran deep, especially in the exiled governments of the German-occupied countries who had fled to London. Public attention after the Second World War was primarily concentrated on the famous

Nuremberg and Tokyo trials, with many other trials simultaneously taking place all over the world in both Europe and the Asia-Pacific region. Until these trials, the prosecution of war crimes and grave breaches of international humanitarian law had yet to become a state practice. Before the Second World War, national legislation did not provide legal tools to punish the unimaginable atrocities committed as war crimes. Therefore, it was to be expected that the free world community could now apply to the Moscow Declaration the national structures for a law enforcement programme that it had been preparing during the war. In 1941, the first attempts at international cooperation were made, of which the first significant result was the January 1942 St James Agreement (London). In a public statement, the exiled governments, Great Britain, the Soviet Union and the United States declared that German war crimes would not go unpunished.[1] War criminals should and would pay for their guilt 'through the channel of organised justice'.[2]

In the months that followed, the Allied efforts to create a functioning collaborative administrative framework became increasingly intense. Initially, this was to be discussed on 7 October 1942 at a session of the House of Lords in London. 'Lord Maugham, who had contributed actively to the deliberations of the London International Assembly,[3] had announced his intention to bring the subject up in Parliament, but the date of the discussion had been twice postponed until the Lord Chancellor would be in a position to reply on behalf of the British Government.'[4] Exactly one year later, on 7 October 1943, it was time.[5] Lord Maugham summarized the discussions of the past months: if the international community did not want to fail again, then it was necessary that war criminals should not disappear, courts should be opened for their punishment, and everything should be done for a smooth administrative and judicial process. However, this would only be possible with the adoption and implementation of national legal regulations. Two weeks later, on 20 October 1943, the British Foreign Office sent an invitation to a diplomatic conference of Allied countries' and dominions' representatives in London to make arrangements for the establishment of a United Nations Commission for the Investigation of War Crimes (UNWCC), chaired by the British Lord Chancellor's Viscount Simon (Sir John Allsebrook). Twenty-eight representatives from seventeen nations attended.[6]

The newly established Commission had two primary purposes: (1) to investigate and record evidence of war crimes, identifying where possible the individuals responsible; and (2) to report to the governments concerned cases in which it appeared that adequate evidence might be expected to be forthcoming. The first aspect was divided into collecting evidence and providing justice. However, for everyone present, it was important that a clear distinction be drawn between the preparatory investigation work of the UNWCC and the procedure of the trial of war criminals after the end of the war.[7] For China, the establishment of a Far East subcommission or special panel was essential.[8]

On the eve of the Moscow Conference, international cooperation was paramount. It was clear to all involved that only a joint effort would lead to success. Two days after the Conference, the first unofficial meeting of the UNWCC in the Royal Courts of Justice took place.[9] All of the nations participating in the conference of 20 October 1943 were present, except for the representatives from South Africa and Canada.[10] The Commission's primary task was to search for and collect, investigate and record evidence of war crimes, reporting to the governments concerned those instances where the sources available appeared to disclose a *prima facie* case.[11] In this function, the UNWCC was assisted by national offices established by each of the Commission's members. Summaries of evidence were submitted to the Commission by the national offices. The UNWCC took no part in the detention of war criminals or bringing them before court. In the end, only a small proportion of individuals listed as war criminals by the UNWCC were ever prosecuted.

The UNWCC established three main committees:

(1.) Committee I: Facts and evidence. This studied the charges made by governments and prepared listings of war criminals.
(2.) Committee II: Enforcement. This comprised measures to ensure the detection, apprehension, trial and punishment of individuals guilty of and responsible for war crimes and crimes against humanity (in the case of German victims).
(3.) Committee III: Legal. The function of this was to advise the UNWCC and the member governments on legal questions.

Defining and Documenting War Crimes

The first point of discussion at the UNWCC was the question of what constitutes a war crime. Several participants at the conference had already prepared lists of common war crimes. It was agreed that a standard definition had to be found so that national procedures could be compared internationally: 'by defining a War Crime as an act which is in violation of the laws of war it might be possible to determine the facts in a particular case and decide whether those facts justified a trial'.[12] However, the category of war crimes should not be too narrow. The Czechoslovakian delegate Bohuslav Ecer favoured the term 'Axis Crimes' because '*War Crimes* was a conception of the past, and it had been surpassed by the method of total war'.[13] There were already surveys of the actions that were considered to be war crimes, but the discussion seemed to be more in the direction of developing a new, updated universal standard that would do justice to the events of the war.

Another central task of the UNWCC was to identify and safeguard evidence for future war crimes trials. The type of evidence that might be admitted in court was another central issue discussed by the committees. In this regard:

> Sir Cecil Hurst [a senior British international lawyer and judge to the Permanent Court of International Justice in The Hague] pointed out that it was not the task of the Commission to collect evidence in a technical sense of the term, but to obtain information ... The question of the form that such information should take and how it should be considered would come later ... In order to follow a common policy, there ought ... to be uniformity of action. There were some 10–15 Nations represented on the Commission, each with its own system of courts and evidence. For a common policy there must be some sort of assimilation ... There was no reason why the United Nations should not all be at work collecting information about particular individuals.[14]

It was also important to clarify which courts would have jurisdiction for war crimes. Would the existing procedural law be used or should ad hoc tribunals be set up? Should ad hoc courts be identical everywhere or be accessible to every country requiring their services? UNWCC members also discussed the question of a permanent international court.[15] In this regard, the UNWCC provided guidance to member states and formulated recommendations on how cases could be prosecuted. It thus helped shape the development of international law in areas such as jurisdiction, extradition, personal responsibility for acts of state, the protection of human rights of civil populations against violations by their own government (crimes against humanity) and other similar issues.

If evidence were to be collected and processed, a standard would inevitably have to be found that would allow it to be brought before all Allied courts. They required a proper system, not directly bound to a specific existing one. Already in the first session of the UNWCC, it became clear that there was a need for a sophisticated notification procedure. All issues dealt with should be individually prepared and discussed by representatives of the member states. The UNWCC had a chance of achieving success only if the results of the investigation were circulated among the participating states. The best way to organize this was through a Central Collection Agency, which in turn would create war crimes lists to be submitted to all involved. Crime lists only made sense if an intra-commission flow of information about prepared and executed trials was guaranteed (intercommunication between nations).

As a first step, there would be a survey of the member states to ascertain their ideas regarding their courts and laws. Such an approach aimed to bring to light a number of aspects that the UNWCC as a whole would need to address. In the end, a complex system of reporting protocols, memoranda, written templates for meetings, wanted lists and most importantly procedural summaries was established. In addition, the UNWCC developed a multilayered filing system with a Central Registry of War Criminals and Security Suspects (CROWCASS) and tribunal materials, including reports of national military tribunals and the transcripts and proceedings of the International Military Tribunal for the Far East (IMTFE).[16] For the task of identifying alleged war criminals, the UNWCC reviewed and examined evidence supplied by member countries through their respective National Offices. Once the UNWCC determined that there was sufficient evidence to prosecute alleged war criminals, it compiled lists of such individuals, sending these lists back to the National Offices. National governments then had the charge to arrest the suspects and hand them over for prosecution, according to the Moscow Declaration, to the country where the war crimes had taken place. This led the national commissioners to enquire about the status of prisoners, as in the case of the Belgian representative to the UNWCC: 'My national office have [*sic*] written to inform me that some Germans, who are responsible for committing war crimes on Sunday, 3rd September 1944 at Frameries, were taken prisoner, the same day, by the Americans at Flénu. My National Office further writes to ask me if it is possible to ascertain what happened to these prisoners.'[17]

A Complex Multilayered Filing System

The following section analyses the structure and indexing of administrative files, including meeting minutes, documents, reports and related materials. Between October 1943 and March 1948, the

UNWCC produced over 1,700 different circulars, ranging from one to more than one hundred pages. Unfortunately, the central collection of the Commission is incomplete. Additions can be found in the relevant record groups held in the British, Australian and US archives. Except for a few isolated cases, where it is not always clear whether each consecutive number was assigned, most of the minutes and documents were reconstructed from the record of the International Research and Documentation Center War Crimes Trials (ICWC) at the University of Marburg (Germany).[18]

The overview given below offers a rough idea of the scope of these documents and of who created them within the UNWCC. Several series consist of just a few documents. For example, the series Minutes of Meetings of the Legal Publications Committee (LPC) of the Legal Committee only documents five meetings between 16 July 1947 and 20 January 1948. It deals with the publication of important cases for the general public. In total, fifteen volumes with eighty-nine cases were published.[19] According to the last LPC protocol from January 1948, four volumes with twenty-four cases had been issued and another ten procedures were discussed by the Preparatory Committee and released for printing. At this time, the dissolution of the UNWCC was already scheduled for 31 March 1948. Those working on the final edition would be held responsible for subsequent volumes.[20]

Table 4.1 provides an overview of the existing series, their dates and number of documents, as well as the missing records.

At the time, the Commission's proceedings were published on a regular basis in its weekly bulletins, listing documents that might be of interest to National Offices. Further details or extracts could be sent following an application to the research office. The weekly bulletins contained details of the venue and administrative jurisdiction of the national courts, a very brief summary of the charges, the names of the defendants and the verdict. Some bulletins would also provide information about special directories or overviews. For example, on 9 February 1948, it was noted that under file number E-4(P)-R8/P20/1, there was a list of war criminals extradited from the British Zone to Poland along with the trial outcomes.[21]

The 'TL' series deals with selected war crimes trials that can additionally be found in the fifteen volumes of the UNWCC Law Reports, including the first Dachau concentration camp case (*US v Kramer et al.*),[22] the so-called Peleus Case,[23] the trial of Takashi Sakai in Nanking (China),[24] the Yamashita trial in Manila (the Philippines)[25] and the French trial in Strasbourg of Robert Wagner.[26] In some cases, there are also overviews of several cases in a single TL report.[27]

The most extensive series bears the abbreviation 'C'. The first of the 303 documents is a subcommittee report that was commissioned at the UNWCC's first official meeting to organize its work and initial administrative structures. It presents a summary of the UNWCC's tasks and a brief outline of the history of international criminal law as well as the advantages and disadvantages of establishing a list of war crimes.[28] The final document 'C-267' of 21 April 1948 is the Final Statistical Progress Report (Committee I) from 1 February 1944 to the end of March 1948.[29] It would take a separate chapter to deal with the wide range of topics addressed in this series. They cover areas from Internal Rules (C-2), Reports of the Financial Administration (C-4), Establishment of a Far Eastern Panel or Branch of the Commission (C-13), UNWCC Progress Reports of (C-48), Memos about Collective Responsibility for War Crimes (C-85), Notes of National Representatives (C-98), Cooperation with the Union of Soviet Socialist Republics (C-142/1), Statement of Cases by Committee III (C-185), Composition of Committees (C-192) to discussions about offences such as Crimes against Humanity (C-201).

Searching the UNWCC Records

The task of developing finding aids to these series in order to conduct thematic searches was immediately taken up. The UNWCC itself provided various forms of access to its files (see Figure 4.1). The most straightforward tool was a list of headings or titles of the document in question. This list facilitated at the very least an overview of the topic being covered; a specific search for single aspects, topics, contexts, place names or persons mentioned was not possible. However, there are alternative search strategies available. For example, using the chronological list of documents contained in Commission 'C', one can create an approximate list of topics discussed per commission. The entire series are unfortunately not always developed according to such a detailed chronological list. In the records, there is only a subdirectory of the documents from the series 'Misc.' (Miscellaneous Documents: War Crimes Commission), which covers the period from 3 December 1945 to 17 June 1946 (nos. 1–33).[30] For a total overview, four subdirectories must be considered together.

Individual series like the War Crimes News Digest were indexed by the UNWCC staff with a single index. It includes entries such as *Amnesty in the U.S. Zone* to *Wright, the Hon. Lord*. Names, institutions (UNWCC), places (Therezin, Theresienstadt), case names (Subsequent

Table 4.1. UNWCC minutes and documents

Series	Description	Document Number	Dates	Missing
A	War Crimes Commission 'A' Documents	1–67	May 1946 10 March, 1948	5, 13, 19
C	War Crimes Commission Documents	1–267 A and B or (1), (2) 303 docs	2 December, 1943 21 April, 1948	
D	Unidentified Documents	1–17	1944–45	1–4, 6–11, 14
Detention Circular	Detention Circular (Committee on Facts and Evidence)	1–54	November, 1944 July, 1947	
Detention List	Detention Lists (Committee on Facts and Evidence)	1	August, 1945	
Doc Com. I	Documents of Committee I (Committee on Facts and Evidence)	1–102	24 April, 1945 9 February, 1948	
Doc Com. II	Documents of Committee II (Enforcement Committee)	1–51	14 February, 1944 22 June, 1945	
Doc Com. III	Documents of Committee III (Legal Committee)	1–118	18 March, 1944 17 November, 1947	
Doc Series	Documents Series: Research Office	1–55 57 documents	August, 1945 August, 1947	
FEC	Unidentified Documents from the Far Eastern & Pacific Sub-Commission	1–5	4 Mai, 1944 15 February, 1945	
Finance	Minutes of Meetings Finance Committee	1–24	12 April, 1944 20 January, 1948	2–11, 13–18, 20–23
LPC	Minutes of Meetings of the Legal Publications Committee (Legal Committee)	1–5	16 July, 1947 28 January, 1948	
LR	Publication of Reports of War Criminals	1–2	5 October, 1945 15 May, 1946	
M	War Crimes Commission Minutes of Meetings	1–135	26 October, 1943 3 March, 1948	

Meetings	Weekly Notice of Meetings Committee I–III	1–80	18 March, 1944 13 April, 1946	
Meeting Com. III	Meetings of Committee III (Legal Committee)	1/1945 11/1947 53 documents	20 August, 1945 17 November, 1947	3/1947
Meeting Com. I	Meetings of Committee I (Committee on Facts and Evidence)	1–141	9 February, 1944 31 March, 1948	
Misc.	Miscellaneous Documents: War Crimes Commission	1–126 A and (1) 128 documents	3 December, 1943 30 April, 1948	
NOC	Documents of the National Office Conferences	1–10	16 May, 1945 19 June, 1945	3, 10
RC	Research Circular: Research Office	1–30	July, 1945 1 March, 1948	
SM	Minutes of Meetings of the Far Eastern & Pacific Sub-Commission	1–38	29 November, 1944 4 March, 1947	
SI	Summary of Information: Research Office	1–55 59 documents	September, 1944 December, 1947	
SFEC	Minutes of the Special Far Eastern and Pacific Committee	1–2	13 August, 1945 27 August, 1945	
TL	Trial and Law Reports Series (Legal Committee)	1–55	5 October, 1945 19 April, 1948	
WB	Weekly Bulletins. Documents recently received by the Research Office	1–124	30 July, 1945 9 February, 1948	
WCND	Press New Summary (1–7), War Crimes News Digest (8–36): Research Office	1–36 42 documents	31 October, 1945 4 March, 1948	
	Several unnumbered documents			

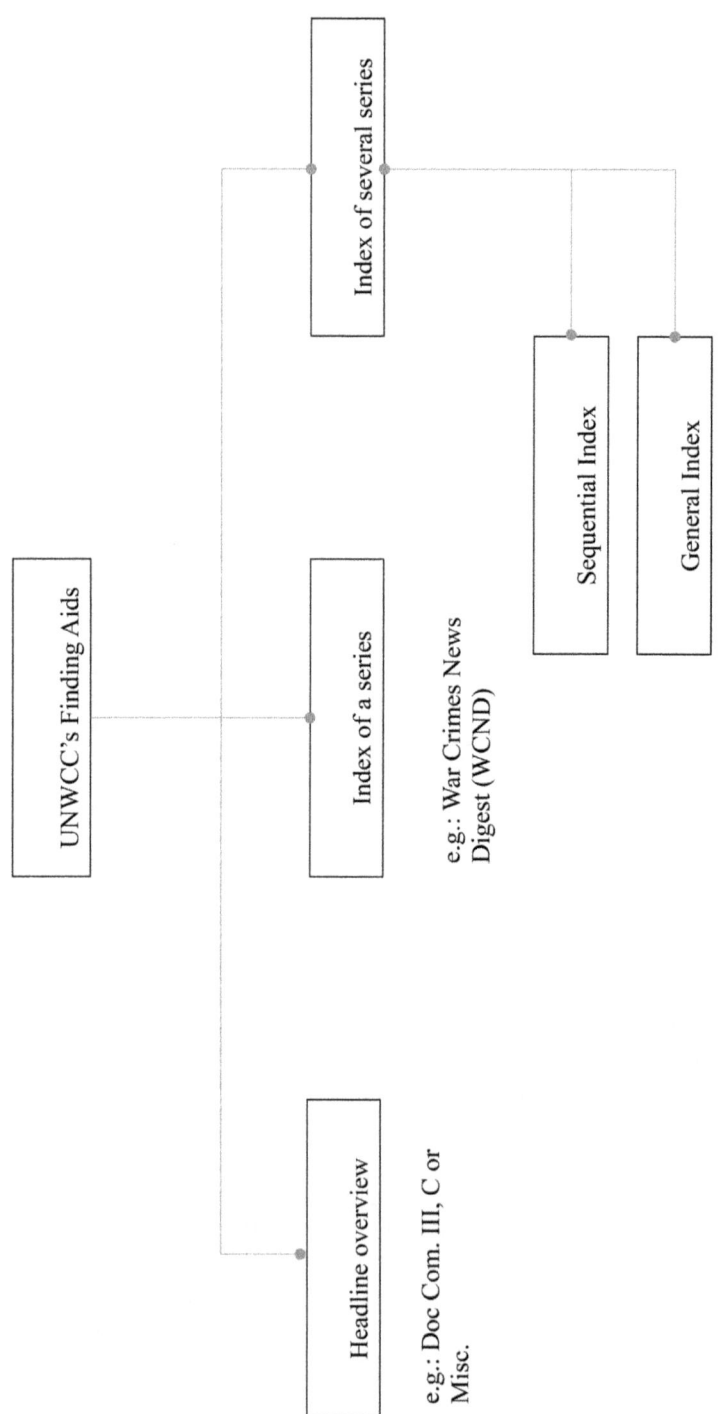

Figure 4.1. Structure of the UNWCC index. © Wolfgang Form

Proceedings), incriminated acts (Sterilization), special crime scenes (STALAG Luft – Stammlager Luftwaffe – Main Camp for P.O.W. Air Force), countries (Poland) and charges (Killing of POWs) were all indexed. In addition, the index refers to other courts and cases, stating for example 'see also Leipzig Trial' or 'Hadamar Trial'. Moreover, there are always partial indexes to the War Crimes News Digest.[31]

Indexes with greater detail were created later. 'The Archives of the United Nations War Crimes Commission', transferred in May 1949 to the United Nations (UN), include several series of documents of major importance. Most of these, including the minutes and documents of the Commission itself and its committees, were indexed by the UNWCC. This index, which appeared in six parts, has been consolidated in a single document by the United Nations Archives and has been published as United Nations Archives Reference Guide No. 11[32] entitled *Index to Minutes and Documents of the United Nations War Crimes Commission, 1945–1948.*[33] Not all documents of the UNWCC were included in the UN Archives. The UNWCC destroyed a portion of its records that were considered to have no enduring value. Retrospectively, this is a pity: almost all records on internal structures are missing. In addition, the records of some subcommittees or subcommissions were not received by the UN Archives, such as the Far Eastern and Pacific Sub-Commission, the Finance Committee, the Executive Committee, the Legal Publications Committee and the Committee on Facts and Evidence. This index was not developed by the UNWCC itself; rather, on the basis of the guides to minutes and documents provided by the UNWCC, the UN Archives amalgamated the six indexes into a unique search tool. No additions or alterations have been made and the entries have been listed chronologically under the same headings as those used in the original indexes.[34]

Microfilm reel 171 contains several additional indexes. The first is the index to the twelve Nuremberg U.S. Military Tribunals' Proceedings (in German, the bound volume of the Institut für Völkerrecht at the University of Göttingen).[35] Moreover, a fascinating guide and stack list of records of the war crimes trials held in Nuremberg was prepared in the UN Archives.[36] Perhaps the most consulted document is an index of the Tokyo trial, published in 1957 by Paul S. Dull and Michael Takaaki Umemura:[37] 'The authors have compiled this functional index of the Proceedings of the International Military Tribunal for the Far East to enable the serious researcher to find his way through some fifty thousand pages of the subject material.'[38]

The index card series is a unique source. Here, the UNWCC wrote a very concise but clear summary: The last series of films, the Index

Card series, contains cards that cross-reference two portions of the collection. The 'Index Cards of War Criminals' cross-references defendants named in series 1, the 'Charge File' series, using a system of abbreviations and numbers that correspond to the country from which the charges were filed, the nationality of the defendant, and the 'registered number' of the case. For example, the index card for defendant Otto Abel, found on reel NDX-1, is given the number 4145/UK/G/604. This reference corresponds to the Charge File with registered number 604, from the file group 'United Kingdom vs. Germans', found on microfilm reel 21,[39] which includes cases with registered numbers ranging from 491 to 630. Similarly, the index card for Ludwig Abel, also found on reel NDX-1, is given the number 5492/B/G/360, which corresponds to a Charge File with the registered number of 360, from the charge file group 'Belgium vs. Germans, Registered Number 261–399' located on microfilm reel 2. The entry for this case includes the rank of the defendant, dates and places of alleged crimes as well as charges: murder, torture of civilians, deportation of civilians, internment of civilians under inhumane conditions.[40] The index cards of the subseries 'Reports of the National Military Tribunals' (NDX-9) contains cards arranged in alphabetical order by the name of defendant, and which appear to be cross-referenced to the contents of the series 'Reports of National Military Tribunals', which are primarily arranged by country of tribunal, in reels 59 to 117, and therein by case numbers.'[41]

Table 4.2. Index cards of war criminals (based on UNWCC documents, microfilm NDX1-9)

NDX01	A	C
NDC02	D	Go
NDC03	Gr	Ka
NDC04	Kai	Lj
NCD05	Lo	Pe
NCD06	Pf	Schr
NCD07	Schr	We
NCD08	We	Z

Total: about 39,000 individuals

Most of the documents were not produced by the UNWCC, but rather by the prosecution teams of the countries participating in the UNWCC. The index refers to the so-called 'charge files'. In the example cited by the United States Holocaust Memorial Museum on the British case against Otto Abel (and three other defendants), the UNWCC's information sheet contains a summary of dates and locations of the crime as well as the number and descriptions of the crimes in the war crimes list: 'case No. 1; murder and breaches of International Law (Article 2 of the Geneva Convention)'. The information was transmitted to the UNWCC by the British prosecution office of Judge Advocate General (Military Department). The other documents are translations of interrogation protocols (defendants and witnesses). There are no indications of a trial or sentence, although there was a trial before a British military court held in Hanover from 20 to 30 January 1947, in which Otto Abel was sentenced to three years' imprisonment.[42]

Not all 39,000 listed persons were brought to justice. The samples also demonstrate that there were investigative documents that did not lead to a lawsuit. In addition, there are often multiple entries for one person. For example, Lieutenant Colonel Abel had two references to the French 'Charge Files': 1675/FR/G/703 and 6619/FR/G/2123. In the last named case, it is noted that Abel was a member of the 1000° Régiment Motorisé de la Légion Tatare et de la Légion Azerbaidjanaise and was said to have committed crimes in the French departments of Corrèze and Creuse with other German soldiers in July 1944.[43] In the documents of the French military archives in LeBlanc, no case files could be identified for this case. In Case 703, the only references made to Abel's rank and the crimes of which he was accused are based on the 'Rapport en date du 4 août 1945 du délégué régional du S.R.C.G.E.[44] pour la région de Clermont-Ferrand'.[45] Further samples have shown that the approximately 39,000 references do refer to a considerably smaller number of potential war criminals. An index card was created for every single entry, but not all refer to matching names in the 'Charge files', which were necessary to lead to legal proceedings.

Conclusion

The UNWCC archival collection is an exceptional historical source, but one that was not organized according to the rules of contemporary archival science. There are many hundreds of memoranda, protocols and other documents circulating in various series among the UNWCC member states. They have been indexed in different densities as the collection organically grew. The digital recording of all index entries presents a very broad picture of the work of the UNWCC. In the end, about 1,200 entries have been found. The first practical applications show that the tagging was undertaken with a postwar focus. Some relevant entries from today's point of view, such as evidence of sexual violence as a war crime or torture techniques including waterboarding, cannot be found. Using digital-humanity-methods (full-text searches) may facilitate the tracing of relevant documents not indexed as such at the time.[46]

In the five and a half years of its existence, the UNWCC not only provided the legal groundwork in international criminal law but also documented the work of investigating authorities in a hitherto barely realized scope. It can be assumed that a considerable number of Belgian, British, Canadian, French, Yugoslav, Dutch, Polish, Czech and US investigative documents were standardized and indexed by name. There are many descriptions of German war crimes in particular, even those that have not been classified as official war crime trials. Only a full-scale digital index, producing a database with search engine access, will allow full access to the UNWCC collection, thereby revealing its full potential for transnational research on war crimes trials in the wake of the Second World War.

Wolfgang Form studied Political Science, Sociology, Social and Economic History and Public Law in Marburg. He received his doctoral degree on political criminal justice during the National Socialism era in Germany. In 2003, he cofounded the International Research and Documentations Center War Crimes Trials (ICWC). Since 1992, he has been a lecturer in political science, international criminology, peace and conflict studies and gender studies at the University of Marburg, Kiel, Wolfenbüttel (Germany), Changsha (China) and Phnom Penh (Cambodia). His main fields of research are political criminal and military justice, the history of international criminal law, peace and conflict studies, and the local and regional history of National Socialism.

Notes

1. Japan had only been occupying large parts of the Asia-Pacific region for a few weeks and was not yet in the focus of the international coalition for the prosecution of war crimes; however, this would not be long in coming.
2. See Laufer, *Pax Sovietica*, 143; Beigbeder, *International Criminal Tribunals*, 21; Wilson et al., *The Politics of Justice*, 13.
3. Armitage, *Europe in Bondage*.
4. *History of the United Nations War Crimes Commission*, 109 (hereinafter *UNWCC History*).
5. For reason for the delay, see Schwelb in: *UNWCC History*, 110–12.
6. Australia: Rt. Hon. S.M. Bruce, Lord Atkin; Belgium: Vicomte de Lantsheere, General de Baer; Canada: Rt. Hon. Vincent Massey; China: Dr Willington Koo, Dr Liang Yuen-Li; Czechoslovakia: M. Lobkowicz, Dr Bohumil Ecer (Bohuslav Ecer); Greece: M. Aghnides, M. Stavropoulos; India: Sir Samuel Ranganadham; the Netherlands: Jonkheer Michiels von Verduynen, Dr J. M. de Moor; New Zealand: W. Jordan; Norway: M. Colban; Poland: Count Raczynski, Professor Glaser; Union of South Africa: Mr Jones; United Kingdom: George Hall, Sir Cecil Hurst; United States: Mr Winant; Yugoslavia: Mr Yevtić, M Milanovitch; French Committee of National Liberation (France Libre) M. Viénot, Prof. Cassin. UNWCC Series C-229; National Archives Records Administration (NARA), RG 153/Entry 145/228/Folder 150–13; ICWC Marburg RG UNWCC Papers/1447.
7. UNWCC Series C-229, 2; NARA RG 153/Entry 145/228/Folder 150–13.
8. The Far Eastern and Pacific Sub-Commission was established one year later on 29 November 1944. Minutes of the inaugural meeting in Chungking. USHMM Series SM-1, NARA RG 153/Entry 145/222/Folder 150–3A; ICWC Marburg RG UNWCC Papers/1584.
9. Australian National Archives, Canberra (NAC) RG A-2937/275.
10. Notes of Unofficial Preliminary Meeting held at 2.30 PM on 26 October 1943. UNWCC Series M-1; NAC RG A-1067/UN46_WC_11; ICWC (International Research and Documentation Center War Crimes Trials) Marburg RG UNWCC Papers/1.
11. Herlitz, 'The Meaning of the Term "Prima Facie"', 391–408.
12. Notes of Unofficial Preliminary Meeting held at 2.30 PM on 26 October 1943. UNWCC Series M-1. NAC-RG A-1067/UN46_WC_11; ICWC Marburg RG UNWCC Papers/1.
13. Ibid.
14. Notes of Unofficial Preliminary Meeting held at 2.30 PM on 26 October 1943, p. 3. UNWCC Series M-1. NAC RG A-1067/UN46_WC_11; ICWC Marburg RG UNWCC Papers/1.
15. See recommendation in favour of the establishment by the Supreme Allied Military Command of Inter-allied Tribunals, appointed on 19 September 1944. UNWCC Series C-51. NARA RG–238/Entry 52Q/1/Folder 6; ICWC Marburg RG UNWCC Papers/1245. Explanatory Memorandum to accompany the draft convention for the establishment of a United Nations War Crimes Court, 6 October 1944. UNWCC Series C-5. NAC RG A-2937/284; ICWC Marburg RG UNWCC Papers/1254.
16. Afterwards the UNWCC's work documents were transferred to the UN Archive in New York. For decades, using these materials was difficult. Since 2014, a set of 187 microfilm reels has been hosted at the United States Holocaust Memorial Archive, including a complete digital collection of 456,156 images, USHMM RG 67.047M.
17. Excerpt from the letter by the Belgian representative, 7 October 1946. NARA, 238/ Entry 52K/1-Belgian Representative.

18. See www.icwc.de (retrieved 27 April 2021).

19. *Law Reports of Trials of War Criminals*, vols I–XV (hereinafter *UNWCC Law Reports*). Volume XV includes no cases, but is rather a digest of law and cases, starting with sources of international law: Legal basis of courts administrating international criminal law, parties to crimes, types of victims of crimes, types of offences (including inchoate offences, war crimes, crimes against humanity, membership of criminal organizations, almost all listed in the Charter of the Nuremberg International Military Tribunal), defense pleas (e.g. pleas of superior orders, having acted in an official capacity, alleged offences carried out as a judicial act or under the principle of nullum crimen sine lege, nulla poena sine lege), procedure of the courts and last but not least punishment of criminals.

20. *UNWCC Law Reports XV* notes on a meeting held on Tuesday 20 January 1948. UNWCC Series LPC-5. NAC RG A-4311/746-4; ICWC Marburg RG UNWCC Papers/146.

21. Weekly Bulletin No. 124, 9 February 1948. NAC RG A-4311/743-2; ICWC Marburg RG UNWCC Papers/394.

22. UNWCC Series TL 1–3. NARA RG 238/Entry 52M - 52-P/1/Folder 1; ICWC Marburg RG UNWCC Papers/484-486.

23. UNWCC Series TL 5 and TL 10. NAC RG A-2937/289; ICWC Marburg RG UNWCC Papers/488, 493. Trial of Kapitänleutnant Heinz Eck and four others for the killing of Members of the crew of the Greek Steamship PELEUS, sunk on the high seas. British military court for trial of war criminals held at Hamburg, 17–20 October 1945. See The National Archives Kew, London (TNA) RG WO 235/5.

24. UNWCC Series TL 27. NAC RG A-2937/289; ICWC Marburg RG UNWCC Papers/507.

25. UNWCC Series TL 50. NAC RG A-4311/743-2; ICWC Marburg RG UNWCC Papers/533.

26. UNWCC Series TL 22–23. NAC RG A-4311/746-4; C-506.

27. For example, UNWCC series TL 34. NAC RG A-4311/746-4; ICWC Marburg RG UNWCC Papers/517.

28. UNWCC Series C-1. Report of the Sub-Committee, adopted on 2 December, 1943. NARA RG 238/Entry 52Q/1/Folder 6; ICWC Marburg RG UNWCC Papers/1188.

29. Legal Tools Database (http://www.legal-tools.org/en/go-to-database/record/6c35c0, retrieved 27 April 2021); ICWC Marburg RG UNWCC Papers/1854.

30. Legal Tools Database http://www.legal-tools.org/en/go-to-database/record/ba8318 (retrieved 27 April 2021).

31. War Crimes News Digest: Vols. I –X, and Vols. XI–XX: NAC RG A-2937/319; Vols. XI–XX: Vols. XXI–XXIV: NAC RG A-4311/743-2; Vols. XXV–XXX: NAC RG A-2937/319.

32. United Nations Archives Reference Guide No. 11, 17 October 1949.

33. Legal Tools Database (https://www.legal-tools.org/en/doc/c7654a, retrieved 27 April 2021). Not all documents of the UNWCC were included in the UN Archives. In addition, the records of some subcommittees or subcommissions were not received by the UN Archives, e.g. the Far Eastern and Pacific Sub-Commission, the Finance Committee, the Executive Committee, the Legal Publications Committee and the Committee on Facts and Evidence. See also Introduction of UNWCC records at the UN Archives, UNHMM 67.041M, UNWCC microfilm reel 171/image 1.290-2.

34. UNWCC microfilm reel 33/image 15.

35. All indexes edited by Hans Günter Seraphim.

36. Prepared October 1949. UNWCC microfilm reel 171/image 1.274ff.

37. Dull and Takaaki, *The Tokyo Trials*.
38. Ibid., Preface.
39. This appears to be from the USHMM microfilm finding aid on UNWCC records (RG-67.041M).
40. USHMM RG-67.041 microfilm reel NDX01, image 9.
41. Finding aid on Unites Nations War Crimes Comission Records, 1943–1949 [microform and digital copy] 2014.26, RG-67.041M. Digital source: https://collections.ushmm.org/findingaids/RG-67.041M_01_fnd_en.pdf (retrieved 27 April 2021).
42. Database of the ICWC, University of Marburg. TNA RG WO 235/279.
43. UNWCC microfilm reel 21/image 1.359.
44. Service de recherche des crimes de guerre ennemis. For more information, see Moisel, 'Les procès pour crimes de guerre allemands en France', 80, 90–101.
45. UNWCC microfilm reel 6/image 1.400.
46. Form, 'UNWCC Policy on the Prosecution of Torture', 323–48.

Bibliography

Published Sources

Armitage, John (ed.). *Europe in Bondage: Reports of the London International Assembly.* London: Lindsay Drummond, 1943.

Beigbeder, Yves. *International Criminal Tribunals: Justice and Politics.* New York: Palgrave Macmillan, 2011.

Dull, Paul S., and Michael Takaaki Umemura. *The Tokyo Trials: A Functional Index to the Proceedings of the International Military Tribunal for the Far East.* Ann Arbor: University of Michigan Press, 1957.

Form, Wolfgang. 'UNWCC Policy on the Prosecution of Torture 1943–1948'. *Criminal Law Forum: The Official Journal of the Society for the Reform of Criminal Law* 25(1–2) (2014), 323–48.

Herlitz, Georg Nils. 'The Meaning of the Term "Prima Facie"'. *Louisiana Law Review* 55(2) (1994), 391–408.

History of the United Nations War Crimes Commission and the Development of the Laws of War, Edited by the United Nations War Crimes Commission. London: His Majesty's Stationery Office, 1948.

Laufer, Jochen. *Pax Sovietica. Stalin, die Westmächte und die deutsche Frage 1941–1945.* Cologne: Böhlau, 2009.

Law Reports of Trials of War Criminals, Selected and Prepared by the United Nations War Crimes Commission. London: His Majesty's Stationery Office, 1947–49, vols I–XV.

Moisel, Claudia. 'Les procès pour crimes de guerre allemands en France après la Seconde Guerre mondiale'. *Usages politiques du droit et de la justice, Bulletin de l'Institut d'histoire du temps présent* (2002), 90–101.

United Nations Archives Reference Guide, No. 11, 17 October 1949.

Wilson, Sandra et al. (eds). *Japanese War Criminals: The Politics of Justice after the Second World War.* New York: Columbia University Press, 2017.

Archival Sources

ICWC, UNWCC Papers: 1, 394, 484–86, 507, 533, 1245, 1254, 1447, 1584, 1854.
NAC: RG A-1067/UN46_WC_11; RG A-2937 # 275, 284, 289, 319; RG A-4311 # 743-2, 746-4.
NARA: RG 153 Entry 145 Box 222, 228; RG 238 Entry 52M – 52-P Box 1; Entry 52Q Box 1.
TNA: WO 235 # 5, 279.
USHMM: RG 67.041M.

CHAPTER 5

LEGAL IMAGINATION AND LEGAL REALISM
'CRIMES AGAINST HUMANITY' AND THE US RACIAL QUESTION IN 1945

Guillaume Mouralis

Introduction

This chapter focuses on the ways in which 'atrocities' and 'persecutions' on 'racial grounds' were defined and legally conceptualized during the Second World War.[1] It seeks to revisit the genesis of 'crimes against humanity' as a category of international law. As many authors have shown since at least the 1970s, the core of the definition laid down in the International Military Tribunal (IMT) Charter arose from a complicated, nonlinear process initiated in the United States War Department during the summer of 1944, driven by a team of well-established East Coast lawyers.[2] This genealogy does not imply that reflection on this topic has not been carried out in other arenas and by other actors. However, the proposals made by the latter were generally not seriously taken into consideration by the policy makers in charge of these issues.

A significant number of Nazi crimes were not punishable under the existing laws of war, especially the 'atrocities on racial grounds'[3] committed by the Axis Powers before or during the war against their nationals. Consequently, various experts, most of them outsiders within the academic legal field, have proposed adapting international law to this new situation.

While most attempts made until 1944 to examine such atrocities helped broaden the well-established concept of war crimes *stricto sensu* (and more rarely creating a new category *ex nihilo*), the solution originally devised within the American administration and ultimately retained was substantially different. It subordinated those atrocities ultimately included in the category of 'crimes against humanity' to other war-related crimes, among which the conspiracy to wage aggressive war occupied a prominent place. This subordination[4] had, for two intertwined reasons, significant restrictive effects: it made the burden of proof especially difficult, as observed by the French assistant representative André Gros during the inter-Allied negotiations in London[5]. It also made it more difficult to universalize the new category in general.[6] Furthermore, to quote French Judge Henri Donnedieu de Vabres, 'the category of crimes against humanity, which the statute had brought in by a tiny door, was, as a result of the [IMT's] judgement, volatilized'.[7]

This chapter aims to understand how this somewhat puzzling legal device was developed and why it was ultimately adopted in the IMT Charter. From my point of view, the mainstream and somewhat disembodied history of legal and political ideas, which pays little attention to the social groups involved in innovation processes, cannot address these issues in an entirely adequate way. Indeed, it would benefit from being combined with a social and professional history of the actors involved in the war crimes discussions as well as with a broader examination of the way in which they justified their actions. I argue that, among other things, two sets of constraints weighed heavily on the process of legal innovation: on the one hand, a sort of professional constraint arising from the specific legal experience accumulated by the actors before and during the war; and, on the other hand, a form of internalization of the state's cause(s) with regard to the principle of sovereignty and its domestic implications. This self-restraint[8] specific to government lawyers or 'legists' precluded legal innovation.

Furthermore, as will be shown here, targeting a policy based on statutory racism was likely to raise domestic questions given the existence of legal segregation (the 'Jim Crow' laws in the Southern states and similar provisions in the North) as well as endemic violence (lynchings) against African Americans condoned by local authorities.

After Adolf Hitler came to power in 1933, African-American publications, especially newspapers, regularly documented anti-Jewish persecutions in Nazi Germany and highlighted parallels between the Nuremberg and Jim Crow laws,[9] and from 1942 indicated the contradiction between domestic and foreign policy.[10] However, although widely circulated, these newspapers represented a relatively isolated part of a highly segregated public space. As for the legal experts in charge of the war crimes policies in the administration, some were aware of the potential domestic implications of the war crimes policy and warned explicitly (albeit never publicly) against any overly broad definition of crimes against humanity.

The elaboration of legal categories during the Second World War was not only a constrained process; it was also often confrontational, even if this was rarely admitted. Seemingly purely legal or technical controversies did not unfold in the smooth space of 'epistemic communities' harmoniously working towards the development of international criminal law.[11] The outcome of the more or less discrete struggle for legitimate and effective expertise in this area depended in particular on the positions the protagonists held within (or in some cases out of) the 'allied' field of power during the war – a very differentiated and asymmetric social space[12] – and on the unequal distribution of professional, political and academic resources among them.

Towards a Legal Category

How were persecutions and atrocities on racial grounds conceptualized? It is evident that before being transformed into a category of international criminal law in 1945, the expression did not encompass a stable meaning and therefore did not necessarily refer to atrocities on racial grounds (to which the London definition is also not limited).

In this respect, it is useful to distinguish 'crimes against humanity' from 'atrocities'. The first expression had a long and complex history before the Second World War, having been marked by a tentative juridification since the end of the nineteenth century.[13] It often referred, albeit not exclusively, to mass crimes (slavery, the lynching of African Americans, anti-Jewish pogroms, massacres of Armenians) partly based on racial ideology. In contrast, the meaning of the term 'atrocities' was profoundly shaped by the experience of the First World War when used in a context of international conflict.[14] However, its racial dimension was not as central as it (belatedly) became during the subsequent war. Furthermore, in the Second World War, the

Nazi crimes were long perceived through the distorting prism of this memory.[15]

I propose to examine in greater detail the trajectory of 'atrocities on racial grounds' as a criminal notion over the last two years of the Second World War, until its integration into the category of 'crimes against humanity'. As far as possible, the analysis links this trajectory to that of the actors involved in the definition, promotion and transformation of the idea into a workable and binding criminal category. This process is particularly difficult to describe in its complexity for various reasons. First, it involved numerous actors acting in various arenas, whether domestic or international, governmental or nongovernmental, academic or activist. Second, the Allied field of power was asymmetrical: on the one hand, intergovernmental bodies such as the United Nations War Crimes Commission (UNWCC) as well as previously created semi-official commissions certainly contributed to global reflection, but their discussions and proposals had a limited impact on the effective drafting of war crimes policies.[16] On the other hand, nongovernmental organizations, be they academic, professional (such as national or international lawyers' associations) or religious (especially American Jewish organizations), were also not in a position to decisively influence Allied policies. Due to the disintegration of the prewar international system and the correlative domination of national states supporting the war effort, legal experts serving the British and American governments played a much more important role than their counterparts in nongovernmental or international organizations.

In this respect, two phases can be distinguished: high-profile experts in the Foreign Service, typically possessing considerable political, diplomatic and legal resources, dominated the first phase. They were reluctant to give substance to the public commitments of the Allied powers. They made clear, especially from 1942, that the punishment of Nazi war crimes was one of their main war aims. However, the US government hesitated until 1944 to go beyond the restrictive definition of 'war crimes' in international law. Despite growing concern over Nazi mass crimes against European Jews, the various proposals that included persecutions on racial grounds within this definition were rejected. For example, State Department officials – in the first place Legal Adviser Green Hackworth, to whom we shall return later on – undermined the initiative of Herbert Pell, the American representative to the UNWCC (whose role is further developed by Kerstin von Lingen and Wolfgang Form in Chapters 3 and 4 of this volume respectively), who instead sought to promote the following resolution:

> It is clearly understood that the words 'crimes against humanity' refer, among others, to crimes committed against stateless persons or against any persons because of their race or religion; such crimes are judiciable by the United Nations or their agencies as war crimes.[17]

For this and other reasons, Pell was dismissed from his position in January 1945. His resignation concluded a conflict where questions of professional legitimacy in the legal and diplomatic fields played a much more significant role than is generally admitted by historians of war crimes policies.[18]

As will be developed in the following section, another type of legal expert – practising lawyers mainly based in the US War Department – took over in the second phase, beginning in the summer of 1944. While they proved to be more imaginative and creative than the members of the previous group, they were no less dependent on their professional rationales as well as on the partly internalized state cause.

The Space of Experience of Practising Lawyers

In August and September 1944, a well-documented struggle took place within President Franklin D. Roosevelt's administration to control the pacification of Germany, whose defeat now seemed imminent. Treasury Secretary Henry Morgenthau argued for a Carthaginian peace including summary executions of the Nazi leaders. For various reasons – a desire to gain leadership in German affairs, a conservative legalism in international relations inherited from Elihu Root and a less confrontational relationship towards Germany – Henry Stimson, his colleague in the War Department, opposed the so-called Morgenthau Plan and and advocated with President Roosevelt a trial of the major war criminals. The desire for leadership in German affairs could explain to some extent the somewhat unexpected conversion of leading War Department officials to a far more ambitious war crimes policy than they had previously envisioned, as in the case of John McCloy.[19]

Stimson and his deputy McCloy encouraged the lawyers of their department to develop a workable plan. On 15 September, Colonel Murray C. Bernays (1894–1970), a New York trial and appellate lawyer, forwarded them a memorandum entitled *Trial of European War Criminals*.[20] Bernays aimed to solve the legal problems posed by the bureaucratic organization of the Nazi crimes and the large number of perpetrators. It introduced two concepts hitherto absent from academic discussions on war crimes: 'conspiracy' and 'criminal organization'. The first facilitated the targeting of the small group of leaders charged with the inception of a criminal plan, while the second stimulated the prosecution of numerous agents of the crime through mere membership in criminal organizations such as the Geheime Staatspolizei (Gestapo), the Sturmabteilung (SA) and the Schutzstaffel (SS). In his memorandum, Bernays proposed linking the prewar atrocities on racial or religious grounds to a criminal plan or 'conspiracy' that had been devised by the Nazis since at least 1933 to achieve world domination. This proposal is interesting insofar as it was consistent not only with the experience of Bernays as a prac-tising lawyer in the interwar period but also with that of his chiefs McCloy and Stimson.

To understand Bernays' proposal, it is worth recalling some biographical elements:[21] he was born in the Russian Empire (Bielorussia today) and arrived in the United States as a child. He later served in the American Expeditionary Forces during the First World War. He was likely to have heard of 'German atrocities' given the importance of this topic as justification for American involve-ment in the conflict.[22] After the war, beginning his career as a 'cause' lawyer, he first defended left-wing activists. He then quickly rose to become a prominent Wall Street lawyer, specializing in civil litiga-tion on behalf of corporate clients and companies; in this capacity he often had to deal with the category of (civil) conspiracy, which was therefore familiar to him.[23] During the Second World War, as an officer performing his military duty in the Pentagon, Personnel Division (G-1), he was first involved in matters regarding enemy as well as American prisoners of war. This activity increased his sensi-tivity to the question of possible retaliation and probably explains his originally cautious approach to war crimes. From July 1944, he was then assigned to design war crimes policies as chief of the Legislative and Special Project Branch, G-1. Without belonging to the first circle of War Department elite lawyers, Bernays had access to influential officials (Samuel Rosenman, Green Hackworth and John McCloy) thanks to his reputation as a lawyer and to prewar contacts (he met Rosenman while studying at Columbia Law School). His social capital certainly helped advance his conspiracy plan. Furthermore, Bernays was conscious of the fate of European Jews[24] despite having only superficial knowledge of the genocide:[25] in this sense, he seemed to have been more interested in law and legal 'creativity' than in the crimes themselves. Also noteworthy was Bernays' subsequent conservatism in international law, as he defended rather orthodox positions on human rights and genocide after the war,[26] reinforcing the impression of self-restraint, a disposition shared by those experts having internalized the State's traditional sovereign interests.

The shared professional experience of Bernays and his chiefs explains to a large extent their enthusiastic support for his plan. In his diary, Stimson recounted his first meeting with Bernays as follows:

> Colonel Bernays ... gave an interesting talk on the possibility of bringing charges against the whole scheme of Nazi totalitarian war, using for the promotion of its end methods of warfare, which were in conflict with the established rules of war. This was virtually upon the theory of a conspiracy and I then told them of my experience as United States Attorney in finding that only by conspiracy could we properly cope with the evils, which arose, under our complicated development of big business. In many respects the task, which we have to cope with now in the development of the Nazi scheme of terrorism is much like the development of big business.[27]

As a partner of the law firm Root and Clarke since 1893, Stimson learnt the evolving legal practices related to the Sherman Antitrust Act (1890), which made 'every contract, combination in the form of trust or conspiracy in restraint of trade or commerce' illegal (section 1). In 1906, he was appointed US attorney for the Southern District of New York by the President with the primary task of fighting against the transgression of antitrust legislation.[28] In this position, he famously tried a case of customs fraud on a large scale involving, among other defendants, the American Sugar Refining Company. In 1909, Stimson succeeded in achieving the conviction of the company for conspiring against the Federal Government.[29]

After Bernays' memorandum was accepted by the Secretary of War, it was subjected to a drafting process from October to December 1944, involving a wide range of officials and legal experts, more or less expressing reservations towards an approach of German war crimes in terms of conspiracy and criminal organizations. While some criticisms had something to do with struggle over professional juris-dictions[30] (as in the case of the Judge Advocate General, traditionally entrusted with war crimes matters), others were more substantial. One of the main points of criticism was the link between conspiracy and 'atrocities on racial grounds' against Axis nationals, as some of them had been committed before the outbreak of the war.

In a first phase, this criticism led to a narrowing of the definition of such atrocities to violations of the penal laws of Axis countries.

Indeed, in the ensuing drafting process of Bernays' proposal, experts with considerable academic resources played a significant role. This was true, for instance, of Herbert Wechsler (1909–2000). This professor of constitutional law at the Columbia University Law School was appointed Assistant Attorney-General in charge of the War Division in February 1944. In a memorandum written in December 1944, he attempted to give a stronger legal basis to the Bernays project, devoiding it somewhat of substance. In a retrospective testimony, the professor highlighted the lawyer's lack of rigour:

> It became evident to me that Bernays himself was confused between conspiracy as a crime and conspiracy as a mode of complicity in substantive offenses, committed by one of the conspirators … My first challenge to the Bernays memo was on that point, and I challenged both its legal acceptability and its wisdom.[31]

After being appointed American Chief Prosecutor by President Harry S. Truman, Robert Jackson retained, in a first step, a definition of atrocities as being limited to violations of Axis penal laws. However, several factors led Jackson and his team to broaden this definition. In particular, Jewish organizations intervened in June 1945, claiming that strict reliance on German laws would prevent the prosecution of crimes against German Jews. Jacob Robinson, director of the Institute of Jewish Affairs (an emanation of the World Jewish and the American Jewish Congresses), had since 1943 developed a plan to charge the Nazi leaders with what he called from December 1944 a broad 'conspiracy against the Jewish people'.[32] He met Jackson with other representatives of Jewish organizations on 11 June 1945 to share his expertise on the topic and to suggest a broader definition of 'atrocities on racial grounds'. The intervention of Robinson at the crossroads of international law, human rights activism and advocacy of Jewish interests is noteworthy because it highlights the complexity of the innovation process, which took place in different overlapping arenas. Due to this intervention and other legal considerations, Jackson and his team broadened the original definition again, abandoning any reliance on Axis laws. However, at the same time, they more strictly connected atrocities with the conspiracy charge to wage aggressive war. This connection was reinforced in particular towards the end of the London Conference, as Robert Jackson made clear that atrocities on racial grounds were a concern for the Allies only because they were part of a common plan to wage aggressive war, thereby hardening the subordination of the former to the latter.[33]

A Distant Relationship to 'Law in the Books'

In seeking to apprehend Nazi crimes through legal means, the War Department officials resorted to notions and arguments that were familiar to them given their professional experience as members of prestigious law practices and as corporate lawyers. Through their academic training and their experience as practising lawyers, they were flexible and open to legal innovations. They maintained a distant and sometimes suspicious relationship to academic knowledge, valuing 'law in action' more than 'law in the books'.[34]

In their retrospective accounts of their involvement in war crimes policies, most described their initial incompetence in international law. For instance, Bernays later wrote to his wife: 'there were too many so-called "international lawyers" on this job. That remark is not directed against the individuals but against their craft ... The trouble was that [they] were thinking traditionally, whereas international law, which is statesmanship taking form in law, can only be handled by men who think creatively.'[35] Bernays liked to portray himself as a pioneer[36] moved by pure inspiration.[37] Remaining rather discreet about the sources of his plan, he nevertheless found – he later wrote – confirmation of his ideas in subsequent academic readings.[38] For example, in October or November 1944, David (Mickey) Marcus provided him with an advance copy of Raphael Lemkin's *Axis Rule in Occupied Europe*.

Sidney Alderman recalled a discussion with the Attorney General F. Biddle that took place shortly after his appointment by Jackson as his first assistant (3 May 1945):

> I told him that it seemed to me that I was a strange selection, being neither recognized as an expert criminal lawyer nor anything in the way of an international lawyer. [Biddle] smiled and said that that might be one of the main reasons why I was selected.[39]

Indeed, Biddle's remark was appropriate: he was aware of his Justice Department predecessor's reservations about theorists and law professors. As American Chief Prosecutor before the IMT, Jackson sought experienced practising lawyers as his assistants. He called upon very few law professors and entrusted them with technical assignments (in the case of Sheldon Glueck, Professor of Criminology at Harvard University) or the writing of legal opinions on limited questions (Hans Kelsen). Conversely, he frequently dismissed as excessively legalistic the perspectives of continental academics such as the French professor of law and jurisconsult Jules Basdevant. During the negotiations on war crimes matters with the other Allied representatives in San Francisco, Jackson wrote in his diary:

> Professor Bastavant [*sic*], a professor of international law in some French school who is advising the French. He is an international lawyer of the old school. On a study of our plan, he pronounced the plan to punish those who institute aggressive wars as 'très fragile'. This from France who has been the victim of two aggressive wars in my lifetime. God save us from professors![40]

This aspect is important because the whole Nuremberg story is marked by a series of professional tensions, such as the internal stress within the legal field between academics and practitioners: while in the first phase dominated by the prosecution, academic resources took a lesser part, they seemed to become much more central in the final phase, resulting in the judgment. This evolution was mostly due to the very different composition of the respective teams. While the professors took a lesser part in the prosecutor's office, they were better represented among the judges and their 'technical advisers'. From my point of view, this observation is important because it facilitates understanding of how the prosecutors and judges assessed the case in contrasting ways. The far more restrictive approach of the judges was to some extent linked to an academic inclination towards moderate innovation.

Furthermore, those who designed and later implemented the Nuremberg trial plan generally belonged to a limited segment of 'elite lawyers', a group that during the New Deal era was able to take advantage of the rise of the regulatory state.[41] The prestigious law practices of which they were members, mostly located on the East Coast, not only represented corporate clients but also specialized in the defence of public bodies, such as city councils or federal agencies. Based among others on antitrust legislation, such litigation rested on legal concepts devised to deal with a form of criminality involving complex organizations. In addition, these lawyers often held important positions in the judiciary before the war, where they had had to deal with similar legal problems. More generally, they socially and professionally maintained a close relationship with the power elite: they spoke a common language, but also internalized bureaucratic and political rationales (showing a deep understanding of the operating principles of the state); they were further able to act effectively and to anticipate the favourable reaction of their superiors as well as ensure that their proposals reached them. While Bernays had the ear of John McCloy and Green Hackworth, his colleague William Chanler – a former associate with Stimson's law firm – took advantage of a direct channel to President Roosevelt to advance his proposal to charge the Nazi leaders for waging an aggressive war.[42]

Sovereignty and State-Sanctioned Racism

'The Minority Problem'

The narrow definition of atrocities on racial grounds (through connection to other crimes) was not only the product of the professional *savoir faire* shared by the War Department lawyers. The other side of the same coin was the considerable concern among American drafters with the issue of sovereignty; to make legal innovations acceptable and workable, they should not radically challenge this principle. By linking 'atrocities on racial, religious, political grounds' to a legal theory based on conspiracy and criminal organizations, Bernays attempted to solve another problem he termed 'the minority problem':

> Some of the worst outrages were committed by Axis powers against their own nationals on racial, religious, and political grounds. As to these, the offenders can plead justification under domestic law. Also, to call these atrocities war crimes would set the precedent of an international right to sit in judgement on the conduct of the several states toward their own nationals. This would open the door to incalculable consequences and present grave questions of policy.[43]

In an earlier memorandum to President Roosevelt (9 September 1944), Stimson sought to refute the Morgenthau Plan in its various aspects, while admitting 'great difficulty' in finding a legal basis to:

> Try and convict those responsible for excesses committed within Germany both before and during the war which have no relation to the conduct of the war. I would be prepared to construe broadly what constituted a violation of the Rules of War but there is a certain field in which I fear that external courts cannot move. Such courts would be without jurisdiction to try those who were guilty of, or condoned, lynching in our country.[44]

This challenge was difficult to solve without a conceptual framework that would enable atrocities to be linked to the Nazi project of world domination. This may explain why until September 1944, those in charge of war crimes policies, not only in the State Department but also in the War Department, were very reluctant to expand the traditional definition of the rules of warfare. Bernays admitted this himself after changing his mind on the issue during the summer of 1944.[45]

Surprisingly, according to Bernays, one of the earliest supporters of his plan was Green Hackworth,[46] who served as long-running Legal Adviser of the State Department (1925–46) and later as Judge of the International Court of Justice (1946–61). However, his support was far from evident. Hackworth was, by his duties, particularly sensitive to issues of sovereignty. During the war, he worked actively if not to neutralize the international commitments to human rights made by the US government, then at least to limit their effects.[47] Furthermore, he consistently opposed initiatives by the American representative to the UNWCC to expand the definition of war crimes beyond its traditional boundaries.[48] Two contextual points are worth underlining here. On the one hand, Bernays mentioned that he met Hackworth at the time of the Dumbarton Oaks Conference,[49] where he told him about his conspiracy plan. As a key member of the American delegation to this Conference, Hackworth helped carefully circumvent colonial and racial questions through nonbinding commitments on human rights.[50] On the other hand, and at the very same time, he was urged (by Herbert Pell, the officials of the War Refugee Board, and Stephen Wise, head of the American Jewish Congress)[51] to take a stand on Nazi crimes against the European Jews: these figures openly raised the question of whether the American authorities contemplated punishment for atrocities on racial grounds. One can assume that Hackworth was seeking a solution to reconcile conflicting aims (i.e. not leaving unpunished mass crimes committed by the Nazis while preserving the sovereign interests of the United States). This adjustment is precisely what the Bernays Plan provided. Hackworth was probably not entirely satisfied with the inclusion of prewar atrocities in the conspiracy plan, as evidenced by a draft memorandum he wrote for Assistant Secretary of War John McCloy in November 1944.[52] Nevertheless, he did not send this document, refusing to inform McCloy of his reservations. I hypothesize that from Hackworth's point of view, human rights and international criminal law similarly challenged sovereignty; rather than frontally objecting to the new principles claimed by his government, he deemed it wiser to neutralize them.

Undoubtedly Bernays showed 'creativity' as he himself said, but one should not misunderstand the meaning of his project: he found an astute way of punishing the perpetrators of atrocities on racial grounds against Axis nationals without creating a new universalizable category. Given his consummate sense of 'neutralizing' international law, this could only seduce Green Hackworth, not to mention John McCloy and Henry Stimson.

Imperial, Colonial and Racial Constraints

To sum up, Hackworth perfectly embodied the self-restraint of the government lawyers examined at the beginning of this chapter, a self-restraint that was partly conscious (in the case of sovereignty) and partly internalized (for its racial implications). These two inter-twined dimensions can be seen in the criticisms that Bernays' plan received from the Administration in general and the War Department specifically. Indeed, another set of concerns may help to explain the reservations about the inclusion of atrocities on racial grounds in the charges to be brought against Nazi leaders, especially when these crimes were not obviously connected to the war: the fear of shaping a universal legal tool that would likely pave the way for international scrutiny of the American racial unequal order.

Few legal experts involved with war crimes policies verbalized or made the point explicit. William Chanler, another imaginative War Department lawyer who advocated the prosecution of Nazis for aggressive war, belonged to this group. Indeed, nearly two months after Bernays formulated his plan, Chanler criticized it as follows:

> Aren't we inviting objections from every one of a nationalistic turn of mind, including many who are not at all isolationists, on the basis that we would be establishing a precedent that, for example, lynching or Jim Crow Laws are matters of international concern? Perhaps it would be a very good thing if they were, but I doubt if we would get very far suggesting it at present, and I fear that this proposal would raise that issue and might cause unnecessary opposition to the whole plan. The British, of course, would have similar objections concerning their colonies and so no doubt would the French, Belgians and Dutch.[53]

Interestingly, in his reply Bernays stated that the objection was irrel-evant, for 'the basic paper' – as he called his original memorandum – had expressly anticipated this criticism in the aforementioned pas-sage on the 'minority problem'. Here is one additional indication of a self-restrained legal innovation through the conscious neutralization of its potential domestic effects.[54] Furthermore, Chanler's observation about the possible objections of European powers is entirely relevant when one considers, for example, the positions taken by the British representatives concerning colonial issues in the subsequent San Francisco Conference.[55]

During the negotiations of the IMT Charter at the London Conference (26 June–2 August 1945), Jackson himself stated without ambiguity to his British, French and Russian counterparts that 'the way Germany treats its inhabitants, or any other country treats its inhabitants, is not our affair any more than it is the affair of some other government to interpose itself in our problems'.[56] He then added:

> We have some regrettable circumstances at times in our own country in which minorities are unfairly treated. We think it is justifiable that we interfere or attempt to bring retribution to individuals or states only because the concentration camps and the deportations were in pursuance of a common plan or enterprise of making an unjust or illegal war in which we became involved. We see no other basis on which we are justified in reaching the atrocities which were committed inside Germany, under German law, or even in violation of German law, by authorities of the German state. Without substantially [sic!] this definition, we would not think we had any part in the prosecution of those things.[57]

Ironically, the only representative to object was the French Professor André Gros, fearing that the link between atrocities and conspiracy (to wage aggressive war) would practically hinder future humanitarian interventions to protect minorities along the lines of those carried out in the nineteenth century.[58] Obviously Gros did not see the advantages of a narrow definition of persecutions and atrocities on racial grounds. Indeed, one might think that such a definition objectively served the colonial interests of his country, especially in Algeria, where an apart-heid-like system flourished. By referring to interventions of a colonial or at least imperial nature,[59] Gros conveyed the impression of being at odds with Jackson. In fact, his humanitarian concerns were not very far from the 'imperial internationalism' widely professed and internalized in parts of the Western field of power. Thus, during the San Francisco Conference, 'to [South-African] Field Marshal Smuts [who helped draft the human rights dispositions of the UN Charter], the term "civilization" meant imperial internationalism— clearly a whites-only proposition'.[60] Conversely, Jackson, who incidentally was later as a Supreme Court Justice involved in the famous civil rights case *Brown v Board of Education* that ruled high school segregation unconstitutional (1954),[61] showed himself aware of American contra-dictions: while lamenting, as Chanler did before him, 'some regrettable circumstances', he nevertheless placed national sovereignty over moral and political considerations.

In other cases, concerns about an overly broad legal definition of atrocities on racial grounds certainly reflected internalized racial structures. These concerns then met the specific fears of Southerners such as Jackson's assistant Sydney Alderman, who was personally committed to an unequal racial order or, alternatively, they met practical political considerations. For example, Secretary of War Stimson himself was acutely aware of the issue, for he regularly had to manage the problems raised by racial segregation in the military.[62] The same observation applies to Assistant Secretary John McCloy, who, as chairman of the 'Advisory Committee on Negro Troop Policy', was reluctant to put an end to discriminatory provisions in the US Army.[63]

Finally, the preceding analysis underlines what a 'workable' legal category either consciously or unconsciously meant. 'Workable' meant that the innovation should not threaten the sovereignty of the prosecuting powers. African-American publications often highlighted the 'irony' of a situation in which the US government was internationally advocating principles that were not domestically observed. For instance, on 29 September 1945, the *Pittsburgh Courier*, an African-American newspaper, headlined 'What Irony! U. S. Signs Agreement [under which] 'Racial Persecutions' [are] A Crime Against International Society'.[64]

However, civil rights lawyers very rarely invoked the new principles of international law (such as 'crimes against humanity') in domestic court cases, where they unveiled and challenged entrenched racism, from lynching to segregation. Indeed, in a wide range of so-called 'test-cases' before the Supreme Court, they more often based their argumentation on international human rights than on international criminal law.[65] This choice was clearly illustrated by an early civil rights case, where three prominent National Association for the Advancement of Colored People (NAACP) lawyers, including Thurgood Marshall, successfully contested before the Supreme Court the racial segregation of passengers on interstate transport. Irene Morgan, an African-American woman, was found guilty in the first instance for having refused to change her seat on a Greyhound bus according to a Virginia segregation law. Concluding their brief for Irene Morgan, filed on 2 March 1946 – while the Nuremberg trial was still ongoing – Marshall and his colleagues stated:

> Today we are just emerging from a war in which all of the people of the United States were joined in a death struggle against the apostles of racism. We have already recognized by solemn subscription to the Charter of the United Nations, particularly Articles One and Fifty Five thereof, our duty, along with our neighbors, to eschew racism in our national life and to promote 'universal respect for, and observance of, human rights and

fundamental freedoms for all without distinction as to race, sex, language, or religion'.[66]

The Supreme Court Justices decided on 3 June 1946 in favour of Irene Morgan by a majority of seven to one. As soberly noted in the opinion, Jackson, on leave of the Court as Chief Prosecutor in Nuremberg, 'took no part in the consideration or decision of this case'.[67]

As evidenced by this and subsequent cases challenging segregation laws, human rights law appeared much more efficient than international criminal law to civil rights lawyers as well as to other African-American activists outside the courts.[68] While they regularly referred to the principles of the UN Charter agreed upon by the United States, they seldom mentioned the IMT Statute in their legal briefs submitted to the Supreme Court.[69] The main reason for this was that the definition of 'persecutions on political, racial or religious grounds' laid down in Article 6(c) was particularly 'locked in', i.e. limited in scope through connection to other war-related crimes. Furthermore, the IMT judges interpreted even more restrictively this nexus and the so-called successor Nuremberg trials, despite their broader legal basis, did not address the issue in a convergent way.[70] Ultimately, if Nuremberg was not a resource for civil rights activists and cause lawyers in multilevel mobilizations against statutory racism and segregation, it was also due to the patient (almost year-long) work of neutralizing the potential effects of a legal innovation: through limitation and subordination, persecutions on racial grounds, as finally included in the new category of 'crimes against humanity', could hardly be universalized.

Conclusion

As I have sought to demonstrate in this chapter, the restrictive definition of crimes against humanity in August 1945, a definition narrowed even further by the IMT judgment, was the result of a complicated drafting process in which professional and social factors played a much more significant role than is often admitted. First, the prewar experience of the legal practitioners involved in American war crimes policies and then in trial preparation was of primary importance. War Department legal experts resorted to their professional *savoir faire* when seeking to build a workable plan to try the Nazi leaders for their unprecedented crimes. The idea behind linking persecutions and atrocities on racial grounds (especially those committed by the

Axis Powers against their nationals) with a broad conspiracy charge was congruent with their previous praxis as elite lawyers acting on behalf of private companies or public bodies. Second, as we have seen, the subordination of atrocities to other, higher crimes could be explained by more substantial reasons: concerns about sovereignty often reflected the self-restraint of government lawyers or 'legists' having deeply internalized state rationales.[71] Here the service of the state accompanied the assimilation not only of the bureaucratic and legal rationality (as a means to achieving state ends), but also of the very reasons of the national state (as an end in itself), which objectively were – in this case at least – in open conflict with international (criminal) law. Third, these general concerns about national sovereignty could meet more specific ones: the fear that too broad a definition of atrocities on racial grounds might result in international scrutiny of domestic discriminatory practices. Few legal experts and officials of the US government – Stimson, Chanler and Jackson – expressed this fear explicitly in the course of the intra-administrative and later diplomatic drafting process leading to the creation of the IMT. None did so publicly, except for Jackson insofar as he subsequently decided to publish a redacted verbatim of the London Conference, including his remarks on the Jim Crow laws and lynchings as 'regrettable circumstances'. However, it is reasonable to assume that these considerations were shared – although not verbalized – by other legal experts. In this sense, the internalization of racial structures by (white) actors also helped to narrow the definition of persecutions and atrocities on racial grounds.

Certainly, for colonial and imperial reasons, the British and French, not to mention the Russians, should have known what a 'workable' category implied, but positions cannot be reduced to national interests reconstructed retrospectively. In fact, it is not clear whether they understood each other, as evidenced by the reservations expressed by André Gros on the American plan linking atrocities to conspiracy and aggressive war.

Other factors also played a role in the year-long drafting process of 'crimes against humanity', such as the acute struggles of professional jurisdictions within the Federal Administration, the effective advocacy of nongovernmental organizations or the more or less distant personal and familial relationships that legal experts maintained with Central and Eastern Europe.[72] This aspect would play a more significant role during the trial itself, given the significant portion of Jewish-German exiled lawyers within the American team.

In conclusion, the analysis outlined in this chapter may enable us to reflect on the significant discrepancies between Nuremberg and longer-term processes. First, it illuminates the partial disconnection between Nuremberg and the history of international law,[73] insofar as with some notable exceptions (such as Hersch Lauterpacht) very few actors involved in the trial and its preparation participated in the development of international law before, during and after the war. Those professors of law and jurisconsults who became judges of the International Court of Justice after 1945 were either reluctant towards innovation during the conflict (Arnold McNair and Green Hackworth) or played a minor role in the definition of crimes (André Gros). Second, the proposed analyses may also prove useful to understanding why Nuremberg was largely disconnected from the history of human rights, their universalization and their juridification.[74] As we have seen, the narrow definition of persecutions on racial grounds prevented the universalization of crimes against humanity and its use as a legal tool by civil rights lawyers, who deemed it more useful to invoke human rights in court cases challenging racial segregation. Third, examination of this controlled, self-restrained innovation, which proved scarcely universalizable, sheds light on the unique position the Nuremberg moment holds in the history of the American relationship with international criminal justice in the twentieth century. It is known that before and after Nuremberg, the US government opposed war crimes trials as well as the creation of an international criminal court. This was the case in the aftermath of the First World War and then again from the late 1940s until the present day.

Guillaume Mouralis is a research professor (Directeur de recherche) in history and sociology at the National Center for Scientific Research (CNRS, France). He is member of the Institut des sciences sociales du politique (Nanterre) and is associated with the Centre Marc Bloch (Berlin). His research interests include the recent history of Germany, the history and sociology of law, postwar justice, purges and mass crimes trials.

His most recent publication is *Le moment Nuremberg. Le procès international, les lawyers et la question raciale* (Presses de Sciences Po, 2019). His other publications include *Une épuration allemande. La RDA en procès, 1949–2004* (Paris: Fayard, 2008); *Dealing with Wars and Dictatorships. Legal Concepts and Categories in Action* (Springer/ Asser Press, 2014, coedited with L. Israël); and 'The Nuremberg Trials: New Perspectives on the Professions', special issue of *Comparativ* (26(4), 2017, (coedited with M.-B. Vincent).

Notes

1. This chapter presents some of the analyses developed in more detail in Mouralis, *Le moment Nuremberg*.
2. On the American war crimes policy, see in particular Smith, *The Road to Nuremberg*; Kochavi, *Prelude to Nuremberg*, 138–71; Cox, 'What Irony!', 301–472.
3. During the drafting process, the terms most often used were 'atrocities' (more rarely 'persecutions'), usually followed by the complement 'on political, religious or racial grounds'. They are subject of the second part of Article 6(c) of the IMT Charter ('persecutions on political, racial, or religious grounds in execution of or in connection with any crime within the jurisdiction of the Tribunal').
4. The accessory nature of the crime against humanity as a whole was strengthened by a later typographical revision of the Charter: through the replacement of a semicolon by a comma, the first part of the definition laid down by Article 6(c) ('murder, extermination, enslavement, deportation, and other inhumane acts...') was also subordinated to the other crimes 'within the jurisdiction of the Tribunal'.
5. Jackson, *Report of Robert H. Jackson*, 361.
6. Robinson, 'The Nuremberg Judgment', 6–8; Robinson, 'The International Military Tribunal and the Holocaust', 12–13.
7. 'Ainsi, la catégorie des crimes contre l'humanité, que le statut avait fait entrer par une très petite porte, s'est, du fait du jugement, volatilisée': Donnedieu de Vabres, *Le procès de Nuremberg devant les principes modernes du droit pénal international*, 526–27.
8. I use this term by analogy with Norbert Elias' analyses in the *Process of Civilization*.
9. See, for example, Du Bois, 'The Future of Africa in America', 183 ('With all our tumult and shouting and pious rage against Hitler, we are perfectly aware that his race philosophy and methods are but extreme development and application of our own save that he is drawing his race lines in somewhat different places'); Jack, 'On Nuremberg Laws in America', 289.
10. See e.g. Lerner, 'Nuremberg and the Dream of Law', 4.
11. On this notion, see Haas, 'Introduction', 1–35.
12. On the concept of 'field of power' elaborated by Pierre Bourdieu, see Denord, Lagneau-Ymonet and Thine, 'Le champ du pouvoir en France', 24–57.
13. The activists fighting for humanitarian causes generally did not use 'crime against humanity' as a legal concept with a precise definition. Concerning early attempts to define the notion in international law, see, for example, Holquist, 'The Russian Empire as a "Civilized State"'; Segesser, 'Die historischen Wurzeln des Begriffs, Verbrechen gegen die Menschlichkeit', 75–101.
14. Horne and Kramer, *German Atrocities, 1914*, 1–6. The authors consider 'atrocities' both as violations of the laws of war and as the construction of a meaning by the Allies.
15. Ibid., 410–18.
16. Even if it has long been neglected by the literature; see Plesch and Sattler, 'Before Nuremberg', 437–73.
17. Resolution moved by Mr Pell on 16 March 1944, United Nation War Crimes Commission, Committee II, United Nations Archives, Predecessor Archives Group, UN-WCC 1943–49, https://www.legal-tools.org.
18. Mouralis, 'Nuremberg, 1945', 215–19.
19. Wyman, *The Abandonment of the Jews*, 235, 294–95; Bird, *The Chairman*, 201–27.
20. Memorandum. Subject: Trial of European War Criminals (by Colonel Murray C. Bernays, G-1), 15 September 1944, reproduced in Smith, *The American Road to Nuremberg*, 33–37.

21. Bernays, *The National Cyclopaedia of American Biography,* 604–5; Conot, *Justice at Nuremberg,* 10–26.
22. Horne and Kramer, *German Atrocities, 1914,* 249–61.
23. See, for example, the case *Irving Trust Company v Deutsch,* 73 F.2d 121 (1934), Circuit Court of Appeals, Second Circuit. 17 September 1934 (rehearing denied 30 October 1934).
24. Bernays attached to his original memorandum of 15 September 1944 a 'statement on war criminals' submitted by the American Jewish Conference to the Secretary of State on 25 August, urging the US government to guarantee the severe punishment of authors of atrocities against European Jews regardless of their citizenship. See Smith, *The American Road,* 6 and 227 (note).
25. Smith, *Reaching Judgment at Nuremberg,* 26–27.
26. Within the Association of the Bar of the City of New York (1948), see *American Bar Association Journal* 34, p. 23 and *New York Times,* 9 March 1949, 4.
27. Henry L. Stimson's diary, 24 October 1944, in August–October 1944, Yale University Library, p. 180.
28. Stimson and Bundy, *On Active Services in Peace and War,* 3–14 and, on his support to the conspiracy theory during the war, 586–88.
29. Ibid., 11.
30. Abbott, *The System of Professions,* 2.
31. Silber and Miller, 'Toward "Neutral Principles" in the Law', 894.
32. One can assume that Robinson was informed of the Bernays plan. While he highlighted a Nazi conspiracy to achieve world domination, this notion did not fulfil the same function in both plans (Bernays conceived persecutions and atrocities as accompanying crimes to this conspiracy, whereas for Robinson, the planned destruction of the European Jews was its central feature). See Lewis, *The Birth of the New Justice,* 164.
33. Jackson, *Report of Robert H. Jackson,* 333. The connection between atrocities and common plan to wage aggressive war appeared for the first time in a draft definition of crimes submitted by the American delegation on 25 July 1944; see ibid., 374.
34. According to the classic distinction of the legal realists (first suggested by Roscoe Pound in 1910) that they seemed to have been uncritically accepted.
35. Letter to Louise (Easton) Bernays, 10 June 1945, Box 1, Correspondence, in: Murray C. Bernays papers, American Heritage Center, University of Wyoming (Laramie), p. 2 (scanned copies ordered through Molly Marcusse, January 2016).
36. McCarten, 'The Man behind the Gavel', 4.
37. In the sense that Max Weber uses this term, as opposed to mere intuition (working through identification): *Economy and Society: An Outline of Interpretive Sociology.*
38. Letter to Louise (Easton) Bernays, 10 June 1945, Box 1, Correspondence, in: Murray C. Bernays papers, American Heritage Center, University of Wyoming (Laramie), p. 5. In addition, Bernays papers contained excerpts from several important publications on war crimes (by Hersch Lauterpacht or Aaron Trainin).
39. The Reminiscences of Sidney Alderman, Oral History Research Office, Columbia University, 1955, p. 808.
40. Diary kept by Robert H. Jackson, 10 May 1945 (Robert H. Jackson Papers, Library of Congress, Reel 95).
41. Shamir, *Managing Legal Uncertainty,* 93–112.
42. Bush, '"The Supreme ... Crime" and Its Origins', 2363.
43. Memorandum. Subject: Trial of European war criminals (by Colonel Murray C. Bernays, G-1), 15 September 1944, reproduced in Smith, *The American Road to Nuremberg,* 33–37 (at 34).

44. Stimson, H.L. (1944, September 9). Memorandum for the President. (6 p.), p. 3, in: Morgenthau Presidential Diaries, pp. 1437–42, FDR Presidential Library & Museum.
45. Letter to Louise (Easton) Bernays, 10 June 1945, Box 1, Correspondence, in: Murray C. Bernays papers, American Heritage Center, University of Wyoming (Laramie), p. 3.
46. The State Department official 'was so enthusiastic over my plan that he wanted to arrange immediately for him and me to lunch with Sir William Malkin'; ibid.
47. He was actively involved in the framing of the international bill of rights arising from the Atlantic Charter: see Brucken, *A Most Uncertain Crusade*, 29–38.
48. Blayney, 'Herbert Pell', 335–52; Cox, 'Seeking Justice for the Holocaust', 77–110.
49. He later wrote 'at the end of [the] Dumbarton Oaks [Conference]' (the first phase of which ended on 28 September), but the discussion most likely took place earlier, in the beginning of September, before the completion of Bernays' original memorandum.
50. On the sidelining of human rights issues during the Dumbarton Oaks talks, see Borgwardt, 'Race, Rights, and Nongovernmental Organizations', 190–193.
51. Letter from Rabbi Wise to Assistant Secretary of State, 1 September 1944 and draft reply prepared by Mr Hackworth (furnished by Lt. Colonel Bernays), in National Archives at College Park (Maryland), RG 107, Entry 180, Box 1.
52. Cox, 'What Irony!', 360–61.
53. William C. Chanler, memorandum to John J. McCloy, 1 December 1944, National Archives at College Park (Maryland), RG 107, Entry 180, box 3, p. 1.
54. Murray C. Bernays, memorandum for John J. McCloy, 1 December 1944, National Archives at College Park (Maryland), RG 107, Entry 180, box 3, p. 1
55. Sherwood, '"There is No New Deal for the Blackman in San Francisco"', 91.
56. Jackson, *Report of Robert H. Jackson*, 331.
57. Ibid., 333.
58. Ibid., 361.
59. He most likely referred to the humanitarian interventions of the nineteenth century aimed at protecting the Christian minorities of the Ottoman Empire. For an overview, see Rodogno, *Against Massacre*, 18–35.
60. Borgwardt, 'Race, Rights, and Nongovernmental Organizations', 200.
61. Shimsky, 'Hesitating between Two Worlds', 207–19; and *Brown v Board of Education*, 427 et seq.
62. Cox, 'What Irony!', 107–59.
63. Taylor, *Freedom to Serve*, 28–34.
64. *Pittsburgh Courier*, 29 September 1945, p. 1, quoted by Cox, 'What Irony!', 466.
65. Mouralis, *Le moment Nuremberg*, 151–59.
66. Brief for Appellant, filed by William H. Hastie, Leon A. Ransom and Thurgood Marshall on 2 March 1946, in *Irene Morgan v Commonwealth of Virginia*, Supreme Court of the United States, p. 28.
67. *Morgan v Virginia*, 328 U.S. 373, 2 June 1946.
68. Von Eschen, *Race against Empire*, 78–84; Anderson, *Eyes off the Prize*, 58–112 (on African-American petitions to the United Nations).
69. For example, in a series of Supreme Court cases challenging racial covenants on real estate (1948–50).
70. Heller, *The Nuremberg Military Tribunals*, 231–50.
71. Bourdieu, 'Esprits d'État', 61.
72. Unlike other experts such as William C. Chanler, Murray C. Bernays was born in Lithuania and maintained relations to his family, especially the mother's side, who was Jewish. He presumably lost several members of his family in the Holocaust.

73. On this history, see, for example, Koskenniemi, *The Gentle Civilizer of Nations*.
74. Borgwardt, *A New Deal for the World*, 196–249; Moyn, *The Last Utopia*, 82.

Bibliography

Published Sources

Abbott, Andrew. *The System of Professions: An Essay on the Division of Expert Labor*. Chicago: University of Chicago Press, 2009 [1988].

Anderson, Carol. *Eyes off the Prize: The United Nations and the African American Struggle for Human Rights, 1944–1955*. Cambridge: Cambridge University Press, 2009.

Bird, Kai. *The Chairman: John J. McCloy. The Making of the American Establishment*. New York: Simon & Schuster, 1992.

Blayney, Michael S. 'Herbert Pell: War Crimes and the Jews'. *American Jewish Historical Quarterly* 65(4) (1976), 335–52.

Borgwardt, Elizabeth. *A New Deal for the World: America's Vision for Human Rights*. Cambridge, MA: Harvard University Press, 2005.

———. 'Race, Rights, and Nongovernmental Organizations at the UN San Francisco Conference: A Contested History of "Human Rights … without Discrimination", in Kevin Kruse and Stephen Tuck (eds), *Fog of War: The Second World War and the Civil Rights Movement* (Oxford: Oxford University Press, 2012), 188–207.

Bourdieu, Pierre. 'Esprits d'État. Genèse et structure du champ bureaucratique'. *Actes de la recherche en sciences sociales* 96(1) (1993), 49–62.

Brucken, Rowland. *A Most Uncertain Crusade: The United States, the United Nations, and Human Rights, 1941–1953*. DeKalb: Northern Illinois University Press, 2013.

Bush, Jonathan A. 'Essay: "The Supreme … Crime" and Its Origins: The Lost Legislative History of the Crime of Aggressive War'. *Columbia Law Review* 102(8) (2002), 2324–424.

Conot, Robert E. *Justice at Nuremberg: The First Comprehensive, Dramatic Account of the Trial of the Leaders*. New York: Carroll & Graf, 1983.

Cox, Graham. 'What Irony! Herbert C. Pell, Crimes against Humanity, and the Negro Problem'. Ph.D. dissertation. Houston: University of Houston, 2008.

———. 'Seeking Justice for the Holocaust: Herbert C. Pell versus the US State Department'. *Criminal Law Forum* 25(1–2) (2014), 77–110.

Denord, François, Paul Lagneau-Ymonet and Sylvain Thine. 'Le champ du pouvoir en France'. *Actes de la recherche en sciences sociales* 190(5) (2011), 24–57.

Donnedieu de Vabres, Henri. *Le procès de Nuremberg devant les principes modernes du droit pénal international*. Leiden and Boston: Brill and Nijhoff, 1947, 526–27.

Du Bois, William Edward Burghardt. 'The Future of Africa in America' (April 1942), in H. Aptheker (ed.), *Against Racism: Unpublished Essays, Papers, Addresses, 1887–1961* (Amherst: University of Massachusetts Press, 1985), 173–83.

Haas, Peter M. 'Introduction: Epistemic Communities and International Policy Coordination'. *International Organization* 46(1) (1992), 1–35.

Heller, Kevin Jon. *The Nuremberg Military Tribunals and the Origins of International Criminal Law*. Oxford: Oxford University Press, 2011.

Holquist, Peter. *The Russian Empire as a 'Civilized State': International Law as Principle and Practice in Imperial Russia, 1874–1878*. Washington DC: National Council for Eurasian and East European Research, 2004.

Horne, John, and Alan Kramer. *German Atrocities, 1914: A History of Denial*. New Haven: Yale University Press, 2001.

Jack, Homer A. 'On Nuremberg Laws in America'. *A Monthly Summary of Events and Trends in Race Relation* 3 (1946), 289.

Jackson, Robert H. *Report of Robert H. Jackson, United States Representative to the International Conference on Military Trials, London, 1945: A Documentary Record*. Washington DC: Division of Publications, Office of Public Affairs, 1949.

Kochavi, Arieh J. *Prelude to Nuremberg: Allied War Crimes Policy and the Question of Punishment*. Chapel Hill: University of North Carolina Press, 1998.

Koskenniemi, Martti. *The Gentle Civilizer of Nations: The Rise and Fall of International Law 1870–1960*. Cambridge: Cambridge University Press, 2002.

Lerner, M. 'Nuremberg and the Dream of Law'. *St Petersburg Times*, 29 November 1945.

Lewis, Mark. *The Birth of the New Justice: The Internationalization of Crime and Punishment, 1919–1950*. Oxford: Oxford University Press, 2014.

McCarten, John. 'The Man behind the Gavel [interview with Murray C. Bernays]'. *The New Yorker*, 17 November 1945.

Mennel, Stephen, Eric Dunning, Johan Goudsblom and Richard Kilminster (eds). *On the Process of Civilization: Sociogenetic and Psychogenetic Investigations. Collected Works of Norbert Elias*: Volume 3. Trans. Edmund Jephcott (Dublin: University College Dublin Press, 2012 [1939]).

Mouralis, Guillaume. 'Nuremberg, 1945. L'engouement tardif des professeurs pour la justice pénale internationale', in Sandrine Lefranc and Guillaume Mouralis (eds), *De quel(s) droit(s) la justice internationale est-elle faite? Deux moments de la constitution hésitante d'une justice de l'après-conflit. Socio* 3 (2014), 215–19.

———. *Le moment Nuremberg. Le procès international, les lawyers et la question raciale.* Paris: Presses de Sciences Po, 2019.

Moyn, Samuel. *The Last Utopia: Human Rights in History*. Cambridge, MA: Harvard University Press, 2010.

Plesch, Dan, and Shanti Sattler. 'Before Nuremberg: Considering the Work of the United Nations War Crimes Commission of 1943–1948', in Morten Bergsmo, Wui Ling Cheah and Ping Yi (eds), *Historical Origins of International Criminal Law: Volume 1* (Brussels: Torkel Opsahl Academic E-Publisher, 2014), 437–73.

Robinson, Jacob. 'The Nuremberg Judgment'. *Congress Weekly: A Review of Jewish Interests* 13(1946), 6–8.

———. 'The International Military Tribunal and the Holocaust: Some Legal Reflections'. *Israel Law Review* 7(1) (1972), 1–13.

Rodogno, Davide. *Against Massacre: Humanitarian Interventions in the Ottoman Empire, 1815–1914*. Princeton: Princeton University Press, 2011.

Segesser, Daniel Marc. 'Die historischen Wurzeln des Begriffs, Verbrechen gegen die Menschlichkeit'. *Jahrbuch der Juristischen Zeitgeschichte* 8 (2007), 75–101.

Shamir, Ronen. *Managing Legal Uncertainty: Elite Lawyers in the New Deal*. Durham, NC: Duke University Press, 1995.

Sherwood, Marika. '"There is No New Deal for the Blackman in San Francisco": African Attempts to Influence the Founding Conference of the United Nations, April–July, 1945'. *International Journal of African Historical Studies* 29(1) (1996), 71–94.

Shimsky, S. 'Hesitating between two Worlds: The Civil Rights Odyssey of Robert H. Jackson'. Ph.D. dissertation. New York: City University of New York, 2007.

Silber, Norman I. and Geoffrey Miller. 'Toward "Neutral Principles" in the Law: Selections from the Oral History of Herbert Wechsler'. *Columbia Law Review* 93(4) (1993), 894–900.

Smith, Bradley F. *Reaching Judgment at Nuremberg*. New York: Basic Books, 1977.

———. *The Road to Nuremberg*. New York: Basic Books, 1981.

————. *The American Road to Nuremberg: Documentary Record 1944–1945*. Stanford: Hoover Institution Press, 1982.

Stimson, Henry L., and McGeorge Bundy. *On Active Services in Peace and War*. New York: Harper & Brothers, 1947.

Taylor, Jon. *Freedom to Serve: Truman, Civil Rights, and Executive Order 9981*. New York: Routledge, 2013.

Von Eschen, Penny M. *Race against Empire: Black Americans and Anticolonialism, 1937–1957*. Ithaca, NY: Cornell University Press, 1997.

Weber, Max. *Economy and Society: An Outline of Interpretive Sociology*. Berkeley: University of Carolina Press, 1978 [1921].

White, James T. 'Bernays, Murray C.', in *The National Cyclopaedia of American Biography* (New York: J.T. White, 1973), 604–5.

Wyman, David S. *The Abandonment of the Jews: America and the Holocaust, 1941–1945*. New York: Pantheon Books, 1984.

Archival Sources

Circuit Court of Appeals, Second Circuit, *Irving Trust Company v. Deutsch*, 73 F.2d 121 (1934), 17 September 1934.

Columbia University, Oral History Research Office, The Reminiscences of Sidney Alderman.

FDR Presidential Library & Museum, Morgenthau Presidential Diaries.

Library of Congress, Robert H. Jackson's diary.

National Archives at College Park (Maryland), RG 107, Entry 180, box 1; box 3.

Supreme Court of the United States, *Irene Morgan v. Commonwealth of Virginia*. 328 U.S. 373 (1946).

United Nations Archives, Predecessor Archives Group, UNWCC 1943–1949, Committee II. https://www.legal-tools.org.

University of Wyoming (Laramie), American Heritage Center, Murray C. Bernays papers.

Yale University Library, Henry L. Stimson's diary.

Chapter 6

Filling the Legal Void
Jewish Victims, German Offenders and Belgian Judges, 1942–52

Marie-Anne Weisers

Introduction

The prosecutions of German war criminals in Belgium were conducted over a rather short period of time: from 1948 to 1952. Overall, they have been considered a failure by a number of observers, as the outcomes of the convictions did not match the initial ambitions of 1944–45.[1] Over 4,400 individuals were placed on the lists of the Belgian War Crimes Commission, many of whom were never found. Of the 533 Germans who were extradited, only 103 were tried in 35 trials.[2] As far as convictions are concerned, sentences were often harsh at the initial trial and reduced after appeal. In 1951, during the Cold War period, most of the convicts were freed and sent back to Germany.

We could stop here and only take into account the legal classifications and final penalties ordered by the courts, as is often the case. That was precisely the conclusion a Belgian newspaper recently presented in an article devoted to the seventieth anniversary of the

Nuremberg trial and its consequences in Belgium. The article, entitled
'The Soft Punishment of German War Criminals in Belgium', reflected
the common opinion that the outcomes of the postwar trials conducted
in Belgium were disappointing.[3] The way in which the Belgian judiciary operated in the wake of the Second World War, specifically in
relation to the genocide of the Jews, has been negatively portrayed for
decades. It is said that Belgian courts turned a blind eye to how the
German occupation treated the country's Jewish population, failing to
sanction those who participated in the persecution, deportation and
extermination of 25,500 of them.

However, analysis of the Belgian court records offers a very different interpretation.[4] While the final results can indeed be deemed
disappointing, a careful reading of the documents sheds light on the
reasons for this negative legacy and reveals the true will some magistrates exhibited in trying to convict the former German occupiers for
the racial policy they enforced.

The Origins of a Frustrating Legal Response

Four key reasons account for why the conclusions of the Belgian judicial responses to the crimes committed against the Jews have been
judged harshly, two attributable to the Allies and two to the Belgian
authorities. The first reason lies in the national implementation process of the Moscow Declaration, which took place at the end of October
1943 during the Moscow Conference between the foreign secretaries of
the United Kingdom, the United States and the Soviet Union, and that
formalized the priority principle by which national courts would have
sole jurisdiction to try war criminals. Indeed, the final Declaration on
Atrocities stated that 'those German officers and men and members
of the Nazi party who have been responsible for or have taken a
consenting part in the above atrocities, massacres and executions will
be sent back to the countries in which their abominable deeds were
done in order that they may be judged and punished according to
the laws of these liberated countries and of free governments which
will be erected therein'.[5] Those whose crimes could not be precisely
located in one place and who held the greatest responsibility would be
subject to a later decision. However, the Allies did not set up any plan
or policy to tackle the complex issue of aligning national legal norms
with international legal norms. The second reason is that the Belgian
government in exile in London focused on preparing to punish collaboration, while leaving the punishment of war crimes undiscussed.

Third, after the war, the Belgian government and Parliament devised a poorly conceived law that was unable to sanction the atrocities committed by the occupiers. Finally, a fourth reason behind the failure can be linked to the fact that in 1948, the United Kingdom and the United States decided to stop extraditing German war criminals.[6] This put an end to any hope of judging men like Kurt Asche or Fritz Erdmann, who headed the Jewish section of the Geheime Staatspolizei (Gestapo) in Brussels, which was responsible for the deportation of more than 25,000 Jews in Belgium.

The main obstacle when trying war criminals is the principle of the non-retroactvity of the law, which means that for an act to be sanctioned, its punishment must be found in the law before it is committed. However, when the war began, national criminal laws were incomplete; the execution of hostages, compulsory labour, persecutions, deportation and extermination were crimes of international concern that were not covered by the national penal codes. Each government in exile in London had to make choices about the legal measures to be implemented. The Belgian government primarily focused on punishing collaboration.[7] As far as war crimes were concerned, only two legislative measures were taken by Hubert Pierlot's government: the Decree-Law of 29 April 1943 concerning the interruption of the limitation period during the occupation and the Decree-Law of 5 August 1943 concerning the jurisdiction of courts outside of Belgian territory. Aside from these two procedural provisions, no article of the Belgian Criminal Code was to be amended in order to facilitate the trials of German war criminals as effectively as possible.[8] Indeed, only laws of jurisdiction and procedure could be retroactive. The Belgian authorities wrongly assumed that the Penal Code was entirely adequate.

After the war, in June 1947, Belgium passed a law on war crimes that assigned competence over these matters to military courts. The authors of the text were thus obligated to negotiate the problem of the nonretroactivity of the laws. They thought they had found a solution when adding that the act committed needed to be both a violation of the laws and customs of war (as set out in The Hague Convention of 1907) and a breach of the Belgian Criminal Code. As a result, the law of 1947 did not create any new offence. However, The Hague Convention only specifies that the occupier must respect the governing laws of the country and religious convictions and practice, but no article covers the execution of hostages, persecutions or deportations. In addition, although Belgium signed the London Charter of Nuremberg in which Article 6 covers crimes against peace, war crimes and crimes against humanity, its Parliament did not pass a law of content to incorporate

it into Belgian domestic law. Therefore, Belgian magistrates had to
prosecute war criminals using legal tools that were unfit to condemn
the acts committed during the German occupation. Both national and
international applicable legislations were thus incomplete and failed
to match the nature or the new scope of the crimes.

The Measures Taken by the Magistrates

The magistrates' actions can be split into two phases: first at the
implementation level of the prosecution policy and then during the
trials.

Three months after the publication of the law, Walter Ganshof
van der Meersch, the Judge Advocate General and Head of Military
Justice, sent a circular to all military courts in the country.[9] This
crucial document indicated how he intended to prosecute German war
criminals, above all regarding the persecutions against the Jews. He
considered that only articles of the Criminal Code related to threats to
the external security of the state and in particular Article 118bis could
fairly condemn crimes of that nature:[10]

> We should not hide the fact that only the application of these articles will
> effectively punish the acts of those who have executed or personally partici-
> pated in the general policy of the Occupier in one of its following criminal
> aspects: racial persecutions, deportation policies, barbaric and inhuman
> investigation methods, economic pillaging, etc. This general criminal policy
> against the laws and customs of war has provoked, as a direct consequence,
> the death of thousands of Belgians or foreigners living in Belgium. If we
> could not resort to articles with a general scope such as article 118bis of
> the Criminal Code, those responsible for this policy would not be reached
> because of the current non-existence of an international law that would
> sanction such crimes integrated into internal Belgian criminal law. Such
> consequence would outrage the opinion and the requirements of morality
> and justice.[11]

At the time, the general definition of Article 118bis sentenced to death
those who had committed acts affecting the external security of the
state. However, the terms used as well as the preparatory work behind
the article underlined how in the legislator's mind, it primarily targeted treason, which involved an act committed by a Belgian citizen
against the Belgian state rather than concerning foreign enemies.
At no point did the Belgian government in exile in London or the
legislator in the course of the adoption of the law of 1947 propose an
amendment to address this shortcoming, even if merely by adding a

phrase to render Article 118bis applicable to foreign enemies, as the Luxembourgish legislator did in the law of 2 August 1947.[12]

The archives of the Auditorat Général (the General Military Prosecutor's office), which was in charge of prosecuting German war criminals, reveal a debate within the Auditorat regarding the difficulties of applying the new law. Some magistrates were opposed to the application of Article 118bis as it had been recommended by the Judge Advocate General and they sensed a risk of future failure.[13] Nevertheless, this did not prevent them from testing the available legal tools and to make different attempts to apply them.

On 20 August 1948, a huge joint trial against twenty-one members of the Sicherheitspolizei-Sicherheitsdienst (Security Police and Security Service (SIPO-SD)) in Charleroi was held before the Military Tribunal of Charleroi. Among those members was the head of the local Jewish section, Heinrich Knappkotter. The court decided to follow the public prosecutor and most defendants were convicted under Article 118bis. The judges used this article to sanction enhanced interrogation techniques, security arrest in concentration camps and Jewish persecution. However, on appeal, the Military Court of Appeal of Brussels partially amended the judgment. According to the Court of Appeal, the preparatory work of Article 118bis (drawn up in 1917) indicated that the legislator of the time had intended to sanction political collaboration with the enemy, that is, crimes committed by Belgians. Moreover, Article 118bis was not amended by the law of 20 June 1947.[14] One year later, in July 1949, the Cour de cassation (Supreme Court) definitively closed the debate by refusing to follow Ganshof van der Meersch and confirming the arguments of the Cour militaire de Bruxelles (Military Court of Appeal) by adjudging that Article 118bis refers to treason, which is linked to a duty of loyalty to which an enemy alien is not bound:

> Whereas the idea of treason is characteristic of the offence of knowingly assisting the enemy to conduct his policy and to achieve purposes, repressed by Article 118bis of the Code; whereas treason implies a breach of the duty of loyalty to the State, and cannot therefore exist on the part of an enemy national only if he has contracted such a duty towards Belgium.[15]

From that date, the magistrates in charge of the prosecutions within the Auditorat Général were obligated to identify grave and precise facts to support the charges against the German defendants – a difficult task. There were very few survivors, some were living abroad, and few of them reported to the judiciary, being busy rebuilding their lives.

It was in this context that five months later, in December 1949, the Siegburg case began. Analysis of this case sheds light on the substantial involvement of the investigating magistrate as well as on the attempts of the judges to create a precedent and punish German war criminals for the specifically racial character of Nazi policy implemented in the country during the occupation.

The defendant, Otto Siegburg, arrived in Brussels in early 1943 and was assigned to the Jewish section of the SIPO-SD in Brussels, where his main activity was to hunt Jews by travelling throughout the city, accompanied by a driver and an informer, a Jew in charge of locating and identifying other Jews. The people he arrested were immediately brought to the Gestapo headquarters. Some of them were beaten up. As soon as their number was sufficient, they were driven by truck to the assembly camp in Mechelen, from where they were deported, mainly to Auschwitz. The activities of this Jew-hunter operating on Belgian soil were thus part of the programme of the destruction of the Jews of Europe. The principal difficulty faced by the Belgian prosecutors was to find applicable legal articles under which they could prosecute former agents of the German occupation for crimes that had not been provided for by the Belgian Criminal Code. However, the possibilities were eventually limited to arbitrary arrest and detention, assault and battery, and murder; there were no articles in the Criminal Code condemning persecution, deportation or extermination.

Siegburg was extradited to Belgium in April 1947 by the British authorities. The investigation would then last for two and a half years. In the first two years, it was easily proven that the accused's main activity was to arrest Jews. This he admitted with no trouble, explaining that he did so because they did not respect German laws: they did not wear the Star of David, they lived illegally at a false address or they evaded compulsory labour. He claimed that he was doing his job as a police officer, obeying his superiors' orders. Jacques Warnant, the prosecutor in charge of the investigation, failed to find strong evidence proving Siegburg's involvement in murder. Warnant was therefore only able to prosecute him for arbitrary arrests and detentions, leading to a ludicrous penalty ranging from three months' to two years' imprisonment. Given that Siegburg had already been remanded in custody for two years, Warnant would have to free him, as also happened to many other war criminals. But in April 1949, suddenly a testimony dramatically changed the case. The witness account stated as follows: on the night of 11–12 June 1943, a Jew named Hillel Erner was arrested in Wemmel (a municipality of Brussels) at his clandestine address, where he was hiding under a false name. This man had lived off the black market and had amassed a small fortune. He was severely beaten by a SIPO-SD team composed of six individuals: four Flemish Belgian Schutzstaffel (SS) and two Germans. Three people, the Duvivier family (a mother, daughter and son) where Erner lived hidden, witnessed this event. Erner was subsequently put in the trunk of the car and taken to the Gestapo offices, where he was thrown in the cellars, where he would die an hour later. Another Jew, Menashe Brunner, was also present in this cellar. He had been arrested in the morning by Otto Siegburg and two Flemish SS members, taken to the headquarters of the SIPO-SD and beaten up. Both Erner and Brunner lived in Antwerp before the war, so they knew each other. Six years later, in April 1949, the investigating magistrate, Jacques Warnant, found Menashe Brunner. In one of his statements, Brunner explained to the magistrate that during the night of 11–12 June 1943, Siegburg, accompanied by two individuals, brought in a man in a very bad state, threw him in the cell and said to him: 'Look at what will happen to you.'[16]

This important statement was the new starting point of the Siegburg investigation after months of stagnation owing to a lack of strong and precise evidence. Brunner would help the prosecutor to identify Erner, as well as the location and the witnesses of his arrest. After numerous difficulties, the prosecutor would finally discover the address of the crime scene and therefore identify the Duvivier family who witnessed the events. Later, during the trial, the prosecutor would also find two other very important witnesses: two employees of a funeral services company used by the Gestapo to remove Erner's corpse. These two men testified that Siegburg was present in the cellar and that he had kicked the dead body while angrily insulting him in German.

When confronted with all these witnesses, Otto Siegburg systematically denied having seen any of these people. However, Brunner was able to recognize him because he had seen him several times; Siegburg was responsible for the transport convoy to Buchenwald, the camp where Menashe Brunner was deported from Mechelen. This was the only fact that Siegburg would admit during the trial, although he was not prosecuted for it by the War Council in Brussels.

The investigation was conducted by Jacques Warnant, who was also in charge of the cases involving SIPO-SD members in Brussels and the Mechelen transit camp. Warnant was born in 1915 in Great Britain. He was close to the Communist party when studying at the University of Brussels and moved to Spain after his graduation. He took part in the Battle of Belgium in May 1940; he was subsequently taken prisoner and sent to Germany, where he stayed until January 1941.

When he returned to Belgium, he participated in the distribution of clandestine communist newspapers and worked until late 1944 as a legal counsel in a mining company. In May 1945, he joined the General Military Prosecutor's office, where he worked in the central war crimes unit. He devoted his whole career to military justice.[17]

The documents available on Siegburg demonstrate Warnant's skills: he was an excellent investigator who battled to the end. Thanks to his hard work and perspicacity, he finally found the witnesses and presented material evidence to drag Siegburg before the War Council, unlike other defendants who were released due to a lack of evidence of a sufficiently serious crime.

The trial was held before the War Council in Brussels, which was made up of five people: two civil judges (Achille Maréchal and Joseph Dautricourt) and three servicemen. The two judges were also involved in other cases related to antisemitic persecutions: the trials of Max Boden (Deputy Chief at the Mechelen camp), Alexander von Falkenhausen and Eggert Reeder (who headed the German military administration) and Constantin Canaris (Head of the SIPO-SD in Belgium).

The presiding judge was Achille Maréchal. He was born in 1907, studied law at the University of Brussels and graduated in 1929. Three years later, he became a magistrate. When the war broke out, he was an examining judge for the Court of First Instance in Brussels and took part in the distribution from 1941 of a clandestine conservative and Catholic newspaper, *La Libre Belgique*. Late in 1944, he joined the General Military Prosecutor's office, and in 1947, he joined the bench, where he was appointed President of the War Council of Brussels in 1948. In 1951, he left the military justice department to pursue a career within the civil justice system. He had been involved throughout his life in social issues. From 1944 and for the next thirty years, he was President of the Public Assistance Commission in the Brussels district of Ixelles.[18]

Joseph Dautricourt, the second judge, was also born in 1907. He studied law at the Catholic University of Louvain (Belgium) and worked as a lawyer in Bruges until 1945. In 1942, he started collecting all the legal materials he could find on the punishment of collaboration with the enemy, and published two books in 1945, a crucial and first tool for military jurisdictions, which were responsible for the interpretation and enforcement of criminal law on that matter. After the war, he became a magistrate. In late 1945, he was appointed as a judge of the Court of First Instance, and in August 1947, he became a civil judge at the War Council in Brussels. He had been involved in international criminal law and in 1946 was appointed Director of the *Journal of Criminal Law and Criminology*, one of the most prominent legal journals in Belgium. He was the General Rapporteur of the eighth Conference for the Unification of Criminal Law, which took place in Brussels on 10–11 July 1947 and dealt with crimes against humanity. This conference would be referred to in Siegburg's judgment by using its definition of crimes against humanity. In the early 1960s, he started teaching a course on criminal law at the Catholic University of Louvain.[19]

All of these biographical elements help clarify the attitude and determination shown by the magistrates in this trial. For once, the judges did not sentence the accused only for war crimes, as was the general rule in Belgium and in other formerly occupied countries (except for the Netherlands); instead, Siegburg was also sentenced for crimes against humanity, which until today historians and legal experts working on the Belgian trials have ignored.

In its decision on 29 December 1949, the court determined that the fact that the victim had been beaten to death and that he had suffered mistreatment must have been driven by only two motives: either to force him to reveal where he had hidden his gold, money and jewellery, or due to racial hatred. The War Council favoured the racial crime rather than the heinous crime theory, and condemned Siegburg to the death penalty for crimes against humanity. As they could not refer to Article 6 of the Nuremberg Charter, the judges demonstrated an impressive degree of imagination by referring to the definition of crimes against humanity formulated by the International Conference in which Judge Dautricourt was General Rapporteur. This definition was also brought forward to support the ruling of the US military court in Nuremberg in the Flick trial of 22 December 1947.[20]

However, on appeal, the military court judges (the appellate court) feared setting a precedent. They did not rule for a crime against humanity as they adjudged that there had not been premeditation. They modified the judgment by replacing the charge of murder with one of manslaughter, thereby restricting the act to a mere war crime, resulting in a sentence of fifteen years of forced labour.[21] As the first instance ruling was never confirmed, it has never been published in any legal journal, which is why lawyers have not been aware of it. Moreover, Joseph Dautricourt never mentioned it in any of his writings, the rule being that one is not supposed to comment on one's own rulings.

After Siegburg's trial, Justices Maréchal and Dautricourt had to find other solutions. They needed to search for other legal means in their toolbox in order to convict Germans for the crimes they had committed against the Jews.

In the trial of Max Boden, Deputy Chief of the Mechelen assembly camp, the accused was prosecuted for manslaughter, for several cases of assault and battery as well as for around one hundred body searches of victims when they arrived at the camp with the objective of finding valuables and jewellery hidden in their private parts. Again, there was no article in the Criminal Code that could sanction the participation of the accused in the genocide against the Jews in Belgium. In August 1950, the military tribunal convicted him to twelve years' imprisonment for manslaughter, assault and battery, and indecent assault. On appeal, the sentence was reduced to eight years in prison.

In subsequent trials – especially those of von Falkenhausen, Reeder and Canaris – the Brussels War Council incorporated deportation into the section of the Criminal Code on arbitrary arrest and detention. Under this section, von Falkenhausen and Reeder were sentenced to twelve years in prison after being found responsible for the arbitrary arrest, detention and deportation of 25,437 Jews. Canaris was sentenced to twenty years in prison and was held responsible for the arbitrary arrest, detention and deportation of 1,654 people, with the physical torture of some victims deemed an aggravating factor.

Conclusion

To conclude, court records represent a valuable tool for researchers. They help piece together parts of the historical truth. In this investigation of how the Belgian judiciary worked on cases involving crimes committed against the Jews, court and political records have allowed us to establish the causes behind the feeling of failure that the trials left many years later. These reasons were to be found in the complex historical and legal context in the wake of the war, especially regarding the issue of the universally accepted principle of the non-retroactivity of the laws. By studying a specific trial, it has also become possible to highlight the enormous amount of time and effort spent by some members of military jurisdictions, even though this failed to bear fruit in the long term. The case revealed a pugnacious investigating magistrate who eventually managed to find unlikely witnesses thanks to his persistence. Then, two quite inventive judges pushed the limits of the laws. Unlike widespread opinion, these trials demonstrated the existence of a true will to defeat impunity and promote justice. Other magistrates, on the other hand, were much more reluctant to acknowledge this attempt to innovate and to review the laws. Instead, they preferred sticking to conventional judiciary, which led to these egregious results.

Given that the Brussel War Council's judgment in the Siegburg case on 29 December 1949 was not confirmed on appeal, it did not set a precedent and was not published in legal journals at the time. For sixty years, this exceptional decision remained unknown. Only through careful and patient analysis of the archives has it been possible to uncover its existence. Finally, the records of the Otto Siegburg case have also offered new material to study individual arrests and everyday violence, a lesser known aspect of the genocide against the Jews in Belgium.

Marie-Anne Weisers has a Ph.D. in contemporary history and is a researcher at the Centre Mondes Modernes et Contemporains of the Université libre de Bruxelles (ULB). Her most recent work, *La justice belge, les bourreaux allemands et la Shoah* (Editions de l'Université libre de Bruxelles), was published in 2020. Her work focuses on the history of the trials against German war criminals and the crimes committed against Jews in Belgium.

Notes

1. Steinberg, 'Le génocide au rendez-vous du palais', 13–27; Steinberg and Gotovitch, *Otages de la terreur nazie,* 55–57; Van Goethem, *Kazerne Dossin,* 12; Wouters, 'La persécution des Juifs devant les juges belges', 817–1052.
2. For more details, see *Rapport sur l'activité de la Commission d'enquête sur les violations des règles du droit des gens,* 15; *History of the United Nations War Crimes Commission,* 92 and 509.
3. P. Havaux, 'Le doux châtiment des criminels de guerre allemands en Belgique', *Le Vif,* n. 47, 20 November 2015.
4. I further refer here to my doctoral research and book: Weisers, *La justice belge, les bourreaux allemands et la Shoah.*
5. B. B. Ferencz, *An International Criminal Court,* 62 (document 12).
6. *Rapport sur l'activité de la Commission d'enquête sur les violations des règles du droit des gens,* 13.
7. Fayat, *Législation belge en exil*; Gilissen, 'Étude de la répression de l'incivisme', 513–628; Aerts, et al., *Papy était-il un nazi?*; Van Haecke, *Repressie en epuratie.*
8. The decree-law of 29 April 1943 (*Moniteur belge,* 8 May 1943) provides for the interruption of limitation periods for criminal offences whose prosecution was made impossible during the period of occupation, either because they benefited the enemy or because the perpetrators were protected by the enemy. The decree-law of

5 August 1943 (*Moniteur belge*, 20 September 1943) extends the jurisdiction of Belgian courts to wartime crimes committed by Belgians and foreigners outside Belgium against nationals of Allied countries.

 9. CEGES (Centre d'Etudes et de Documentation Guerre et Sociétés Contemporaines), AA1882, G/5-11-6, circulaire no. 1903, 22 September 1947.

10. Article 118bis: 'Shall be put to death, he who takes part in transformation by the enemy of legal entities or organizations, who staggers citizen's loyalty in wartimes towards the King and the State, or who knowingly serves the policy and purpose of the enemy.'

11. Translation from French by the author.

12. 'En aucun cas l'application des lois visées à l'art.1er ne pourra être écartée sous le prétexte que les auteurs, co-auteurs ou complices des infractions y prévues auraient agi en qualité de fonctionnaire, soldat ou agent au service de l'ennemi': Loi du 2 août 1947 sur la répression des crime de guerre, *Mémorial du Grand-Duché de Luxembourg*, no. 38, 11 August 1947, 756. Retrieved 4 May 2021 from http://legilux. public.lu/eli/etat/leg/loi/1947/08/02/n1/jo.

13. CEGES, AA1882, G-5-11-6, Avis des auditorats sur l'application de l'article 118bis.

14. AAG (Archives de l'Auditorat Général), Procès Sipo Charleroi, dossier 252/48, dossier Réserve, arrêt Cour militaire, p. 44.

15. *Pasicrisie belge*, 1949, 514: 'Attendu que l'idée de trahison est caractéristique de l'infraction de servir sciemment la politique et les desseins de l'ennemi, réprimée par l'article 118bis du Code ; que la trahison suppose un manquement au devoir de fidélité envers l'État, et ne peut donc exister dans le chef d'un ressortissant ennemi que s'il a contracté un tel devoir envers la Belgique.'

16. AAG, Dossier Otto Siegburg, Farde II/C/1, PV 14 June 1949, pièce 48.

17. AGR (State Archives of Belgium), M.J, services généraux, Personnel, Dossiers des magistrats 1953–1980, dossier no. 2837; SVG (Service Victimes de guerre), dossier Jacques Warnant.

18. AGR, M.J, services généraux, Personnel, Dossiers des magistrats 1953–1980, dossier no. 1691; Archives ULB, dossier personnel; SVG, dossier Achille Maréchal; Archives de la commune d'Ixelles, dossier personnel.

19. AGR, M.J, Services généraux, Personnel, Dossiers des magistrats 1953–1980, dossier no. 485; Archives de l'Université catholique de Louvain (UCL), dossier personnel.

20. AAG, dossier répressif Otto Siegburg, Farde V, *Jugement et appel*, Jugement du Conseil de guerre du 29/12/1949.

21. AAG, dossier Otto Siegburg, Farde *Cour Militaire*, pièce 16.

Bibliography

Published Sources

Aerts, Koen et al. (eds). *Papy était-il un nazi? Sur les traces d'un passé de guerre*. Tielt: Racine, 2017.

Fayat, Hendrik. *Législation belge en exil. Aperçu de l'action législative et exécutive du gouvernement belge en exil (16 mai 1940–8 septembre 1944)*. Brussels: Fondation Hubert Pierlot, 1994.

Ferencz, B.B. *An International Criminal Court, a Step toward World Peace: A Documentary History and* Analysis. New York: Oceania Publications, 1980.

Gilissen, Jean. 'Étude de la répression de l'incivisme'. *Revue de droit pénal et de criminologie* (1950–51), 513–628.

History of the United Nations War Crimes Commission and the Development of the Laws of War. London: His Majesty's Stationery Office, 1948.

Rapport sur l'activité de la Commission d'enquête sur les violations des règles du droit des gens, des lois et coutumes de la guerre instituée par arrêté du Régent en date du 21 décembre 1944. Brussels: Moniteur belge, 1948.

Steinberg, Maxime. 'Le génocide au rendez-vous du palais', in *Juger ('Justice et barbarie 1940–1944')* 6–7 (1994), 13–27.

Steinberg, Maxime, and José Gotovitch. *Otages de la terreur nazie. Le Bulgare Angheloff et son groupe de Partisans juifs. Bruxelles, 1940–1943.* Brussels: VUB Press, 2007.

Van Goethem, Herman. 'Kazerne Dossin, le musée', in *Kazerne Dossin. Holocauste et droits de l'homme* (Mechelen: Kazerne Dossin, 2012), 9–13.

Van Haecke, Lawrence. 'Repressie en epuratie. De bescherming van de uitwendige veiligheid van de Staat als politiek-juridisch probleem tijdens de Belgische regimecrisis (1932–1948)'. Ph.D. dissertation, Ghent: Ghent University, 2014.

Weisers, Marie-Anne. *La justice belge, les bourreaux allemands et la Shoah.* Brussels: Editions de l'Université libre de Bruxelles, 2020.

Wouters, Nico. 'La persécution des Juifs devant les juges belges', in Rudi van Doorslaer et al. (eds), *La Belgique docile. Les Autorités belges et la persécution des Juifs durant la Seconde Guerre mondiale* (Brussels: Luc Pire, 2007), 817–1052.

Archival Sources

AAG File of Sipo Charleroi; File of Otto Siegburg.

AGR, M.J, services généraux, Personnel, Dossiers des magistrats 1953–1980, dossier no. 2837; dossier no. 1691; dossier no. 485.

Archives de l'Université catholique de Louvain (UCL), dossier Joseph Dautricourt.

Archives de la commune d'Ixelles, Achille Maréchal.

Archives ULB, dossier personnel Achille Maréchal.

CEGES, AA1882, G/5-11-6

Mémorial du Grand-Duché de Luxembourg, no. 38, 11 August 1947.

Pasicrisie, 1949.

SVG, dossier Jacques Warnant; dossier Achille Maréchal.

CHAPTER 7

SOVIET FOOTAGE OF WAR CRIMES, 1941–46

BETWEEN PROPAGANDA AND JUDICIAL EVIDENCE

Vanessa Voisin

Introduction

The Second World War was not the first conflict in which warring nations resorted to the power of images to mobilize their citizens or international public opinion. Besides the best-known example – the Spanish Civil War[1] – all contemporary wars have witnessed the development of this form of mobilization, at first through photographs, drawings, postcards and posters, and later through cinema.[2] However, the Second World War marked a shift both in terms of quality thanks to technical progress (especially the distribution of the mobile camera) and quantity. The footage shot during this war by the most active countries – Germany, the United States, the Soviet Union and the United Kingdom – amounted to millions of metres of film.[3] Moreover, the films and newsreels distributed came to hundreds of units. Residents of the Allied countries rushed to the theatres to see the war on screen and until the end of 1942, they especially followed operations on the Eastern Front.[4]

What did these images show? Victorious defences or attacks on the front, the unity of their own nation and the devotion of workers on the home front, and a more or less articulated presentation of the war goals. From the end of the nineteenth century, in parallel to the accelerated development of international law, one of the main arguments for waging war had become the defence of the assaulted and violated nation against a barbaric and cruel enemy.[5] The genocidal and predatory Nazi occupation policy of Soviet territory provided numerous instances of illegal and wanton violence against disarmed prisoners of war (POWs) and civilians. These acts of cruelty fed a hate propaganda symbolized by the famous 1942 poems of the war correspondents Ilya Ehrenburg ('Kill!') and Konstantin Simonov ('Kill him!'), calling on Soviet soldiers to beat and kill the enemy without mercy.[6] A specificity of Soviet war propaganda was that the first territorial recoveries occurred at the end of 1941, facilitating the visual documentation of the crimes of the enemy from the first months of the Soviet–German conflict.

Archives in Kiev, Moscow, Riga and Minsk contain thousands of metres of footage, both raw and edited, showing Nazi crimes on Soviet and Polish territory. However, the methods of filming and editing varied from case to case, revealing both the professionalization of this practice and the fast-shifting political stakes related to it. This chapter raises several hypotheses as to the purposes of these images, their editing and their possible distribution. Beyond the propagandist agenda of the Soviet authorities, what can the films add to our knowledge of the war when their historicity is taken into account? By cross-referencing the material and political conditions of the gathering of the images, the formatting of the editing and the distribution policy, it is possible to shed light both on the archival value and the use of atrocity footage, while building understanding of the Soviet ambivalence towards movie images being seen as 'documents'.

This chapter is based on an analysis of the images themselves and on written material from the funds of the studios involved in these productions, the funds of political institutions and some private funds of filmmakers such as Aleksandr Dovzhenko and Aleksandr Kuznetsov.[7] It builds on recent literature on related topics[8] and on the collective and personal work carried out for the exhibition *Filming the War: The Soviets and the Holocaust (1941–1946)* in 2015.[9] First, the instructions given to the cameramen on the field in the initial stage of the war are recounted, a period dominated by the urgency of broad mobilization and consequently by an emotional denunciation of the enemy's cruelty. Next the chapter presents the surge in 1943 of new priorities related to the historical meaning of the war, leading to the creation of the first state-centralized film archives. Finally, the ambiguity of the status of judicial evidence in the Soviet policy pertaining to atrocity footage from 1944 to 1946 is questioned.

Mobilization or Documentation?

The precocity of the first Soviet films showing Nazi crimes and destruction played a major role in generating considerable ambivalence around these images: perceived and labelled as 'documents', they were actually intended as weapons of mobilization, thus neglecting accuracy and fact-stating. Another striking feature of the early practice of recording these crimes on film was related to the absence of precise and concrete instructions on how to carry out the filming.

As specialists have demonstrated in recent monographs, footage of atrocities and destruction appeared on Soviet screens after the Red Army recorded its first victories on 23 December 1941 in a newsreel dedicated to the liberation of Rostov at the end of November.[10] However, as early as 2 August 1941, the Political Directorate of the Red Army had transmitted to cinema groups on the front line an instruction signed by its Chief, Lev Mekhlis, demanding that all cameramen possessing a private camera photographed '1. The exactions of the fascists against the Soviet civilians and soldiers, the looting of the population', to be immediately sent to the Political Directorate of the front along with the necessary identification of the subjects photographed.[11] The point was obviously to use these photographs in the Army newspapers in order to foster the fighting spirit of the troops.[12] However, no instructions about filming Nazi crimes can be found prior to December 1941, when the same Mekhlis signed a directive emphasizing the value of movie images for mobilization both inside the country and abroad:

> The universal significance of the Great Patriotic war strongly demands the creation of annals of cinematographic documents about the on-going events and the showing of the offensives of the Red Army, the beginning of the crashing of the hitlerite Germany.

> The films edited on the basis of these documents are powerful weapons for the political education of the soldiers of the Red Army and for numerous generations of Soviet people.

> A quality cinematographic account, when shown on foreign screens, is a convincing means of propaganda and popularization about the strength and the power of the Red Army.[13]

In highlighting several flaws of the cinema work on the front, the Chief of the Political Directorate evoked the filming of Nazi atrocities: 'The face of the German army of looters, its mass atrocities in the districts liberated by the Red Army, the destruction of artifacts of Russian culture and civilisation are shown poorly, impersonally, with no documentation, and there are no shots of the moments of the recording of atrocities.' He recommended paying special attention to these shootings.

Indeed, the Rostov newsreel did not comprise images of *aktirovanie* (officials certifying the crimes in the presence of legists and witnesses), even though they existed.[14] However, judging from the Rostov newsreel of December 1941, Mekhlis' criticisms were not entirely fair. Jeremy Hicks has provided an in-depth analysis of this newsreel, revealing the emotional power of the visual report on Nazi atrocities in Rostov. Of course, much of its strength is based on the editing and the soundtrack (extracts from Pyotr Ilyich Tchaikovsky's *Pathétique*, which would become the 'consistent musical trigger for such scenes').[15] Nevertheless, the operators in the field had already made significant choices in their filming of these crimes, such as close-ups on the faces of specific victims (notably children) and shots of mothers and sisters grieving. Both operators' and editors' choices strongly affected the documentary and evidential character of the images, dragging them towards a mobilization function. They prioritised relatives' suffering over the recording of witness accounts or official certification of the crimes. Nonetheless, the emphasis placed on emotions did not preclude a demand for authenticity. Certainly, the correspondence between Moscow and the front teams confirmed the strict ban imposed on staging, re-enactment and so on if the 're-enacted' scenes constituted the core of a subject.[16] In other words, re-enactment was tolerated to marginally complete a documentary narrative based on real images from the front. The cinema authorities perfectly understood that staging might discredit the newsreels, damaging the purpose of propaganda.

The state of the studio archives for the war years, notably the loss of several documents produced before and during the mass evacuation of October 1941,[17] precludes certainty as to the definition of film standards for the enemy crimes prior to Mekhlis' December text. The available information points to the operators' reluctance and political bans, as well as the technical impossibility of filming the Soviet retreat and the consequences of German victories (flows of refugees, victims of bombings and so on), although some images of this kind existed and were evacuated eastwards in October 1941. Most likely the authorities directly supervising the work of the cameramen at the front – the political directorates of each army – delivered oral instructions of what to film and how. Once the situation had become normalized in Moscow in late 1941, the Direction of Production of Newsreels (Glavnoe Upravlenie po proizvodstvu kinokhroniki, or 'Glavk') returned to sending regular reviews of the shots coming from the front. Usually signed by the main editor of the Central Newsreels Studio and the Deputy Director of the Glavk, these evaluations reinforced Mekhlis' abstract and general instructions. For instance, an evaluation of Mazrukho and Khikoian's subject 'Atrocities of German Fascists in the Town of Nalchik' dated 17 February 1943 explained:

> This subject shows with great details the 'death ditch' where the Hitlerite hangmen, trying to hide the mark of their atrocities, threw the bodies of more than 600 victims.
>
> The cameramen properly fulfilled their mission. Wide shots of the death ditch testify of the monstrous scope of the crime. Some moments of the footage (the bodies of Soviet civilians and [sic] the moment when relatives identify the victims) contribute to create a cinematographic document striking by its content and intensifying the hate of the enemy, while also unmasking the fascism through its vile crimes.
>
> The photographic quality of the image is satisfactory. The footage will be partially used for the newsreels and retained in the archives.
>
> Katsman, deputy-director of the Glavkinokhroniki
>
> Vaks, head of the redactional department.[18]

The wording of this review suggests a lack of general instructions regarding the way in which Nazi crimes must be filmed: its authors deemed it necessary to explain why wide shots were necessary and the kinds of details to present. Reactions to sound footage were similar in their attempt to educate the cameramen:

> Raw footage also includes a story told by a female witness of the atrocities. The composition of the image is artificial. The woman stands at the forefront; her house and the crime scene are reduced to the function of background setting. The witness' movements repeat themselves constantly: either she speaks to the spectator, either she clumsily leans backward, pointing to things in the background. All these elements produce an artificial, stiff impression. For a documentary picture it would have been more relevant and more interesting to film a testimony right on the crime scene: near the house, the ditch, in which the victim was thrown. The filming of

a complementary sequence showing the woman crossing the background (and not filming exclusively with a fixed camera and with direct sound) would have fulfilled the need of scenery.

... There are also mistakes in the organisation of the sound shots. In the sequence showing the victims prevail wide and three-quarter shots on the group of persons. Portraits with close-ups are very rare. And yet this type of shots is the most interesting, the most direct and true in terms of intonations, facial expressions and composition of the image.[19]

Such reviews appear to be the only instructions sent to the cameramen in the field. As for the cameramen themselves, little information is available concerning their attitudes towards such shootings. Most of the early filming reports written after the filming and attached to the reels sent to Moscow were lost, preventing historians from studying the precise evolution of the composition of subjects of atrocity in the field. Those that were preserved (usually after 1943) exemplify an awareness of the significance of such recordings, compelling the cameramen to put aside their feelings in order to professionally record the horrors they saw. The tone was factual and professional, describing shots of different victims and their injuries. However, the consternation felt by the operators was occasionally filtered through the information they gathered about the reasons behind the killings or through introductory remarks describing them, as in Valentin Orliankin's report about Babi Yar in late 1943:

This is a place of horror and human tragedy.

This is the place of the vilest outrage of the German barbarians in Kiev.

This is the place of a sacred revenge and of the oath shouted by dozens of thousands of our people before their death to exterminate the damned beasts.[20]

The memories of the operators also cast some light on the mixed feelings experienced during these shootings, even where they retrospectively rationalized the decisions made on the spot:

Looking at this tragic sight was unbearably hard. But when you shoot you don't have the right to indulge in personal feelings. I perfectly understood: it was essential to record this for history so that people will never forget the monstrous barbarism of fascism, all the more monstrous as it was beforehand thought through and planned. I read about it later in Germany in a booklet for the German soldier.[21]

Resulting from the screenings at the Central Studio in the presence
of Roman Katsman, a redactor, film directors, newsreel editors and
military 'advisors' (censors), the reviews were not sent to all groups
on the front, but only to the team producing the reviewed images.
Therefore, up to September 1943, there were no centralized instructions about atrocity footage and no protocol for such filming. The
operators originally followed the pattern established in the Rostov
newsreels, and continued in *Razgrom nemetskikh voisk pod Moskvoi*
(*The Defeat of the German Troops Near Moscow*) when the film was
released in mid-February 1942. *Razgrom* initiated a stable scheme of
atrocity footage editing. Wide shots of destruction in various towns
were followed by sequences on the torture and murder of POWs,
and the murder, mutilation and rape of civilians (the presentation of
the latter following a specific scheme in *The Defeat*).[22] Certainly, the
patterns increasingly followed the scheme set by Viacheslav Molotov,
Minister of Foreign Affairs, in his official 'Notes' about Nazi atrocities,
which were widely reproduced in the press and in special brochures.
However, contrary to the latter, the newsreels and films of this period
were built on recurrent calls for revenge that were rendered more
effective by a process of identification between the spectator and the
victims' relatives.[23]

The aiming for the widest identification as well as the effects of
an ongoing process of developing a Soviet identity in a Russian-
dominated culture led to an almost but not complete silence on the
Holocaust on Soviet screens. The victims with whom the spectator
was invited to identify were first and foremost Soviet citizens, regardless of their nationality. One newsreel on the liberation of Livny in
Orel province described the obligations made to the Jews to wear an
armband marked 'Jude' during the Nazi occupation. However, it said
nothing on the Nazi antisemitic ideology or on the mass murder of the
Jewish communities in Soviet-occupied territory.[24] More generally,
whereas Molotov's Note of 6 January 1942 explicitly mentioned the
specific fate of the Jews, the newsreels did not evoke them at all, even
though most of the shots did show Jewish victims or indirectly alluded
to some of them. They also avoided stating that Jews represented
most of the dead. For instance, in the newsreel on the liberation of
Barvenkovo in southeast Ukraine, shot by Leon Mazrukho and edited
by Irina Setkina, the camera goes down from afflicted civilians to the
frozen corpse of a young woman tied up by her wrist to an elder man.
The voiceover explains that Tatiana Reingold was tied and killed with
her father, Iakov. The last name of the victims as well as the surname
of the father point to a Jewish family. However, Setkina cut out the

raw footage, going even lower and stopping in order to show the armband on the girl's arm, where a Star of David is painted.[25]

Similarly, while all the sequences about atrocities linked in the same logic the depiction of the dead and the sight of destroyed buildings, none showed or mentioned synagogues or any other building tied to Soviet Jewish culture. In contrast, visual and written propaganda abundantly covered the destruction of Russian cultural monuments, such as Tchaikovsky's house in Klin, Leo Tolstoy's house in Iasnaia Poliana, the great Orthodox monastery in Istra and so on.[26]

The feature-length film *We Will Avenge!* was released in June 1942, gathering all of the atrocity footage recorded at that time to powerfully convey a call for revenge against an enemy that decided to destroy the Soviet people. By focusing on the diversity of ages, sexes and social activities of the victims, the voiceover completely silenced their ethnocultural identity, while the images suggested a common belonging to a broadly defined Slav culture. This fact is rendered all the more striking when it is considered that at this stage of the war, even the cinema authorities were well aware of the tragic fate of Soviet Jews, as was shown in a telegram sent in April 1942 by Roman Katsman to the Chief of the Southern Front Group, Mark Troianovski: 'When filming victims of fascist atrocities pay attention and send Moscow film documents showing German atrocities against Jewish population.'[27]

Thus, the film documents collected by cameramen in the first stage of the Soviet–German conflict can be considered as documents, for they managed to record both the scope and the dreadful details of Nazi crimes in Soviet territory, even though the cinema groups were not present at all of the crime scenes due to the length of the front. However, they lacked an important component: testimonies of what happened in these places. Moreover, the editing of raw material strove to mobilize people through universally identifying the victims by silencing their national identity. In the absence of clear identification of the victims, the researcher today is forced to cross-reference the images with other media (articles and booklets) and literature on the Holocaust to understand what one is looking at: an organized and systematic genocidal policy against the Jews, or random violence against civilians that would become more and more widespread after the development of the partisan resistance in mid-1942? Consequently, Soviet footage of the Nazi atrocities tells us as much about the authorities' perception and presentation of them as about the crimes themselves.

Nevertheless, mobilization in the country and abroad was not the only goal of Soviet cinema at war. After the victory in Stalingrad cleared the sky and raised hopes for a final victory, the authorities decided to create a special fund of systematic film 'annals' about the war. Therefore, they allowed filming not only for the screen, but also 'for history'.

Images for History ...

In March 1943, Ivan Bolshakov, the President of the Cinema Committee, forwarded to his subordinate Fedor Vasilchenko a recently received report on the state of the 'cinematic annals' (*kinoletopis*)[28] kept in the Central Studio's storehouses. He wrote down a critical note on the document: 'I warned you several times of the necessity to organise the conservation of front images. Obviously, you haven't paid enough attention to this question. Submit me under five days exhaustive propositions to radically improve this matter. March 13th.'[29] Indeed, the inspection ordered by Bolshakov revealed major flaws in the treatment of unused footage. The storehouse on Potilykha Street was not properly heated, part of the reels was spread on the floor, there was no specialist assigned to their maintenance and there was no inventory of the images filmed before the evacuation in October 1941. Moreover, some topics were not visually documented because they did not appear in the newsreels or film production plan.

From then on, the topic remained at the top of Vasilchenko's agenda for 1943. One cannot document the origin of this sudden concern in the Cinema Committee for archival footage. Did Bolshakov receive instructions from the Kremlin in the wake of the Stalingrad victory? Did he eventually – maybe on his own – follow the example of the Commission for the History of the Great Patriotic War created in December 1941 in the Moscow Academy of Sciences?[30] Or was it the creation of the Extraordinary State Commission for recording and investigating Nazi crimes in November 1942 that provoked this new concern?[31] Whatever the reasons, the administration in charge of the newsreels' production set in motion global reflection on 'cinematic annals'. On 24 March, Vasilchenko passed Bolshakov's demands to the Director of the Central Studio, Aleksandr Georgevich Kuznetsov. He gave instructions to put the Potylikha storehouse in order, to repatriate the reels stored in the town of Belye Stolby (south of Moscow), to inventory all the reels belonging to the 'cinematic annals' of the Studio (those kept in Moscow, in Belye Stolby and those evacuated to Novosibirsk) and finally to establish a conservation policy.[32]

The need for such a policy was certainly acute. Formally, the 'cinematic annals' were created in the Central Studio in May 1936, but as an undefined storage deprived of curators. In practice, after their first screening at the studio, images were either immediately selected for a newsreel or a film, sent to the *filmoteka* to be used in the near future, or sent to the 'cinematic annals', both collections being kept by the *filmoteka* staff. According to the available but unsystematic information, it seems that while the *filmoteka* collection retained distributed productions (newsreels and films) and some offcuts of raw footage, the 'cinematic annals' received only offcuts and undistributed edited productions.[33] Moreover, nobody was responsible for sorting and identifying these offcuts, which were carelessly put back in pieces in their original boxes without the images selected for the newsreels. The 'cinematic annals' constituted a kind of second-rate archives of the Studio, physically kept in the *filmoteka* but never treated or classified, with the exception of footage showing Vladimir Lenin (transferred in 1924 to the Lenin Institute). Contrary to the edited productions, which were to be regularly sent to the Central Audiovisual Archives, depending of the archival administration and after 1938 under the remit of the political police (NKVD), the 'cinematic annals' were not recognized as having any value per se as national heritage.[34] They were left to the Studio's policy and needs, which were of course not defined by historical concerns, but by productive goals.

Thus, up to 1943, the archival policy targeted distributed production only. This situation explains the presence at the beginning of the war of old raw or censored footage at the Studio *filmoteka* (but labelled 'cinematic annals'). This old footage, some dating back to the pre-revolutionary years, as well as the first images of the Soviet-German war filmed in the summer and autumn of 1941 were evacuated to Novosibirsk and Belye Stolby in October 1941, while simultaneously the Central Audiovisual Archives were evacuated to Saratov.[35] As footage continued to arrive from the front, in the spring of 1943 the Studio kept in its Moscow storehouses 16,250 reels of prewar and war footage – both edited and unedited. The Novosibirsk Studio of Technical Films provided shelter to another 12,740 reels belonging to the Central Studio, which Kirill Aksiutin, the previous head of the *filmoteka*, began to classify in evacuation.[36] The sudden interest of high-ranking officials in the images as a means of writing a visual history of the war questioned the difference between *filmoteka* and 'cinematic annals', and pointed to the urgency of protecting the reels from an uncontrolled use by the artistic employees of the Studio.

Between March and September 1943, there emerged a perception that this raw footage had intrinsic value, provided that it was thoughtfully selected, reconstituted in its original form and properly annotated.

In fact, this concern was not new to specialists of Soviet cinema. During the heated debate at the end of the 1920s between the supporters of Esfir Shub and Dziga Vertov, a reflection on the historical value, or even purpose, of newsreel shots came to the forefront.[37] Vertov's fast-moving editing of short takes ('life caught unawares') was seen by most critics as 'distorting material reality and as incomprehensible for the masses'.[38] In contrast, Esfir Shub's use of archival images and long takes organized through linear editing was applauded as the best way to truly exploit documentary images as historical documents. According to Josh Malitsky, this new understanding of documentary cinema was linked to the idea that images were primarily filmed for the future rather than for the present, and that their documentary value rested in their intrinsic capacity to record the facts as they were. This justified the preference for long-take shots and the conception of editing as a way to ease the self-expressing power of the image; editing, while obviously guiding the meaning made out of the images, must try to remain as 'objective' and 'distant' as possible: 'Since the film document was the most valued component of the documentary, film archives at this time were valued less as conservators of film culture or preservers of particular styles than as sites of catalogued and classified documents.'[39] However, as I have already indicated, only distributed edited material was kept in the Central Archives and up to 1943, only the footage gathered, bought and treated by Shub was duly catalogued. Furthermore, according to reports and critics in 1943, Shub remained the only documentary director working with copies of original footage in order to preserve their integrity.

However, there was one prominent theorist and filmmaker who repeatedly asked for a better preservation of documentary raw footage. Grigory Boltiansky, one of the fathers of Soviet cinematography and the history of cinema, had been leading several fights since the 1920s in order to create a Museum of the Cinema, then the Cinema Archives and to provide these archives with competent staff. In 1932, he even raised the idea of a 'pan-Soviet *kinoteka*'.[40] He shared with Shub a concern with preserving raw footage in their original length and for their systematic cataloguing. For Boltiansky, Soviet cinema had recorded cinematic documents of paramount historical value. Documentary images were 'a new and unprecedented kind of historical documents', 'reproducing historical facts and processes in a lively and authentic form, in their own movement and dramatic dimension, and forcing us to feel emotions, thus turning us into witnesses of ancient events'.[41] As soon as the summer of 1941, Boltiansky wrote to the Direction of Production of Newsreels with a proposal for a book about Soviet documentary cinema at war. Even before seeing the first images shot by the cameramen at the front, he recognized their salience for history. In July 1942, he asked to be called back from Tashkent, pointing out that he would be of far better use in the Central Studio, acting as an experienced redactor or methodological-scientific advisor.[42]

However, only the first major Soviet victories of the winter of 1942–43 and the development of judiciary and historical projects enabled these proposals to come to fruition.[43] Aksiutin seemed to have been the first person called back from evacuation to work on the organization and principles of the future Department of Cinematic Annals. He participated in a meeting held at the Central Studio on 14 June 1943. Grigory Boltiansky joined the team a month later and wrote the first detailed history of the cinematic annals and proposals about the department and the periodization of the war footage.[44] The new team prepared a work plan for August to September 1943, already including special shots for the cinematic annals. Eventually, several meetings at the Direction of Production of Newsreels (11 September 1943) and at the Cinema Committee (14 September 1943) led to an order of the President of the Committee establishing the tasks, initial structure and resources of the new department.[45] The definition of the cinematic annals was to be found elsewhere, in the documents signed by Fedor Vasilchenko on 14 September and 3 December 1943 (see Appendix 7.1). The first document recounted the history of the fund, its currently weak state and the considerable political value of the footage, beginning with the war footage. It approved all of the proposals submitted by Boltiansky in August, though the discussions between the specialists on 11 September had not led to definitive decisions. Three main principles are relevant to this paper. First, a selection of the footage was to be made in order to eliminate duplicates and technically poor footage, but also to select them according to Boltiansky's definition of the 'authentically historical cinematic annals':

> Only those images reflecting quietly, but vividly, truly (refusing artistic personalisation and dramatisation) and *by essence* the major phases as well as precise events of all the life of the USSR – its fight, accomplishments, difficulties and their overcoming in their *typical traits*, or those images representing *typical processes* of the socialist construction of the

country. These events, facts and processes partially or completely out-
last their temporary topicality after a certain amount of time after their
release in the form of films (and even right when they are recorded) and
they acquire a lasting, stable, constant significance.[46]

Second, the cinematic annals had to be organized into primary units
('reels-units'), gathering relevant images about a topic, edited with
explanatory title cards. These reels-units were to be compiled by
the redactors of the Department, assisted by historical, military and
political advisers. To produce these reels-units, the redactors and
editors of the Department needed to select historically meaningful
images according to the aforementioned definition, either from raw
footage (original negatives) or edited newsreels and films, Soviet or
foreign (copies). Thus, the Department not only represented an organ
for storing and classifying, but also produced its own material, which
was composed of thematically edited and mute reels-units catalogued
and indexed according to an overall classifier organized by phases
of the war and then subthemes. This unprecedented productive
attribute of a fundamentally archival organ probably justified the
special resources – both in terms of staff and material – given to the
Department. Another interesting aspect of this production was its pli-
ability: Boltiansky explained that the reels-units could be modified if,
for example, new interesting images were discovered or, in contrast, if
some of their content lost significance over time. The offcuts of these
reels-units could sometimes be kept as stock, second-rate footage.[47]

Third, a new rule was established: from then on, the negatives of
the cinematic annals became inaccessible to the editors of the newsreels and the film directors, who could only work with contratypes
(copies) of the original negatives. In truth, this rule was difficult to
put into practice until the end of the 1940s, but at least it recognized
the archival value and purpose of the cinematic annals, besides any
productive goal.

A fourth proposition was made, but, according to the available
documentation and to my own experience of Moscow's visual archives,
was not realized. It is nevertheless interesting for the present reflection as it proposed the production of collections of visual annals in
each phase of the war, selecting the best images from the reels-units
and involving in this work historians, officers, front writers, front
cameramen and film directors. These collections would have to select
in approximately twenty reels of ten-minute footage the most meaningful images in order to produce a timeless narrative of the war,
thanks to the absence of artistic editing tied to present concerns.[48] In
other words, it intended to fulfil the old utopia of the formalist critics

of the late 1920s: the writing of a comprehensive visual history of a paramount event in Soviet history, 'objective' in its ambition, but in reality guided by a political interpretation of the event. The potential public of this collection was not very clear: perhaps directors several decades after the war seeking to produce a truthful documentary about it?

Regardless, atrocity footage occupied a central place in the project of cinematic annals at its early stage. On 8 September 1943, before the meetings mentioned earlier, Vasilchenko addressed a circular to all the cinema front groups, stating the salience of such images (see Appendix 7.2). For the first time, concrete and precise instructions on how to film the traces of Nazi crimes were provided. The footage kept today in the Krasnogorsk archives demonstrates that these principles were strictly followed thereafter. This move was initiated by a request from the Extraordinary State Commission on Nazi Crimes asking for a regular recording of such proofs. It probably also received an impetus from the preparation of the second main trial of war criminals held in public, in Kharkov from 15 to 18 December 1943. The high profile of the defendants – three of them being German POWs – and the substantial press coverage of this event both in the Soviet Union and abroad entailed a thorough investigation resulting in the gathering of a huge amount of documents, textual as well as visual. The documentary film about the trial, released in Moscow in mid-January 1944, opens with several minutes of atrocity footage.[49]

Another project was set in motion at approximately the same time. The 1944 film production plan mentions a documentary by Dziga Vertov and Elizaveta Svilova entitled *Counts [to Be Presented] to the Enemy*.[50] The film, which was never produced, was supposed to be released in the Soviet Union and abroad immediately after the end of the war as a means of drawing up a visual report of the Nazi occupation of Soviet territory. Moreover, the directors' proposal stated: 'This film will serve as an indictment against the fascist Germany and, more broadly, against fascism. At the same time, this picture will prove to the world the high cost of our victory.' This project may explain why on 9 December 1943, Vasilchenko ordered Aksiutin to collect a series of atrocity footage, an order he repeated on 10 January 1944.[51]

Simultaneously, the Extraordinary State Commission on Nazi Crimes asked Vasilchenko to make an inventory of and annotate all the available footage pertaining to atrocities (see Appendix 7.2). At the end of 1943, the mobilizing function of this kind of footage had receded in favour of its historical and judicial aspects.

... or Images as Evidence?

The use of film in judiciary procedures was first studied by Christian Delage in relation to the Nuremberg trial.[52] Since then, the literature has steadily expanded.[53] While examining the first films on the Holocaust, Jeremy Hicks devoted two seminal chapters to the Soviet compilation film screened on 19 February 1946 in Nuremberg and to Roman Karmen's film on the trial. Some material enables us to draw a hypothesis regarding Soviet thought on the relationship between film and justice *before* the production of *Cinematic Documents on the Atrocities Committed by the German-Fascist Invaders on Soviet Territory* (1946).

Despite the obvious role played by the Extraordinary Commission in the attention devoted to atrocity images in late 1943,[54] no special procedure was created to certify the authenticity of atrocity footage shot at the liberation by Soviet cameramen. This dearth stands in sharp contrast to the practices followed by the English and American cameramen accompanying the armies during the liberation of Western Europe.[55] It also differs from the scheme quickly adopted for the Commission's 'akty' (certificates) duly signed by officials and numerous witnesses, which mentioned with precision the place of the crime, the names of the victims if known and so on. Similarly, the first trial movies of the war years, produced in the summer (Krasnodar trial) and in late 1943 (Kharkov trial), used atrocity footage in an illustrative rather than a judicial way. For example, the lengthy introduction of *The Kharkov Trial*, released in early 1944, shows images taken in various parts of the Soviet Union, not even always in the Ukrainian Soviet Republic. The images seek to create a dramatic atmosphere as opposed to providing the spectator with evidence. They thus stand on a different level from the excerpts of witnesses' testimonies or the reading of parts of the Extraordinary Commission's certificates. In fact, most likely more than half of the atrocity footage shown in this documentary film does not concern the defendants' crimes in any way. Instead, they are used to literally *show* the cruelty and the number of Nazi crimes in Soviet territory.

The same can be said of the film made for the Krasnodar trial (14–18 July 1943), although its use of atrocity footage is more discrete and does relate to the Krasnodar province.[56] The illustrative function still prevails: the spectator can see the building where the Gestapo established its headquarters, the yard where arrested people were executed and so on. The images are intended to illustrate rather than prove. Obviously, this was the stance adopted by the film editors in

Moscow at that time, in contrast to the understanding of their role by some front cameramen. For example, shortly afterwards, Mark Troianovskii, the senior cameraman at the Krasnodar trial, delivered an inspired speech to his team regarding their documentary mission:

> Nobody saw as much as we did. Nobody saw as many exploits of our fighters. Nobody saw as much suffering of our people as we did when we retreated between the Prut River [running through Moldavia and Romania] and the Caucasus heights.

> We witnessed countless abuses committed by the fascist murderers. We witnessed remarkable achievements of the Red Army soldiers. We are still to witness events of paramount historical significance.

> ...

> Moscow filmotheques keep thousands of metres of film resulting from our work. A large part of it has already been shown, a large part will durably be kept in the archives. All of them constitute a valuable documentation on the Great Patriotic War.[57]

A major ambiguity lies at the core of the Soviet use of atrocity footage to prove the reality of the Nazi crimes. The first full-length documentary produced by the Soviets to this end was a forgery. *A Tragedy in the Forest of Katyn*, released in late February 1944,[58] attempted to convince Western audiences of the responsibility of the Germans in the mass murder of Polish soldiers at the beginning of the war. Resorting to awkward and dubious scenes of witnesses' testimonies as well as to images of scientific expertise regarding the bodies and documents said to be found at the site, this film helped instigate long-term suspicion towards Soviet documentaries in the West. Indeed, *A Tragedy in the Forest of Katyn* used the same patterns of conviction as those used in Babi Yar in 1943 and later in *Majdanek* (1944). In these two scenes of actual Nazi mass crimes, the Soviet authorities organized special visits of journalists (both nationals and foreigners) and foreign diplomats. Raw footage recorded these visits (as well as the Katyn visit) to produce a very different effect on correspondents.[59] Sceptics remained unconvinced, such as Bill (W.H.) Lawrence, who published '50,000 Kiev Jews Reported Killed' [in Babi Yar] in the *New York Times* on 29 November 1943: 'On the basis of what we saw, it is impossible for this correspondent to judge the truth or falsity of the story told to us.' In contrast, Bill Downs was appalled by the visit and the story told by three survivors: 'From what I saw, I am convinced that one of the most horrible tragedies in this Nazi era occurred there between September 1941 and November 1943 ... As substantiating evidence, while walking over the mass graves, I saw bits of hair, bones, and a crushed skull with bits of flesh and hair still attached. Walking down the ravine, I constantly came across shoes, spectacle cases, and in one place found gold bridgework.'[60]

For unclear reasons, the Soviets did not use the footage of these visits to substantiate their assertions about Nazi mass crimes. However, despite the harm produced by *A Tragedy in the Forest of Katyn*, they went on to produce new 'special releases' of newsreels about Majdanek and Auschwitz.[61] Nevertheless, the main contradiction of the Soviet approach to such images remained. Though the images were deemed to constitute 'documents' capturing the crude reality of Nazi violence, they were neither used as evidence nor authenticated for the spectator. This fact is surprising. Moreover, it is plausible that Moscow had not planned to show any film at Nuremberg until the American film *Nazi Concentration Camps* was screened in the tribunal in late November 1945. The first mention of the preparation of the Soviet films appears in mid-December, in a note addressed to Georgy Malenkov by the Head of the Propaganda Department of the Party Central Committee Grigory Aleksandrov and the Chair of the Cinema Committee Ivan Bolshakov.[62] The document reveals that the films were ordered by the Main Prosecutor of the Soviet Union, Konstantin Gorshenin. A production plan of three movies had just been established, the deadline being fixed on 5 January 1946. The best editors and directors of the Central Studio of Documentary Films had been appointed to the task of selecting the images and editing them. Several of them possessed experience of using such footage: Svilova (who had edited the film on Auschwitz), Irina Setkina (editor of the special newsreel edition on the Krasnodar trial) and Roman Karmen, who had spent nearly the entire war on the front and directed the team sent to Majdanek.[63]

At the end of the month, the films remained in production and so Bolshakov suggested to Malenkov the creation of a commission including themselves, Gorshenin and Aleksandrov in order to accelerate the process of validating the films once ready. Finally, on 13 January, with the commission's endorsement, the films were handed over to Andrei Zhdanov as documents for the accusation. In his note to Zhdanov, Aleksandrov specified that they had used available images at the Studio, some of which had already been shown in widely distributed films.[64] The Soviets created three films: *The Destructions of Art Works and Monuments of the National Culture by the Germans on Soviet Territory*; *The Destructions Perpetrated by the Germans on Soviet Territory*; and the longer *Cinematic Documents on the Atrocities*

Committed by the German-Fascist Invaders on Soviet Territory. The latter is probably the best known and consists of an 85-minute compilation of the majority of the atrocity footage that had been filmed since 1941. The others supported two important patterns of Soviet accusation: the idea of the destruction of a culture (mostly Slav, i.e. Russian, Belarusian and Ukrainian) and the colossal material damage inflicted on the country. To certify the authenticity of the images in the absence of documents written and signed in situ during the filming, the five first minutes of *Cinematic Documents* show certificates signed by the director of the Studio, Sergei Gerasimov, as well as by the operators whose images were used in the film. The latter testified that:

> From 1941 to 1945, we accomplished our official duty, working in the ranks of the Red Army, we filmed various episodes of the Patriotic War. In particular, we accompanied the Red Army when it entered localities right after their liberation from the German-fascist troops, and we began filming immediately. We solemnly testify that the images used in the present film are the exact and true reproduction of what we discovered when we arrived in the areas from where were just expelled the German-fascist troops. These filmic images did not undergo any kind of alteration, correction, retouching, distortion or any kind of other modification. They are the exact copy of the originals kept in the filmotheque of the Central Studio of Documentary Films.[65]

The same pattern was used in what was actually the first Soviet film of this kind, entitled *A Trial against Germans in Belarussia*.[66] Its 24 minutes of footage visually summarize the crimes committed in the Belarusian republic by the occupiers. It opens with the exact same certificates from Belarusian studios and cameramen, written in Belarusian. However, just like the five special releases produced on the Smolensk, Minsk, Kiev, Nikolaiev and Leningrad trials of December 1945 to February 1946, this film was never intended for international audiences. Moreover, the five films about the trials – including both atrocity footage and even captured footage from the Minsk trial – were not shown beyond the territories of these republics or regions according to a cross-analysis of regional newspapers.

Conclusion: A Pedagogy through Images?

Despite the broadly shared belief in Soviet cinema circles that the documentary images constituted 'documents', atrocity footage was almost never fully used as evidence in the legal meaning of the word. This fact may have something to do with prevailing – and often contradictory – perspectives concerning what images are and what they suggest. Through decades of thinking and experimenting with documentary cinema, directors and cameramen clearly built a strong professional identity contingent on the social responsibility of the documentary filmmaker in the Soviet Union: accomplish revolution through art and teach the masses by showing them the present as a promised reality. As for the authorities, a long path had been followed since the experiments of the 1920s: art had to serve the socialist state and its current and long-term agenda.[67] Especially during the war, documentary cinema was mobilized, as the rest of society, to achieve shifting goals: developing hatred of the enemy, convincing international audiences of the special burden carried by the Soviet Union, and then sustaining Moscow's claims for the postwar political order. Even within the framework of this broad policy and successive phases, the Soviet use of atrocity footage was not consistent, as shown by the examples of 'images of conviction' in Katyn, Majdanek and Auschwitz. The only common purpose linking these images through the six years under study was the objective of pedagogy in the broadest meaning of the term, with audiences that were not always clearly defined.

Nevertheless, a substantial amount of images were filmed and have been retained to the present day in the audiovisual archives of some post-Soviet states. The edited footage merits historical analysis, both as testimonies of the tragedy of occupation and as documents regarding the Soviet treatment of this legacy.

Vanessa Voisin specializes in the history of the Soviet Union and studied the repressive mechanisms against collaborators set up by the Soviet Party-State during the Second World War and afterwards (*L'URSS contre ses traîtres : l'Épuration soviétique (1941–1955)*, 2015). She then took part in a collective program on Soviet cinema at war (1939–49). She is currently engaged in a research project on Soviet trials of mass perpetrators and is Senior Assistant Professor at Bologna University Alma Mater Studiorum. She is associated researcher at the CERCEC (EHESS, CNRS; Paris) and at the CEFR in Moscow.

Appendices

Appendix 7.1 Circular Sent to the Chiefs of Cinema Front Groups by Fedor Vasilchenko, Director of Newsreel Production, 8 September 1943 (Excerpts)

To the chiefs of cinema front groups[68]

One of the major tasks of the front cameramen in the districts liberated by the Red Army consists of filming the traces of the atrocities and destruction perpetrated by the German fascist invaders. It is essential to explain to all the cameramen that recording the crimes of the Hitlerians is a paramount obligation of the newsreels. Such images are a document of state significance.

In order to record in the most comprehensive way the atrocities and the damage inflicted by the Germans on the Soviet people, you must take into account the instructions of the regional commissions and inspectors of the Extraordinary State Commission for the statement and the investigation of the atrocities committed by the German fascist invaders.

The subjects to be shot must be:

- Monuments destroyed and blown up by the Germans, as well as houses, enterprises, public buildings, bridges and other installations;

- Inner and exterior views of the savagely damaged houses, museums, schools, libraries and churches;

- Places where the fascists perpetrated massacres of Soviet people: Gestapo headquarters, places of executions, corpses of killed and tortured citizens and camps of Soviet POWs;

- Scenes of identification of the victims by their relatives and friends; people who have escaped from fascist captivity and runaways from Germany; children whose parents were killed by the Germans; mothers who lost their children during the occupation;

- Material evidence of German persecutions against the populations of Soviet towns and villages; various kinds of inscriptions: announcements, placards with threats, interdictions or orders of the German command; tokens and armlets that the German slaveholders put on our people;

- Every other trace of atrocities and destruction perpetrated by the occupiers.

You must shoot both panoramas and close-ups showing the most expressive details. Inform the cameramen of the necessity of writing detailed reports providing all the information pertaining to the filming of these subjects.

The Director of Glavkinokhroniki,
Vasilchenko

Appendix 7.2 Circular Sent to the Chiefs of Cinema Front Groups by the Director of Newsreel Production Fedor Vasilchenko, 3 December 1943 (Excerpts)

ABOUT SHOOTS FOR FILMIC ANNALS[69]

During the filming of combat scenes and other significant facts on the fronts of the Great Patriotic War, cameramen often come across events that they do not record either because these events do not fit into the current workplan of newsreel editions, either because images of these events are, for various reasons, not suitable now for newsreels and films.

Meanwhile, such images often possess a unique value for the history of the Great Patriotic War, as cinematic annals. These images will in the future become cinematographic documents of exceptional force, truthfully reflecting all the greatness of the fight of the Soviet people against the German fascist invaders, including all its difficulties.

...

GERMAN ATROCITIES AND DESTRUCTIONS

This section requires specific attention.

At present, cinematographic documents on the German atrocities and destruction are under review/systematisation and edition for the Extraordinary State Commission (on its assignment).

Film the German atrocities and destruction, the most terrible and the hardest, and do not try to adjust them to aesthetic requirements.

While filming these scenes, operators must conform to no other principle than the duty of recording the vile actions and the robbery committed by the Germans on our soil, for which they shall take the punishment.

...

The Head of Glavkinokhroniki,
Vasilchenko

Notes

This research was supported by a French research program 'CINESOV 1939-49' (ANR-12-BSH3-0008) led by Valérie Pozner and by a fellowship from the Fondation pour la Mémoire de la Shoah (Paris).

1. Basilio, *Visual Propaganda*; Crusells, *La Guerra Civil española*; Fontaine, *La guerre d'Espagne;* García López, *Spain Is Us*; Lefebvre-Peña, *Guerra gráfica*; Maspero, *L'ombre d'une photographe, Gerda Taro*.
2. Véray, *Les films d'actualité français de la Grande Guerre*; Véray, *La Grande Guerre au cinéma*; Delporte, *La guerre après la guerre*; Morin, *La Grande Guerre des images*; Rosenheim, *Photography and the American Civil War*; Thomas and Petiteau, *The Great War*; Bertin-Maghit, *Une histoire mondiale des cinémas de propagande*. In the Soviet Union, war also quickly became the subjet of films (e.g. the First World War, the Ethiopian War, the Spanish Civil War and the Sino-Japanese War). See Barbat, 'Une Guerre en marge'.
3. Aldgate and Richards, *Britain Can Take It*; Bennett, *One World, Big Screen*; Chapman, *The British at War*; Coultass, *Images for Battle*; Culbert, *Film and Propaganda in America*; Doherty, *Projections of War*; Fox, *Film Propaganda in Britain and Nazi Germany*; Garden, *The Third Reich's Celluloid War*; Hoffmann, *The Triumph of Propaganda*; Kallis, *Nazi Propaganda and the Second World War*; Roeder, *The Censored War*; Rother and Prokasky, *Die Kamera als Waffe*.
4. Documents in the funds of the Cinema Committee (f.2456, Russian State Archives of Literature and Art, Moscow, hereinafter RGALI) confirm this assertion of historians of British and American cinema during the war. Some of them are reproduced in Fomin, *Kino na voine*.
5. See, for example, the propaganda organized at the beginning of the First World War regarding German atrocities: Engelstein, '"A Belgium of Our Own"', 441–73; Horne, 'Les milieux des sciences humaines et sociales face aux atrocités', 11–20; Horne and Kramer, *German Atrocities, 1914*.
6. On the overall propaganda context during the war, see Berkhoff, *Motherland in Danger*; Livshin and Orlov, *Sovetskaia propaganda v gody Velikoi Otechestvennoi voiny*; Livshin and Orlov, *Sovetskaia propaganda na zavershaiushchem etape voiny*.
7. Besides Dovzhenko's funds in Moscow and Kiev archives (it should be noted that Solntseva's documents are kept within her husband's funds), I used Aleksandr Kuznetsov's fund at the State Central Museum of Cinema (Moscow), and Mark Troianovsky's and Viktor Tëmin's funds at the State Archives of the Russian Federation (Moscow).
8. Fischer, ' Promoting International Criminal Law', 623–53; Gershenson, *The Phantom Holocaust*; Hicks, *First Films of the Holocaust*; Pozner, 'Les actualités soviétiques de la Seconde Guerre Mondiale', 421–44; Shneer, *Through Soviet Jewish Eyes*.
9. See http://filmer-la-guerre.memorialdelashoah.org (retrieved 4 May 2021); Pozner, Sumpf and Voisin, *Filmer la guerre*.
10. Hicks, *First Films of the Holocaust*, 47–48; Voisin, *L'URSS contre ses traîtres*, 213–31; *Soiuzkinozhurnal* no. 114, released on 23 December 1941. Central Newsreels Studio (Moscow). Editor: Roman Gikov. Cameramen: Aslan Kairov, Arkady Levitan, Georgy Popov and Andrei Sologubov. Russian State Archives of Film and Photograph, Krasnogorsk (hereinafter RGAKFD), no. 4672.
11. State Central Museum of Cinema, Moscow (hereinafter TsGMK), fund 56, inv.1, file 25, leaf 65.

12. See, for example, the early releases of *For the Glory of the Motherland* (*Vo slavu Rodiny*), the newspaper of the South-Western Army.
13. Russian State Archives of Sociopolitical History, Moscow (hereinafter RGASPI) 17/125/71/229-231, quoted in Fomin, *Tsena kadra*, 154–55.
14. Similarly, raw footage of such scenes shot in the spring of 1942 was not used in the edited documentaries: RGAKFD, no. 6226, silent footage. The second subject shows a military commission certifying crimes committed in the Kalinin province; the third is certification of crimes committed in the Leningrad province (cameraman: Fedor Ovsiannikov, April 1942).
15. Hicks, *First Films of the Holocaust*, 49–58.
16. GARF 10094/1/91/113. The complete version of this telegram is published in French and Russian in Voisin, 'Mark Troïanovski, chef d'équipe cinématographique', 129–60. See also Pozner, 'Les actualités soviétiques de la Seconde Guerre Mondiale'.
17. When Moscow was partly evacuated, the cinema administration and several departments of the Central Studio left the capital and settled in Novosibirsk, Kuibyshev and various towns in Central Asia.
18. RGALI 2451/1/129/18.
19. RGALI 2451/1/127/24: review of the footage shot on the Southwestern front by the cameraman Semenov and the director Avdeenko for Dovzhenko's documentary *Ukraina* (known as *The Battle for Our Soviet Ukraine*, released in late October 1943), 28 July 1943.
20. Fomin, *Tsena kadra*, 602–3. See also Rodnichenko's report dated late September 1943, in Nizhnepetrovsk: ibid., 578–80.
21. Ibid., 574, excerpt of Vladimir Tomberg's memories published in 2003.
22. In this widely distributed feature-length film (an American re-edited version of which received a prize in the United States in 1942), the rape is not only evoked incidentally by the commentary accompanying the image of a dead woman; several shots show a crying girl being consoled, suggesting more than naming the rape.
23. For a detailed analysis of this pattern, see Hicks, *First Films of the Holocaust*, 49–74.
24. *Soiuzkinozhurnal* no. 9, released on 30 January 1942. Central Studio. Editor: Roman Gikov. Cameramen: A. Elbert, V. Tsesliuk, B. Vakar, M. Goldbrikh, N. Mukhin and G. Ostrovsky. RGAKFD, no. 4680.
25. Raw footage: RGAKFD, no. 6042. Cameraman: Leon Mazrukho. Newsreel: *Soiuzkinozhurnal* no. 27, 30 March 1942. Editor: Irina Setkina (Central Studio). The subject was also integrated into the Kuibyshev newsreel dated 28 April 1942. RGAKFD, no. 4759.
26. An entire sequence is devoted to these destructions in *The Defeat of the German Troops Near Moscow*, constantly stressing that *Russian* culture was destroyed. In late 1942, a 231-page booklet was edited by the Commission of History of the Great Patriotic War, *Iasnaia Poliana*.
27. GARF 10094/1/91/18.
28. The notion is hard to translate, even for specialists, because the definition of the nature and statute of these images was unclear, as I will explain below.
29. RGALI 2451/1/136/ 35.
30. Guskov et al. (eds), 'Zhivye golosa voiny', 158–68. The Commission aimed to collect as many documents, testimonies and so on as possible regarding the history on the ongoing conflict.
31. Sorokina, 'People and Procedures', 797–831.
32. RGALI 2451/1/136/30-31.
33. Undistributed for political reasons (censorship) or because they were finished too late and lost topicality.

34. This was despite the principles established in the 1926 governmental decree creating a cinema branch in the Central Archives of the Russian Federation and ordering the transmission of all images (negatives and positives, raw footage as edited production) presenting historical interest to the Archives five years after they were recorded. See G. Boltiansky, 'Okhrana dokumentov revoliutsii', *Kino*, 21 January 1940, p. 4.

35. Half of the funds were evacuated to Saratov in 1941: 'Iz istorii RGAKFD', *Vestnik arkhivista*, 9 September 2009. http://www.vestarchive.ru/ubilei/623----1938-2005-.html.

36. RGALI 2451/1/136/26-29: anonymous report entitled 'The State and the Tasks of the Cinematic Annals' (written by Aksiutin, Chudinova, Shingareva or Boltiansky, after 1 April 1943).

37. Pozner, 'La notion de "fait" dans les débats cinématographiques', 91–104.

38. Malitsky, 'Esfir Shub and the Film Factory-Archive'.

39. Ibid.

40. G. Boltiansky, 'Nuzhna vsesoiuznaia kinoteka', *Kino*, 6 December 1932, p. 4.

41. RGALI 2057/1/377/17-32: note written by G. Boltiansky in August 1943 entitled *About Conservation, Preservation and Use of Old Documentary Footage*.

42. RGALI 2057/1/188/1: R. Katsman's answer to G. Boltiansky's letter, 18 July 1942.

43. Voisin, *L'URSS contre ses traîtres*.

44. RGALI 2057/1/387/1-2: chronology of the first two years of work on the department of cinematic annals (1943–44) established by K. Asiutin.

45. RGALI 2057/1/380/7-8: order signed by Bolshakov on 25 October 1943, 'About the Measures to Improve the Work of Organisation and Systematisation of Documentary Cinematic Annals'.

46. RGALI 2057/1/377/24: note written by G. Boltiansky in August 1943 (emphasis added).

47. Ibid. The 14 September 1943 circular does not provide as many details as Boltiansky's August proposals, but clearly follows all of them.

48. RGALI 2451/1/136/17-18: note signed Shingareva (then Head of the Department of the Cinematic Annals), 1 August 1943. Ibid., sheets 9–11ob: anonymous copy of a report entitled 'The state and the tasks of the documentary cinematic annals', undated (after 1 August 1943). It is probable that Shingareva wrote this report for Vasilchenko, using all of Boltiansky's ideas and adding her own one about the collections.

49. *Sud idët!* Sound film, 45 min. 1943. Central Studio. Editor: Ilia Kopalin. Cameramen: A. Lebedev, A. Lapty and V. Frolenko. RGAKFD, no. 5070.

50. RGALI 2456/1/921/28-29: production plans for 1944, attached to the minutes of the work session at the Cinema Committee, 30 March 1944.

51. RGALI 2057/1/387/1-2: chronology established by Aksiutin.

52. Delage, *La vérité par l'image*.

53. Delage and Goodrich, *The Scene of the Mass Crime*; Umphrey et al., *Law and War*, 2–22; Dufour, *Images of Conviction*; Kozlovsky-Golan, 'L'image visuelle de la Shoah et les procès de Nuremberg', 61–104.

54. On 2 April 1943 Aleksandr Dovzhenko was named a member of the main board of the Ukrainian commission (RGALI 2081/1/962/1) and later, in October 1944, the Central Commission mandated the photograph Viktor Tëmin, as a member of the Commission, to shoot various death centres on Polish territory in 1944 (GARF 10140/1/38/17).

55. Delage, *Filming the Camps*.

56. *Prigovor Naroda* (*The Verdict of the People*). Sound film, 12 min. Central Studio. Editor: Irina Setkina. Cameramen: M. Troianovsky, A. Levitan, D. Sholomovich, L. Kotliarenko, G. Aslanov and S. Stoianovsky. RGAKFD, no. 5056.
57. Troianovsky, *S vekom naravne*, 184–85.
58. E. Pomeshchikov, 'Tragediia v Katynskom lesu'. *Literatura i Iskusstvo*, 4 March 1944, p. 4.
59. *The Town of Kiev*. Image: G. Mogilevsky, 22 November 1943. RGAKFD no. 8591. *Maidanek*. Image: R. Karmen et al., July–August 1944. RGAKFD no. 10856.
60. Downs, B., 'Blood at Babii Yar: Kiev's atrocity story', *Newsweek*, 6 December 1943.
61. For an in-depth analysis of these films and their distribution, see Hicks, *First Films of the Holocaust*, 157–85; Liebman, 'Les premiers films sur la Shoah', 145–79; Pozner, Sumpf and Voisin (eds), *Filmer la guerre*. For reflections on the various levels of staging in atrocity footage (re-enactment, staging and fasification), see the work accomplished for the exhibition *Filming the War* and summarized in Pozner, Sumpf and Voisin, 'Que faire des images soviétiques de la Shoah ?', 8–41.
62. RGASPI 17/125/373/235. Malenkov was already one of the major leaders in Stalin's time. He was a member of the State Defence Committee created in June 1941, which was in charge of essential sectors of the war effort, including aviation, re-construction of the liberated areas and dismantling of German industry as war reparations.
63. Barbat, 'Une Guerre en marge'; Barbat, 'Kinooperator na vojne', 275–94. For a French version of this paper, see Barbat, 'Un opérateur en guerre'.
64. RGASPI 17/125/467/1 (Bolshakov's note, 31 December 1945), 17/125/467/373/236-237 (Aleksandrov's note).
65. RGAKFD no. 6820.
66. *Protsess nad nemtsami v Belorussii*. Sound film, 24 min. Belarusfilm. 1946. Cameramen: M. Berov, G. Bobrov, T. Bunimovich, I. Veinerovich and I. Dovnar. BGA-KFFD, no. 901.
67. Laurent, *L'oeil du Kremlin*.
68. Translated from Fomin, *Tsena kadra*, 378.
69. Translated from ibid., 384, 386.

Bibliography

Published Sources

Aldgate, Anthony, and Jeffrey Richards. *Britain Can Take It: British Cinema in the Second World War*. London: I.B. Tauris, 2007.

Barbat, Victor. 'Un opérateur en guerre : Le parcours de Roman Karmen, 1941–1945', in Sylvie Lindeperg (ed.), *Par le fil de l'image: Cinéma, guerre, politique* (Paris: Publications de la Sorbonne, 2017), 109–126.

——. 'Kinooperator na vojne. Maršruty poezdok Romana Karmena, 1941–1945', in Vanessa Voisin, Valérie Pozner and Irina Tcherneva (eds), *Perezhit' voinu. Kinoindustriia v SSSR, 1939–1949* (Moscow: ROSSPEN, 2018), 275–94.

——. 'Une Guerre en marge: Le conflit sino-japonais sur les écrans soviétiques (1938–1941)'. *Conserveries mémorielles. Revue Transdisciplinaire* 24 (2020). Retrieved June 2021 from http://journals.openedition.org/cm/4126.

Basilio, Miriam M. *Visual Propaganda, Exhibitions, and the Spanish Civil War*. New York: Routledge, 2013.

Bennett, M. Todd. *One World, Big Screen: Hollywood, the Allies, and World War II*. Chapel Hill: University of North Carolina Press, 2012.

Berkhoff, Karel C. *Motherland in Danger. Soviet Propaganda during World War II*. Cambridge, MA: Harvard University Press, 2012.

Bertin-Maghit, Jean-Pierre (ed.). *Une histoire mondiale des cinémas de propagande*. Paris: Nouveau Monde éd., 2015.

Chapman, James. *The British at War: Cinema, State, and Propaganda, 1939–1945*. London: I.B. Tauris, 2000.

Mints, I.I., and S.A. Tolstaia-Esenina. *Iasnaia Poliana: Stat'i, dokumenty*. Moscow: Ogiz; Politizdat, 1942.

Coultass, Clive. *Images for Battle: British Film and the Second World War, 1939–1945*. Newark: University of Delaware Press, 1989.

Crusells, Magi. *La Guerra Civil española: Cine y propaganda*. Barcelona: Ariel, 2000.

Culbert, David. *Film and Propaganda in America: A Documentary History, Vol. 3*. Westport, CT: Greenwood Press, 1990.

Delage, Christian. *La vérité par l'image : De Nuremberg au procès Milosevic*. Paris: Denoel, 2006.

———. *Filming the Camps: John Ford, Samuel Fuller, George Stevens from Hollywood to Nuremburg*. Paris: Memorial de la Shoah, 2010.

Delage, Christian, and Peter Goodrich (eds). *The Scene of the Mass Crime: History, Film, and International Tribunals*. Abingdon: Routledge, 2013.

Delporte, Christian et al. (eds). *La guerre après la guerre : Images et construction des imaginaires de guerre dans l'Europe du XXe siècle*. Paris: Nouveau Monde, 2010.

Doherty, Thomas. *Projections of War: Hollywood, American Culture, and World War II*. New York: Columbia University Press, 1993.

Dufour, Diane (ed.). *Images of Conviction: The Construction of Visual Evidence*. Paris: Éditions Xavier Barral, 2015.

Engelstein, Laura. "'A Belgium of Our Own': The Sack of Russian Kalisz, August 1914'. *Kritika: Explorations in Russian and Eurasian History* 10(3) (2009), 441–73.

Fischer, A. 'Promoting International Criminal Law: The Nuremberg Trial Film Project and US Information Policy after the Second World War', in Morten Bergsmo, Wui Ling Cheah and Ping Yi (eds), *Historical Origins of International Criminal Law: Volume 1* (Brussels: Torkel Opsahl Academic E-Publisher, 2014), 623–53.

Fomin, V.I. *Kino na voine: Dokumenty i svidetelstva*. Moscow: Materik, 2005.

———. *Tsena kadra. Sovetskaia frontovaia kinokhronika 1941–1945 gg. Dokumenty i svidetelstva*. Moscow: Kanon+, 2010.

Fontaine, François. *La guerre d'Espagne: Un déluge de feu et d'images*. Paris: Berg international, 2003.

Fox, Jo. *Film Propaganda in Britain and Nazi Germany: World War II Cinema*. New York: Berg, 2007.

García López, Sonia. *Spain Is Us: La Guerra Civil española en el cine del Popular Front (1936–1939)*. Valencia: Publicacions de la Universitat de València, 2013.

Garden, Ian. *The Third Reich's Celluloid War: Propaganda in Nazi Feature Films, Documentaries and Television*. Stroud: History Press, 2012.

Gershenson, Olga. *The Phantom Holocaust: Soviet Cinema and Jewish Catastrophe*. New Brunswick, NJ: Rutgers University Press, 2013.

Guskov, A. et al. 'Zhivye golosa voiny: Arkhiv Komissii po istorii Velikoi Otechestvennoi voiny'. *Rossiiskaia Istoriia* 6 (2015), 158–68.

Hicks, Jeremy. *First Films of the Holocaust: Soviet Cinema and the Genocide of the Jews, 1938–1946*. Pittsburgh: University of Pittsburgh Press, 2012.

Hoffmann, Hilmar. *The Triumph of Propaganda: Film and National Socialism, 1933–1945*. Oxford: Berghahn Books, 1996.

Horne, John. 'Les milieux des sciences humaines et sociales face aux atrocités pendant et après la Guerre. Henri Pirenne, Fernand van Langenhove, Marc Bloch', in Jean-Jacques Becker (ed.), *Histoire culturelle de la grande guerre* (Paris: A. Colin, 2005), 11–20.

Horne, John, and Alan Kramer. *German Atrocities, 1914: A History of Denial*. New Haven: Yale University Press, 2001.

Kallis, Aristotle A. *Nazi Propaganda and the Second World War*. Basingstoke: Palgrave Macmillan, 2005.

Kozlovsky-Golan, Yvonne. 'L'image visuelle de la Shoah et les procès de Nuremberg. Le film Les Camps de concentration nazis et son impact'. *Revue d'histoire de la Shoah* 195 (2011), 61–104.

Laurent, Natacha. *L'oeil du Kremlin: Cinéma et censure en URSS sous Staline (1928–1953)*. Toulouse: Privat, 2000.

Lefebvre-Peña, Michel. *Guerra gráfica. Espagne 1936–1939, photographes, artistes et écrivains en guerre*. Paris: La Martinière, 2013.

Liebman, Stuart. 'Les premiers films sur la Shoah. Les Juifs sous le signe de la croix'. *Revue d'histoire de la Shoah* 2(195) (2011), 145–79.

Livshin, Aleksandr, and Igor Orlov. *Sovetskaia propaganda v gody Velikoi Otechestvennoi voiny: 'kommunikatsiia ubezhdeniia' i mobilizatsionnye mekhanizmy*. Moscow: ROSSPEN, 2007.

———. *Sovetskaia propaganda na zavershaiushchem etape voiny (1943–1945 gg.): Sbornik dokumentov*. Moscow: ROSSPEN, 2015.

Malitsky, Joshua. 'Esfir Shub and the Film Factory-Archive: Soviet Documentary from 1925–1928'. *Screening the Past* (17) (2004). Retrieved September 2016 from http://www.screeningthepast.com/issue-17-first-release/esfir-shub-and-the-film-factory-archive-soviet-documentary-from-1925-1928/.

Maspero, François. *L'ombre d'une photographe, Gerda Taro*. Paris: Seuil, 2006.

Morin, Claude. *La Grande Guerre des images: La propagande par la carte postale, 1914–1918*. Turquant: L'àpart éditions, 2012.

Pozner, Valérie. '"Joué" versus "non-joué". La notion de "fait" dans les débats cinématographiques des années vingt en URSS'. *Communications* 79 (2006), 91–104.

———. 'Les actualités soviétiques de la Seconde Guerre Mondiale: Nouvelles sources, nouvelles approches', in Jean-Pierre Bertin-Maghit (ed.), *Une histoire mondiale des cinémas de propagande* (Paris: Nouveau monde éditions, 2008), 421–44.

Pozner, Valérie, Alexandre Sumpf and Vanessa Voisin. 'Que faire des images soviétiques de la Shoah ?' *1895. Mille huit cent quatre-vingt-quinze* 76 (2015), 8–41.

———. (eds). *Filmer la guerre : Les Soviétiques face à la Shoah, 1941–1946*. Paris: Mémorial de la Shoah, 2015.

Roeder, George H. *The Censored War: American Visual Experience during World War Two*. New Haven: Yale University Press, 1993.

Rosenheim, Jeff L. *Photography and the American Civil War*. New Haven: Yale University Press, 2013.

Rother, Rainer, and Judith Prokasky (eds). *Die Kamera als Waffe: Propagandabilder des Zweiten Weltkrieges*. Munich: ET+K, Edition Text + Kritik, 2010.

Shneer, David. *Through Soviet Jewish Eyes: Photography, War, and the Holocaust*. New Brunswick, NJ: Rutgers University Press, 2011.

Sorokina, Marina. 'People and Procedures toward a History of the Investigation of Nazi Crimes in the USSR'. *Kritika: Explorations in Russian and Eurasian History* 6(4) (2005), 797–831.

Thomas, Ann, and Anthony Petiteau. *The Great War: The Persuasive Power of Photography*. Milan: Five Continents, 2014.

Troianovsky, M. (E. Uvarova-Troianovskaia and N. Venzher, eds). *S vekom naravne. Dnevniki, pisma, zapiski*. 2004.

Umphrey, Marta Merrill, Austin Sarat and Lawrence Douglas (eds). *Law and War*. Stanford: Stanford Law Books, 2014.

Véray, Laurent. *Les films d'actualité français de la Grande Guerre*. Paris: SIRPA/ AFRHC, 1995.

———. *La Grande Guerre au cinéma de la gloire à la mémoire*. Paris: Ramsay, 2008.

Voisin, Vanessa. *L'URSS contre ses traîtres : L'Épuration soviétique (1941–1955)*. Paris: Publications de la Sorbonne, 2015.

———. 'Mark Troïanovski, chef d'équipe cinématographique sur le front, 1941--945', in Emilia Koustova (ed.), *Combattre, survivre, témoigner : expériences soviétiques de la Seconde Guerre mondiale* (Strasbourg: Presses Universitaires de Strasbourg, 2020), 129–60.

Archival Sources

BGAKFFD: Belorusskii Gosudarstvennyi Arkhiv Kinofotofonodokumentov (Belarusian State Archives of Audio and Visual Documents), Dzerzhinsk.

GARF: Gosudarstvennyi Arkhiv Rossiiskoi Federatsii (State Archives of the Russian Federation), Moscow.

RGAKFD: Rossiiskii Gosudarstvennyi Arkhiv Kinofotodokumentov (Russian State Archives of Film and Photograph), Moscow.

RGALI: Rossiiskii Gosudarstvennyi Arkhiv Literatury i Iskusstva (Russian State Archives of Literature and Art), Moscow.

RGASPI: Rossiiskii Gosudarstvennyi Arkhiv Sotsialno-Politicheskoi Istorii (Russian State Archives of Sociopolitical History), Moscow.

TsGMK: Tsentralnyj Gosudarstvennyi Muzei Kino (State Central Museum of Cinema), Moscow.

CHAPTER 8

FROM MAJDANEK TO DEMJANJUK

FAILURES OF JUSTICE IN POSTWAR GERMANY, 1958–2009

Rebecca Wittmann

Introduction

On 21 May 1975, the Federal Republic of Germany, in conjunction with the State Attorney's office in Stuttgart, opened its prosecution against the infamous Rote Armee Fraktion (RAF). The Stammheim Trial, named after the prison built especially for defendants Andreas Baader, Gudrun Ensslin, Ulrike Meinhof and Jan-Karl Raspe, was a national sensation that was closely followed by the West German media and the public. The trial lasted just under two years, during which time virtually every defence lawyer was at some time barred from the proceedings, the chief judge had to step down because of bias, Ulrike Meinhof killed herself, and Siegfried Buback, the Attorney General of West Germany, was shot dead by the second generation of RAF members (whose murder trial I will discuss further below). On 28 April 1977, Andreas Baader, Gudrun Ensslin and Jan-Karl Raspe were found guilty of murder and attempted murder, and were sentenced to multiple life sentences in prison. About six months later, they all committed suicide in their cells, sparking what was and continues to be known as the 'German Autumn', a period of political violence that included kidnappings, more murder, a police clampdown not seen since the 1940s, and a sense of fear and anxiety ratcheted up to a hysterical pitch by a frightened government and a hungry media.

The year 1975 marked the beginning of another important trial: it was intended, by the State Attorney's office in Düsseldorf, to be the largest and most important trial of Nazi perpetrators since the sensational, watershed Auschwitz trial in Frankfurt ten years before. This was the Majdanek trial of camp guards from the slave labour and death camp in Lublin. State attorneys made an effort to bring to trial a representative cross-section of guards from the camp and to demonstrate that these people had committed horrific crimes by shooting or gassing thousands of innocent men, women and children. But the results were in fact dismal. The vast majority of Nazi defendants would not be convicted of murder. The fifteen defendants were mainly charged with crimes of excess and gruesome cruelty, but the prosecution could prove excess crime only rarely – usually when there was evidence that the Nazis themselves had disapproved of a guard's actions because they were not ordered by officials in Berlin. The crimes deemed murderous in Düsseldorf constituted exceptions to the rule in the Nazi period as well, leading to a perverse echoing of Nazi standards for what was legal and what was not in the Düsseldorf courtroom. The trial was also plagued by legal limitations: endless debates about eradicating the statute of limitations on murder; ageing and dying defendants; survivors whose memories were fading and who were increasingly reluctant to appear at yet another trial for fear of being branded 'professional witnesses'; a disinterested press; and a public who felt that these senior citizens who had lived productive lives for the last thirty years were harmless in comparison to the 'state enemies' on trial in Stuttgart at the same time. After all, the Nazi defendants had been acting in the name of the state; a perverted state, to be certain, but they were nothing other than functionaries of that state and therefore not dangerous. Interestingly enough, no systematic comparison of these two trials has ever been undertaken, despite the fact that they occurred during the same time period using the same law – the German Penal Code. My research addresses the question as to why this is, and I will outline the decisions and attitudes that led to an astonishing complacency about Nazi crimes that is only now, and still in a deeply troubled fashion, being addressed; as we shall see, in many ways the latest attempts at Nazi justice create more problems than they solve.

The Prosecution of Former Nazis in the German Federal Republic

After the Nuremberg trials, the German public lost interest in punishing the Nazi collaborators; politicians and the public were focused on building a democracy at any cost, and in order to do so, ex-Nazis had to be reintegrated into society rather than chastised or alienated. Gradually, throughout the early 1950s, they were welcomed back into society. The intensifying Cold War – in which Germany was of course directly on the front line – meant that the Allies were very busy pardoning perpetrators. Bureaucrats from the Nazi period were guaranteed pensions and, in general, both the Allies and the newly formed West German government considered investigations into Nazi crime to be a fading priority. However, there were young prosecutors who were powerfully driven to confront the Nazi past and who made it their mission to bring perpetrators to justice. Fritz Bauer, Attorney-General of the state of Hesse (and a German Jew who had been in exile during the Nazi period), was a main force behind Nazi trials and was the instigator of the Auschwitz trial. And so the new West German justice system slowly got its wheels into motion and investigations into Nazi crimes gained momentum throughout the 1950s.

State public prosecutors felt strongly that an organized and coherent national database for Nazi investigations was crucial, and so in October 1958, the 'Central Office of the Land Judicial Authorities for the Investigation of National-Socialist Crimes' (Zentrale Stelle der Landesjustizverwaltung zur Aufklärung nationalsozialistischer Verbrechen (ZdL)) in Ludwigsburg was established, through an agreement of regional judicial administrations and funded by all of the states. Civil servants at the ZdL investigated Nazi crimes (primarily in the East) and gathered information (documents or witness testimony), which was then forwarded to the appropriate prosecutor's office for criminal prosecution. In 1959 alone, the ZdL initiated 400 new investigations into crimes committed in the east by both the *Einsatzgruppen* and the guards at concentration and death camps.[1]

A new era of judicial investigation into Nazi crimes thus began, and by the late 1980s, the ZdL had launched investigations into at least 13,000 proceedings.[2] By 1992, approximately 103,823 German citizens had been investigated for Nazi crimes. This certainly sounds encouraging, but in fact only 6,487 of these suspects were prosecuted and convicted; worse, 5,513 were for 'non-lethal' crimes of National Socialism – generally aiding and abetting. Very few of these investigations actually pertained to the mass murder of Jews, because racial hatred, the identification of the ethnicity of the victims and the programme of racial annihilation were not central elements to a murder conviction. In all, of these some 6,000 convictions, 'little over seven percent actually related to the mass killing of Jews'.[3] Of the 6,487 convicted defendants, 13 were sentenced to death (before the death sentence was abolished), 163 to life imprisonment (a murder conviction), 6,197 to temporary prison terms and 114 to fines.[4] Why were the results so dismal? A brief examination of the legal code used for Nazi crimes after 1949 is necessary.

Criminal Law and Criminal Lawyers in the Shadow of the Third Reich

First and foremost, the newly formed Justice Ministry rejected the incorporation of the international criminal charges used at Nuremberg into the West German Penal Code, including the important and sweeping 'Crimes against Humanity' charge. Jurists argued that it was important to demonstrate that they could deal with their past using laws that had already existed during the Nazi period (which was certainly not the only motive, as we shall see). They used the national Penal Code, established in 1871, to try former Nazis. The murder charge stipulated that the prosecution prove the subjective inner motivation of the defendant. Elements of intent in murder included lust for murder, sexual drive for killing, treachery, malicious intent, cruelty and, finally, base motives (which the postwar German courts defined as race-hatred for the Nazi trials). There were debates within judicial circles regarding the definition of perpetration of murder as an objective or subjective act. Ultimately the German High Court of Appeals adopted an entirely subjective definition, which determined perpetration entirely by the presence of will, regardless of whether the defendant physically committed the act – thus allowing for the possibility that the person who committed the act not be guilty of murder. The distinction between perpetrator and accomplice in the Penal Code specified that the primary perpetrator must show individual initiative and knowledge of the illegality of the act; this meant that the more a defendant claimed that he believed in and identified with the Nazi worldview, the less likely he was to be convicted, despite the fact that the orders of the Nazi state had already been deemed illegal at Nuremberg.[5]

Why was this subjective definition embraced? The explosion of historical research on the West German confrontation with the past points to an undeniable presence of former Nazis in all parts of public life and, most especially, in the judiciary. Despite the best efforts of the Allies to purge the judicial system of its Nazi members, this seemed to be virtually impossible, as it would have left the justice system without any functionaries. During the reconstruction period of 1945–49, the Allies made more and more exceptions to their initial rule that anyone who had even nominally participated in the Hitler regime should lose their jobs. First, all those who had retired or been fired in 1933 were called back; next, anyone who joined the party after 1937 was given a clean slate; then, for every judge with a clean record, a tainted judge could be hired; and, finally, all judges who had gone through the flimsy denazification process could be brought back. This meant that in the state of Bavaria, for example, 80 per cent of the judiciary were former Nazis; in the city of Schweinfurt, that figure was a full 100 per cent.[6]

It is clear that legal theorists actively introduced roadblocks to the conviction of former Nazis so that jurists could shield themselves from conviction as law makers and law enforcers during the Nazi period. The best proof of the lasting heritage of Nazi law on postwar law is the fact that there were only two judgments of lawyers or judges who instituted and carried out the Nazi programme, and both were before 1949 (by the West German courts). There was certainly a connection between the jurists creating and interpreting the law, and the law itself, as we shall see. It is striking that the main jurist heading the commission for criminal law reform during the 1960s was a man named Edward Dreher. Dreher was the former prosecutor at the 'Sondergericht' – special courts set up by the Nazis that regularly sentenced people to death for the smallest of infractions – in Innsbruck during the Nazi period, and is presumed to have been responsible for the execution of hundreds of innocent people. He represents perhaps the most powerful of many former Nazi jurists in the postwar period, as he wrote the most widely used commentary on the criminal law during the 1960s. Surely Dreher's past and that of so many jurists making reforms to the legal system played a role in their worldview.[7] A recently published monograph entitled *Die Akte Rosenburg* – a historical examination of the Justice Ministry's involvement in Nazi crimes and postwar legacy – demonstrates the extraordinary degree to which lawyers and judges were not only card-carrying members of the Nazi Party, but also architects and enforcers of Nazi policy.[8]

Let me turn briefly to my earlier research focus, the Auschwitz trial. It was intended to be an event of great significance. In the mind of its principal organizer, Attorney-General Fritz Bauer, the trial was to put the entire 'Auschwitz Complex' before the court, not only the 'small men' who had carried out the 'Final Solution', but also those who had created the measures, policies and laws that had given the Holocaust an air of legality. The trial of twenty Auschwitz 'perpetrators' – representing a cross-section of criminals who participated in the atrocities at the camp between 1940 and 1945 – took place in Frankfurt starting in December 1963, and lasted over 180 days. It involved approximately 400 witnesses and produced 30,000 pages of files, not including the trial record itself. The trial was not the first criminal procedure against Nazi criminals in Germany, but it was by far the largest, most public and most important ever to take place in West Germany, using West German judges and West German law. It has emerged as the symbol of West Germany's ongoing confrontation with its past. Much literature on war crimes trials points to the Auschwitz trial as the true turning point in postwar West German understanding of Nazi crimes, as it 'captured the imagination of millions of young Germans as virtually nothing about the country's past had done before'.[9] And yet, the information that the public received was distorted. The sincere effort of the public prosecution to teach lessons about the culpability of all involved in the murder of innocents was hindered by the law as it was defined. Prosecutors had to adhere to rigid interpretations of the murder statute and subjective definitions of perpetrators and accomplices that, in the end, condemned only those who had gone above and beyond ordered acts of murder. Those who carried out the state-ordered genocide were convicted only – if they were convicted at all – as accomplices to murder. The murder of millions in the gas chambers – the main form of murder at Auschwitz, after all – became a lesser crime, with a lighter sentence, than the murder of one person without orders from superiors. The German public learned to chastise and denounce the sadistic 'excess perpetrators' of Auschwitz, and to forgive the order-followers whose crimes of complicity were never the true focus of the trial, the law or the extensive press coverage from which people obtained their information about the trial and, I would argue, about Auschwitz.[10]

The Majdanek and Stammheim Trials of 1975

Ten years after the end of the Auschwitz trial, the same pattern was evident. The Majdanek trial, which began in 1975 in Düsseldorf, had even more shameful results: of the fifteen indicted defendants at the Majdanek trial, nine were men and six were women, and the focus was particularly on the sadistic actions of the female guards, whose excessive cruelty was especially shocking and sensational because of their gender.[11] Otherwise, the trial was seemingly endless. Four defendants were acquitted in 1979 because of a lack of evidence. Only one defendant, known as 'Bloody Brigitte', was sentenced to life in prison in 1981, and of the rest, no one received a sentence longer than twelve years. One of the main reasons that the trial dragged on for six years was the behaviour of one unrepentantly disruptive lawyer named Ludwig Bock, a member of the right-wing extremist German People's Union, who lodged multiple complaints about the main expert witness on the side of the prosecution, the eminent historian Wolfgang Scheffler. What was the charge? That Scheffler could not be objective: his dissertation advisor had been Jewish, and being trained by a Jewish scholar meant that he was biased. In addition, he had the gall to have regular contact with other Jewish scholars. Such antics were indeed reported upon critically by the little press that did show up to comment on the Majdanek trial, but they were not enough to cause Bock's dismissal. Bock removed himself from the trial in April 1978, claiming that he was the victim of a smear campaign. It could be argued that the defence lawyers at the Majdanek trial plainly supported a criminal organization not only with their sympathetic arguments, but because some of them had been members of the Nazi Party and had been responsible for applying the perverted laws of the Nazi state. But at the Majdanek trial, the ban on retroactivity was to be strictly adhered to and the defendants were not to be charged with being members of a criminal organization because the SS in fact had not been one during the Nazi period. This seems just if the ban on retroactivity had been applied universally, but the decisions of the Federal legal officials in cases involving left-wing crimes transgressed it again and again, leading some critics to wonder whether there was a special 'lex RAF'.

What does 'lex RAF' mean? The subjective interpretation of the law – that individual initiative is required to prove perpetration of murder – was used to benefit Nazis, who were deemed less responsible for their beliefs because they were performing state-ordered actions, and to the detriment of left-wing terrorists, whose inner motivation was to destroy the democratic state. The four defendants at Stammheim were judged more harshly than Nazi defendants on the stand at the time because of their knowledge of the illegality of the act and their goal to commit crimes against the state. The Stammheim trial was the greatest public and media sensation of the era. It was also marred by flagrant legal violations that would never have occurred at the Majdanek trial, especially regarding the court's restriction of defence lawyers' rights and access to information.

First, in January 1975, the Federal Court in Karlsruhe decided that defendants could no longer have more than three lawyers and therefore had to quickly drop lawyers – and their defence strategies – just before the trials began. Second, and most astonishingly, a collaborative effort between the Federal Criminal Bureau, the Federal Attorney's office and the Federal Minister of the Interior resulted in a Federal Constitution Court decision in early 1975 to introduce an amendment to the Procedural Criminal Law (Strafprozessordnung (StPO)): judges were now required to dismiss defence lawyers if there was any '*suspicion* of supporting a criminal organization'.[12] Proof of support was not required; suspicion was enough. Of course, this meant that many defence lawyers were dismissed either directly before or at the very beginning of the trial as it was in fact their *mandate* as defence lawyers to support their clients – for the Federal Attorney General (GBA) and the High State Court of Stuttgart (OLG), supporting their clients and supporting the RAF as a criminal organization were one and the same. Klaus Croissant was dismissed as Andreas Baader's lawyer under this charge one day before the trial began; Kurt Groenewold and Christian Ströbele were also dismissed from defending Baader, and then Ensslin and Raspe, on the same charge a few months later. The Federal Attorney's office regularly referred publicly to the defence lawyers in the Stammheim trial as a 'lawyer's collective', conjuring up images of a communist (and therefore illegal) organization. Confidential letters and memos exchanged between lawyers and their clients were seized; when lawyers lodged complaints about the illegality of such measures, the OLG Stuttgart or the GBA simply threw out their objections. The ultimate example of the Federal Attorney Siegfried Buback's reactionary attitude was his proclamation that it was a disgrace simply to serve as a defence attorney for the RAF. What does it say about the new democracy when its highest legal official proclaims the defence of certain defendants – the most basic right in any democratic legal system – to be immoral? It should not surprise us that Siegfried Buback himself became a member of the Nazi Party on 1 July 1940.[13]

The extraordinary bungling of the trial against Siegfried Buback's murderers is another excellent example of the ways in which laws were loosely prescribed to in the case of RAF crimes. In July 1980, Knut Folkerts, a known RAF member, was sentenced to life in prison by the Federal Courts for murdering Buback. From the very beginning of this investigation, there were doubts about the possibility of his involvement, as he had already been serving a twenty-year sentence in the Netherlands for the murder of a Dutch policeman. In 2007, the GBA's reopened the Siegfried Buback murder investigation: Knut Folkerts was convicted as an accomplice, despite the fact that it was never proven that he was involved in the planning, pulled the trigger or was even in Karlsruhe – or Germany – at the time. *Der Spiegel* conducted extensive investigation into the whereabouts of Folkerts during the murder of Buback, and the journalists discovered extraordinary and numerous acts of both police and judicial incompetence, creating 'more evidence gaps than evidence'.[14]

In fact, the court seems to have been more interested in public opinion than in establishing the truth; there was very strong evidence that Folkerts was in Amsterdam at the time of the murder. In fact, two former RAF members, Verena Becker and Peter-Jürgen Boock, accused another former RAF colleague, Stefan Wisniewski, of murdering Buback from the passenger seat of a Suzuki GS750. Becker did so in 1982, in an interrogation in the constitutional courts, and Boock did the same in April 2007 in a conversation with *Der Spiegel*.[15] In fact, the details published by *Der Spiegel* in 2007 had been known to several Federal agencies for decades, but never turned into an investigation or criminal proceedings against Wisniewski. His name had never been associated with the murder of Buback, but he was a convicted RAF terrorist: he had been given two life sentences in 1981 for the abduction and the murder of Hanns Martin Schleyer and was released in 1999 after 'credibly dissociating himself' from 'enforcing political goals by force'. Federal Attorney Monika Harms opened a new investigation in April 2007, this time looking into Wisniewski's involvement in the crime. The state was never able to establish conclusively his guilt. In April 2009, Verena Becker was arrested for involvement in Buback's murder (she had been under investigation ever since she testified against Wisniewski); in 2012, she was convicted as an accomplice and sentenced to four years in prison, of which she served two and a half years. Political scientist Wolfgang Kraushaar is an expert on the subject of Verena Becker's role in the RAF and her subsequent prosecution and conviction; he called the trial against Becker a 'farce' and was extremely critical of the prosecution's handling of the case.[16]

The Stammheim trial and the various different trials regarding the murder of Siegfried Buback demonstrate a malleability and flexibility in relation to terrorist crimes – including a willingness to overlook evidence – that simply does not occur in Nazi trials. In the Majdanek trial, for example, the inability of the state to prove the defendant's physical presence during the commission of the crime, let alone his level of involvement in the shooting, would have completely ruled out a 'co-perpetrator' (Folkert's) conviction. Unless the state could prove that a defendant had acted on his or her individual initiative and the prosecutors adequately showed that the defendant possessed one of the elements of subjective inner motivation stipulated in the murder charge, the most he or she would be convicted of was 'aiding and abetting'. It could very well be that Knut Folkerts had the inner motivation and individual initiative required to make him guilty, but this would have to be proven, not assumed.

The Trials of John Demjanjuk

So how far has Germany come in its judicial reckoning with the past? We can look at a very recent example to see that the answer, sadly, is not very far. In late November 2009, the state court of Bavaria commenced the trial of John Demjanjuk, former camp guard at the Sobibor death camp. Demjanjuk was charged with aiding and abetting murder of 27,900 people. The state attorneys arrived at this number through a process of deduction: it is presumed that Demjanjuk was a guard at Sobibor in 1943 and during that time, as Nazi documents show, the same number of people were brought to Sobibor – mainly from the Netherlands – and murdered there. Demjanjuk presented a problematic case for many reasons. First, he was already (in)famous for his sensational trial in Israel three decades ago. He was extradited from the United States and put on trial there as 'Ivan the Terrible' – a notoriously sadistic camp guard at Treblinka – and sentenced to death (the only other Nazi sentenced to death in Israel besides Adolf Eichmann). Demjanjuk's Israel trial was almost as dramatic as the Eichmann trial in 1961, and was certainly meant to act as a galvanizing force in Israeli identity politics; once again, survivors were brought into the courtroom to describe the horrors of Treblinka, the death camp outside of Warsaw in which Ivan the Terrible was a guard. One by one, they identified Demjanjuk as the very same man who tortured them there. His conviction of crimes against humanity in 1988 carried a death sentence, but, unlike Eichmann, he was not executed right away and spent five years on death row. In 1993, the Supreme Court of Israel suddenly overturned the conviction. New evidence had become available because of the fall of communism and the opening of millions of KGB (secret police) files regarding Nazi crimes. This evidence pointed strongly to the fact that Demjanjuk had in fact been in Sobibor rather than Treblinka.

Demjanjuk returned home to Cleveland, Ohio, while American investigators put together a new case against him. This time he was tried by the Germans, which brings us to the second problem. Demjanjuk was conscripted by the Red Army and fought for the Soviets until he was captured by the Germans in 1942. He was then imprisoned as a prisoner of war (POW), where he faced a few bleak possibilities: murder at a concentration camp (the Nazis killed 15,000 Soviet POWs at Auschwitz alone in 1941), death through hard labour or starvation, or Trawniki, a training camp near the Ukraine border in Poland, set up by the Nazis for POWs like Demjanjuk to do the dirty work of murdering Jews at the Operation Reinhard death camps. So Demjanjuk constitutes a more complex kind of perpetrator than those Germans who joined the SS and worked at camps in order to avoid serving on the front, and the vast majority of those Germans were not tried or were tried and acquitted by German courts, Demjanjuk's superiors included. Demjanjuk was found guilty of aiding and abetting, with a five-year maximum sentence. To be sure, as a participant in the mass murder of thousands of innocent people in the Holocaust, he had to be tried and punished accordingly. The problem lies in the fact that Demjanjuk spent many more years in prison, as an involuntary guard against whom no concrete specific proof of his actions exist, than many thousands of Germans who voluntarily went to death camps and against whom there is copious evidence of participation in crimes of mass murder.

A good example of this flawed legal response to Nazi crimes is the case of SS Captain Karl Streibel, the commander of the Trawniki training camp. Trawniki was a multi-purpose camp that served different functions; while over 5,000 new SS guards were trained at the camp (mainly Soviet POWs, but also some civilians), there were also over 6,000 Jewish prisoners conscripted as forced labourers at the camp. In October 1943, the grisly 'Aktion Erntefest' was carried out: after attempted uprisings at Sobibor and other camps, the SS decided to act swiftly and violently as a deterrent: they shot all 6,000 Jewish prisoners at the camp in a single day, eradicating the entire workforce.[17] Karl Streibel was indicted by the LG Hamburg in 1970 for his role as commander at the camp; after six long years, he (along with five other guards) was acquitted of the mass murder of Jews.[18]

How is it possible that someone like Streibel was acquitted and someone like Demjanjuk was convicted as an accessory? Certainly, the personnel who today constitute the German legal system are not old Nazis trying to protect themselves from incrimination. We are dealing here with a whole new generation of jurists, most of whom genuinely want to address the Nazi past and pursue justice. In fact, in the few Nazi trials that still take place (including the Demjanjuk trial), prosecutors have gotten wise to the fact that it is virtually impossible to get a conviction for perpetration and therefore do not even indict on that charge. This means that there are more convictions that match the charges – of aiding and abetting – but it perpetuates the flawed argument that most people who worked voluntarily at death camps were simply accomplices. But Demjanjuk represents a problem case: first of all, it is unlikely that Demjanjuk joined the SS guard ranks voluntarily. Second, jurisdiction is a problem: the state argued that Demjanjuk could be tried by the Germans, although he is not German and his crimes did not take place in Germany, because he was an *Amtsträger* – an employee who lost his status as a POW because he was paid by the Germans and therefore was a member of the German bureaucracy. This definition of a guard like Demjanjuk is a highly problematic one for two reasons: first, it has been constructed retroactively by the ZdL in Ludwigsburg as a way to prosecute more people like Demjanjuk – non-German former POWs; and, second, as writer Scott Raab has argued: 'These *Wachmänner* were pure products of the most criminally insane nation in human history, Nazi Germany ... And now – now: sixty-five years later – a Ukrainian clump of Red Army fodder, the likes of which the Nazis murdered by the millions, has been transmuted into a German official so that Germans may prosecute him for helping to murder Jews at a German death camp.'[19]

Conclusion

The paradox is that Germany now confronts its past on a daily basis, like no other country, and one could easily hold up the German process as a model for how all postdictatorial societies should reform themselves. But the success of German *Vergangenheitsbewaeltigung* (coming to terms with the past) did not come through trials like that of John Demjanjuk.[20] The law was not the setting in which Germans would come to recognize the complicity of an entire generation; this would occur through different channels, most especially the earnest historical inquiry and an explosion of archival research, sound scholarship, debate and information to a young, curious German public. Indeed, perhaps the deficiencies of these trials are necessary; perhaps their failings are precisely what has led to more dialogue and debate and a more whole-hearted confrontation with the past. The legal approach to Nazi crime remains awkward, tortured and unfinished, and it will remain so even after the last Nazi is dead and gone.

Rebecca Wittmann is Associate Professor of History at the University of Toronto. Her research focuses on the Holocaust and post-war Germany, trials of Nazi perpetrators and terrorists, and German legal history. Her book *Beyond Justice: The Auschwitz Trial* (Harvard University Press, 2005) won the Fraenkel Prize in Contemporary History. Her edited volume *The Eichmann Trial Reconsidered* is forthcoming 2022 with the University of Toronto Press. She is currently working on her second book project entitled *Guilt and Shame through the Generations: Confronting the Past in Postwar Germany*.

Notes

1. Rückerl, *The Investigation of Nazi Crimes*, 53.
2. Rückerl, 'Nazi Crime Trials', 627.
3. De Mildt, *In the Name of the People*, 20–21. De Mildt states that many crimes prosecuted were 'final phase crimes': for example, the execution of German soldiers who had deserted, or 'political denunciation', that is, acting as informants to the Gestapo on fellow German citizens. Few trials actually related to the 'Final Solution' of the Jews in the death camps and gas chambers.
4. Ibid., Appendix A.1, 403.
5. For more on the German Criminal Code (StGB) in relation to Nazi crimes, see Rückerl, *The Investigation of Nazi Crimes*.
6. Mueller, *Hitler's Justice*, 202.
7. For more on Dreher and the lack of legal reforms, see Perels, *Das Juristische Erbe des 'Dritten Reiches'*.
8. Commissioned by the Ministry of Justice, similar to *Das Amt* – a historical exposition on the German Foreign Ministry and culpability during the Nazi era – such state-commissioned studies are part of a larger trend in enlightenment and public accountability, especially for government institutions. See Görtemacher and Safferling, *Die Akte Rosenburg*.
9. Osiel, *Mass Atrocity, Collective Memory, and the Law,* 192–93. Osiel quotes extensively from Hannah Arendt and Ian Buruma on the importance of the Auschwitz trials.
10. For more on the Auschwitz trial, see Pendas, *The Frankfurt Auschwitz Trial, 1963–1965*; and Wittmann, *Beyond Justice*.
11. All references to the Majdanek trial come from Investigation 853 Majdanek, and Landesgericht (LG) Düsseldorf Investigation 869 Majdanek, LG Düsseldorf, Az.: 8 KS 1/75, Rep. 432.
12. Bakker-Schut, *Stammheim*, 135–36.
13. 'Von RAF ermordeter Generalbundesanwalt Buback war NSDAP-Mitglied', *Focus Magazine,* 15 March 2011. Retrieved 5 May 2021 from http://www.focus.de/panorama/vermischtes/nsdap-von-raf-ermordeter-generalbundesanwalt-buback-war-ns-dap-mitglied_aid_608945.html.
14. 'Mehr Lücken als Beweise', *Der Spiegel*, 12 December 2007.
15. Büchel, '"Es ist auch Scham dabei"'.

16. Kraushaar, W., Commentary in *Die Tageszeitung,* 7 June 2011.
17. For more on Trawniki, see http://www.ushmm.org/wlc/en/article.php?Modu-leId=10007397 (retrieved 5 May 2021).
18. Published in Justiz und NS-Verbrechen Vol. XLI, verdict and trial summary online at https://www.junsv.nl, case #833, LG Hamburg 760603, BGH 791009.
19. Raab, 'John Demjanjuk'.
20. For more on the Demjanjuk trial, see Douglas, *The Right Wrong Man.*

Bibliography

Published Sources

Bakker-Schut, Pieter. *Stammheim.* Kiel: Neue Malik, 1989.
Büchel, Helmar. "'Es ist auch Scham dabei'. Ex terrorist Peter-Jürgen Boock, 55, über des Attentat auf Generalbundesanwalt Siegfried Buback, die Strategie der RAF und seine persönliche Schuld'. *Der Spiegel,* 24 April 2007.
De Mildt, Dick. *In the Name of the People: Perpetrators of Genocide in the Reflection of Their Post-War Prosecution in West Germany.* The Hague: Nijhoff, 1996.
Douglas, Lawrence. *The Right Wrong Man: John Demjanjuk and the Last Great Nazi War Crimes Trial.* Princeton: Princeton University Press, 2016.
Görtemacher, Manfred, and Christoph Safferling. *Die Akte Rosenburg: Das Bundesministerium, der Justiz und die NS Zeit.* Berlin: C.H. Beck, 2016.
Mueller, Ingo. *Hitler's Justice: The Courts of the Third Reich,* trans. Lucas Schneider. Cambridge, MA: Harvard University Press, 2001.
Osiel, Mark. *Mass Atrocity, Collective Memory, and the Law.* New Brunswick, NJ: Transaction Publishers, 1997.
Pendas, Devin O. *The Frankfurt Auschwitz Trial, 1963–1965: Genocide, History and the Limits of the Law.* Cambridge: Cambridge University Press, 2006.
Perels, Joachim. *Das Juristische Erbe des 'Dritten Reiches'.* Frankfurt: Campus, 1999.
Raab, Scott. 'John Demjanjuk: The Last Nazi'. *Esquire Magazine,* 11 August 2010. Retrieved 5 May 2021 from http://www.esquire.com/features/john-demjanjuk-1109.
Rückerl, Adalbert. *The Investigation of Nazi Crimes 1945-1978: A Documentation,* trans. Derek Rütter. Heidelberg: C.F. Müller, 1979.
———. 'Nazi Crime Trials', in Michael Marrus (ed.), *The Nazi Holocaust,* vol. 9 (Westport, CT: Meckler, 1989), 612–35.
Wittmann, Rebecca. *Beyond Justice: The Auschwitz Trial.* Cambridge, MA: Harvard University Press, 2005.

Archival Sources

Investigation 853 Majdanek and Landesgericht (LG) Düsseldorf Investigation 869 Majdanek, LG Düsseldorf, Az.: 8 KS 1/75, Rep. 432.
Justiz und NS-Verbrechen Vol. XLI, verdict and trial summary online https://www.junsv.nl/ (case #833), LG Hamburg 760603, BGH 791009.

CHAPTER 9

FORCE OF FACT

MUNICIPAL AUTHORITIES, VICTIM ASSOCIATIONS AND FORENSIC SCIENCE AT THE INTERNATIONAL CRIMINAL TRIBUNAL FOR THE FORMER YUGOSLAVIA

Isabelle Delpla

Introduction

Historians and social scientists have developed substantial interest in international trials as a paradigmatic source of data, archives and testimonies. They even take the existence of such sources for granted, so much so that they have become accustomed to classifying them according to the types of source they have produced or publicized: the Nuremberg trials proved to be the trial of documents, while the Eichmann trial was that of live victim testimonies, paving the way to the era of the witness.[1]

In a linear narrative of the progress of international justice, the International Criminal Tribunal for the Former Yugoslavia (ICTY) marked a crucial step. Reconciling the contributions of the Nuremberg and Jerusalem tribunals, it constituted both the court of witnesses, who represented the first primary evidence when documents were lacking, and subsequently the court of documents. In a new and more striking way, the ICTY used the most sophisticated forensic science to investigate mass crimes. Starting with the ICTY, international criminal justice entered the era of scientific police with a full panoply of the crime scene experts and forensic doctors who have become familiar characters in contemporary detective stories.[2]

In this context, the role and status of victim witnesses has evolved in part. This chapter aims to provide an overview of their role in this process of evidence gathering and in the constitution of archives. It will focus on two features: their mobilization and their diversity in the process of archive constitution. First, it is commonplace to talk about victim mobilization in the aftermath of mass crimes.[3] Such a phenomenon can be observed in Bosnia and Herzegovina from the municipal to the state and international levels.[4] However, while recalling the intertwining of these scales of mobilization, this chapter will challenge the usual connotations of protest and dissidence attached to the term 'mobilization' in descriptions of social movements in Western countries. Second, while these victims and their associations concurred in their search for truth, they exhibited a significant and often unnoticed degree of diversity in their relationship with the production of archives and regarding judicial procedures.

A Step, an Acme or an Exception?

Before addressing these issues, a caveat should be given: we should not take for granted the interest of international criminal courts in scientific precision or even factual truth. Rather, we should depart from a glorious and progressive interpretation of international justice, starting with Nuremberg, to reach the International Court (ICC) thanks to the ICTY's achievements. Instead of representing a step in the continuous progress of international justice and historical knowledge, the ICTY's investigations were actually an acme and have even become an exception in the realm of international criminal justice.

Indeed, the International Criminal Court (ICC) has developed a quite different approach. Its first prosecutor, Moreno Ocampo, has decided to primarily rely on state cooperation rather than on direct investigations. He has also turned away from field criminal investigations and forensic science expertise. Investigator teams were obligated to incorporate nongovernmental organization (NGO) members, who were less trained in the requirements of criminal investigations capable of standing cross-examination. Rapidly, such teams have also been barred from carrying out field investigations. Instead of international investigations, the Office of the Prosecutor has relied on intermediaries to identify witnesses and gather evidence. As a result, police investigators (some of them former ICTY officers) and judicial experts have resigned. Most cases have ended in fiasco at the trial stage due to a lack of serious evidence or credible witnesses. On several occasions, defence lawyers have been able to prove that the victim witnesses had been trained to provide false testimonies.[5]

One of the rare cases that ended up in a condemnation of the accused is quite relevant. Germain Katanga[6] was condemned to twelve years' imprisonment for crimes in Ituri without any precise account of the number of victims (which reduced during the procedures) and without a serious police investigation. The first field investigation took place five years after the opening of the case and three years after Katanga's indictment and incarceration. According to Juan Branco, the hyperinflation of legal and jurisprudential inventions in this case was inversely proportional to the weakness of empirical data.[7]

Not only has there been a lack of progress of international justice in the production of archives and evidence, but the requirements of international justice for the establishment of facts have also become less demanding than those of national courts in most democratic countries. This should be kept in mind before considering the ICTY investigations and production of evidence.

Some Characteristics of the ICTY Investigations: The New Role of Forensic Science

The ICTY's achievements in terms of the gathering of evidence are quite impressive. Without any claim to being exhaustive, this evidence can be said to fall into three main categories: live witnesses, documents and data resulting from forensic science. As stated in its official presentation,[8] the ICTY heard more than 4,650 witnesses on more than 10,800 trial days, which were transcribed in more than 2.5 million pages. In the predominant adversarial procedures at the ICTY and in the absence of an instruction file, all information had to be presented in court. In the first trials, given the lack of documents, eyewitnesses who survived the Prijedor camps were the primary providers of evidence. Their role differed from that of the victim witnesses in the Eichmann trial, who mainly possessed expressive and symbolic value, and hardly added crucial information compared to the documents already available. At later stages, after the end of the war, when field investigations became possible in Bosnia and Herzegovina, the prosecution was also able to rely on documents obtained through search and seizure or other means of investigation.

The ICTY's novelty compared to previous international war crime trials was twofold. First, unlike the Nuremberg tribunal, the ICTY allowed and favoured guilty pleas, a procedure that led several defendants to speak as key eyewitnesses and release crucial 'insider' information, particularly concerning the Srebrenica massacre.[9] Second, forensic science has developed a new role for mass crimes. Criminal investigations started to bring together specialists who traditionally possessed criminal expertise, but were new in mass crime investigations, including crime scene technicians, ballistic analysts, mass grave archaeologists, physical anthropologists, forensic doctors and military analysts. DNA analysis is also now used at a mass scale.

The crucial role played by forensic science could be seen in the Srebrenica investigations in two regards. First, several executions left no survivors or eyewitnesses for the vast operation that took place several months after the killings to displace and hide the corpses in 'secondary' mass graves. Analysis of the objects found at these locations, such as cartridge cases, blindfolds, ligatures and fragments of broken glass, along with the examination of soils and pollens has enabled 'primary' and 'secondary' mass graves to be linked. This phase of evidence concealment was therefore only established through forensic science, given the lack of eyewitnesses or documents.[10] Second, Srebrenica's classification as a crime and as genocide greatly relied on forensic medicine, which became crucial to prove that Bosniak[11] men were defenceless and not killed in combat.[12] A large number of the corpses were found with their hands tied behind their backs. The very fact that these individuals were executed clearly contradicts claims that the victims were combatants. Forensic doctors acquired a new status: they became the dead victims' spokespeople and allowed witnesses from the grave to tell a story that no live witness could or would.[13]

In addition, the ICTY procedures led to the cross-examination of these experts by defence lawyers and to the opposition of experts for the prosecution and for the defence. As a consequence, this new level of precision has tended to become the norm in further trials and investigations, especially with the increased use of DNA analysis for the individual identification of mass crime victims.

International Mobilization

The Srebrenica investigations were particularly representative of an international mobilization of experts and expertise to establish the events and crimes. Such mobilization can be considered in three ways. First, it is that of the international organizations that help search for data, such as to assess the number of refugees (e.g. the United Nations High Commissioner for Refugees (UNHCR)) or war casualties and missing persons (the International Committee of the Red Cross (ICRC) and the International Commission for Missing Persons (ICMP)).[14] Second, it is that of actors such as ICTY staff, journalists, members of international organizations and NGOs who come from all over the world. Third, it is an internationalization of expertise.

This internationalization of expertise is particularly clear in the case of the search for missing persons and the identification of anonymous corpses or bones found by thousands in Srebrenica, as well as on a smaller scale in numerous places across Bosnia and Herzegovina. At the beginning of the investigations for mass crimes, traditional forms of identification prevailed. On the one hand, criminal justice only required mass ethnic identification and not individual recognition; it was sufficient that the victims were women, children or unarmed to classify their killings as a war crime, and that they were Bosniaks (identified as such by their clothes or personal objects) to support classification of the crime as a crime against humanity or genocide. On the other hand, the individual identification of victims was dependent on family recognition of corpses or, in a softer way, of the photographs of clothes or personal belongings gathered in the ICRC books of missing persons.

The search for the missing and their identification progressively attracted foreign forensic doctors gathered in the NGO Physicians for Human Rights who, like Clyde Snow, had worked to find missing persons in Argentina or Guatemala. Later on, the ICMP, which was created in 1996, developed methods of DNA identification in Bosnia and Herzegovina on a large scale, which allowed for individual identification en masse; these were subsequently exported to other countries in Africa, Asia and the Americas. Symptomatic of this internationalization, the ICRC, Physicians for Human Rights, the ICMP and the ICTY collaborated or competed with various methods for the search and identification of missing persons.[15]

State Mobilization at All Levels

In Bosnia and Herzegovina, such international mobilization has not been separable from the state mobilization of Federation[16] and Bosniak authorities, be it at the head of the state or at the local level. First, the ICTY was able to rely on the state apparatus and its resources: the ICTY benefited from its cooperation with the Federation police, the secret service, the army intelligence service and the War Crimes Commission directed by Mirsad Tokača. The exhumations were also realized with the Federal Commission for Missing Persons. According to my own findings in a research project on ICTY witnesses in the area of Prijedor, ICTY witnesses often gave their first statement to the municipal police and not to the NGOs or victim associations. Such state cooperation was also decisive in the Srebrenica investigations: the ICTY could rely on the inventory of the War Crimes Commission and on the huge compilation of witness accounts undertaken by the Tuzla police and the Agency for Information and Documentation (AID), that is, the Bosnian secret service and the radio communications intercepted by the Army of the Republic of Bosnia and Herzegovina.

Such state cooperation was not a matter of mere routine or lip service paid to European Union (EU) requests. Concerning Croatia and in particular Serbia, state cooperation with the ICTY was the result of political pressure and bargaining in the process of negotiating for EU membership.[17] The reluctance was even greater for the Republika Srpska, which for the most part refused to cooperate with the ICTY, except under intense pressure from the Office of the High Representative. On the contrary, the Bosnia and Herzegovinan authorities during the war and the Federation authorities after 1995 made a clear political choice to cooperate with international institutions in an attempt to establish state and national legitimacy regarding international law and justice. They hoped that international justice would prove that the state of Bosnia and Herzegovina was the victim of aggression by Serbia and Montenegro, and that Bosniaks as a nation were the primary victims of war crimes and even genocide. Indeed, on 20 March 1993, the Government of the Republic of Bosnia and Herzegovina (which was named as such from 14 December 1995) filed proceedings against the Federal Republic of Yugoslavia (from 4 February 2003 named Serbia and Montenegro and from 3 June 2006 the Republic of Serbia) for violations of the Convention on the Prevention and Punishment of the Crime of Genocide.[18]

Cooperation with the ICTY therefore proved key in the pursuit of political and moral legitimacy. State institutions cooperated with the ICTY's Office of the Prosecutor at all levels, extending to certain types of victim associations. The associations of former camp inmates were active participants in this process at the national, regional and municipal levels. Camp inmates were the primary eyewitnesses for prosecution cases and their associations helped locate them or collect their testimonies.[19] Several representatives of these associations testified at the ICTY, either as direct eyewitnesses or as representatives of the associations and the voices of others.[20]

Such local mobilization of individual victims and victim associations to gather evidence was reinforced by direct exchanges with ICTY investigators, who were present at the crime scenes in the area. This worked in two directions: victim witnesses helped the ICTY to locate other witnesses, places or data, and in return they expected that the ICTY would arrest their persecutors and help them find their missing relatives. Unsurprisingly, the other type of association that was most often mobilized to gather evidence were associations of the families of missing persons, who also organized at the municipal and state levels with the active support of the ICMP. Over the years, the ICMP succeeded in creating a huge DNA database linking human remains to relatives, which relied on the families' cooperation to provide blood samples.

Culture of Proof and Critical Competence

Such international and state organization at all levels resulted in the creation of a culture of proof and evidence. The state institutions and victim associations that used to work with international organizations often ended up competing to produce the most precise and trustworthy casualty assessment. In other contexts, it was conventional to compete by inflating the number of victims.[21] However, on several occasions in Bosnia and Herzegovina, local victim associations insisted that there were mistakes in their previous records, as some victims had been counted twice. They were prepared to diminish their casualty tolls to prove their seriousness and credibility. This move was accompanied by criticisms of Serb records for having used inflated figures, including people who had died before the war or elsewhere. In the case of Srebrenica, the United Nations (UN) and the ICTY supported this effort. Bosnian Serb authorities defended the massacre as an act of revenge for the genocide committed on Serbs around Srebrenica.

Such an interpretation was based on the claim that over 3,000 Serbs were killed there, while the ICTY and the Bosnian Research and Documentation Center discredited these figures, showing that Serbs actually suffered 151 casualties.[22]

The competition for precision led to a profound revision of the number of war casualties. During the war, the authorities of Bosnia and Herzegovina claimed that there were 200,000 casualties, who were mainly civilians. Convergent studies by the ICTY[23] and the Research and Documentation Center in *The Bosnian Book of the Dead* concurred in establishing that a little under 100,000 people had been killed during the war, a small majority of whom belonged to the military.[24] Significantly, the Research and Documentation Center in Sarajevo, directed by Mirsad Tokača, pursued the work of the War Crimes Commission, thereby symbolizing long-term cooperation between international and national investigations. Nevertheless, such a drastic revision of war casualties triggered violent criticism against the Research and Documentation Center and its director.

Criticism of one's own victim association for inaccuracy, exaggeration or distortion is also common, but less obvious. The difference between witness truth and institutional truth begins with the collection of testimonies by victim associations. There are first cases of outright private or public protest against a distortion of one's testimony to serve a national cause.[25] There is also day-to-day resistance to a national interpretation of one's own experience. The remarkable work of Cécile Jouhanneau on the Brčko association of former camps inmates describes a discreet normalization of the testimonies, erasing individual differences in the collection of data, not because of some malevolent attempt at standardization, but as a result of psychological mechanisms of defence and fatigue by representatives of these associations, who were also victims themselves and lacked professional training.

Internal criticism has also been voiced against the investigative work of international organizations. In different ways, several representatives of victim associations and witnesses, who have become accustomed to interacting with international and national organizations for the gathering of evidence, have also developed a critical competence. Not only are they familiar with the ICTY's proceedings, but they also make a point of analysing them. Of course, lay criticism or denunciation of judicial procedures are common, especially when sentences are either deemed too lenient or severe. Such critical competence differs from lay criticisms in two regards. It combines the usual opposition between witness truth and legal truth with an insider perspective on the ICTY's procedural choices. They do explain what was left aside in the ICTY's investigations, but also try to explain why such choices were made.

In this way, these victims and witnesses have contributed to the debate among historians on the relationship between historical truth and judicial truth. There is clear convergence between the questions that are relevant for witnesses and those of researchers. In particular, victims and witnesses point to the difficulties raised by:

(1.) the timeframe of the indictment, which generally focused on a few days or few months, leaving aside previous and following events that were less lethal but no less important to understanding the dynamics of the events and of the continuous persecutions.

(2.) the choices of the indictment to leave aside not only precise individuals, but also entire categories of perpetrators (for instance, none of the military investigators who led interrogations in the Prijedor camps was indicted).

(3.) the specific or generic crimes left aside by indictments, one of the main complaints of women associations being that rape charges are often dropped.

(4.) the locality under investigation: the focus on well-known mass crimes overshadowed numerous places where exactions were also carried out.

(5.) prosecutors' choice of witnesses: why some individuals were key witnesses for being the only survivor or why others were chosen for their symbolic or social status.

They therefore attempt to explain the success or failure of the ICTY investigations and prosecutions both by the objective availability of evidence or the lack thereof and by the choices made by the Office of the Prosecutor.

Differences among Victims and Victim Associations: Status and National Differences

As a result, there are important differences between victim associations that are largely underestimated. The most striking difference is that of legal categories and status:

(1.) civil victims of war are defined in relation to the Geneva Convention and in opposition to wounded veterans or killed soldiers. They can be direct or indirect victims of violence – in the first case, suffering corporal damage (such as losing a limb) and, in the second case, suffering social damage (losing a family member such as a husband or parent).

(2.) former camp inmates can be civilians or members of the military and share a common fate of severe mistreatment forbidden by international humanitarian law and the law of armed conflicts. They are all direct victims of arbitrary detention (for civilians) and mistreatment.

(3.) there is an ambiguity in the status of missing persons: they can be soldiers missing in action, who are war casualties without being victims of forced disappearance, while missing persons (civilians or military) can also be victims of forced disappearance and therefore defined as victims of humanitarian and human rights violations. Given that all of the wartime missing persons in Bosnia and Herzegovina were dead, the associations that dealt with their cases were associations of the families of missing persons. There is a second ambiguity in the status of victims, who are both the missing ones and their families as vicarious victims.

A second major difference is a national one inasmuch as ethnic or national factors account for the structure of victimhood. Indeed, associations of families of missing persons in Prijedor mainly gather Bosniaks and a few Croats, as Bosniaks and Croats as non-Serbs were frequently the victims of ethnic cleansing by Serb nationalist forces in 1992. Moreover, Srebrenica associations of families of missing persons for the 1995 massacre are entirely Bosniaks because there were no other non-Serbs in Srebrenica at the time.[26] This national factor is also constitutive of their organization on a larger scale: to prove the rights of the Bosniak people as victims of genocide, the Bosniak authorities additionally organize these associations on a national basis.

These differences of status and nationality partially explain the contrasting attitudes that can be seen towards the gathering of evidence. Associations of civilian victims of war are not part of such a process. The status of civilian victims of war is granted by a state commission on the basis of a medical record and does not require criminal investigations. Conversely, proving that mistreatments took place in the camps or searching for missing persons requires legal proceedings and criminal investigations. As a result, victim associations for camp detainees and missing persons were the first to cooperate with the ICTY. However, they did this in accordance with their national or state authorities. As a result, Bosnian-Serb and Serb associations cooperated much less frequently with international organizations than did Bosniak or even Croat associations.

The Degree of Cooperation with International Organizations

However, the major difference is the lack or degree of cooperation with international organizations. The difference between non-Serb and Serb associations of missing persons in Prijedor is telling: the non-Serbs, mainly Bosniaks, have organized themselves into two associations: one specialized in relationships with families (Bridges of Friendship) and the other in the collection of data (Izvor, meaning 'The Source'). Both work in close contact with the ICMP. In the aftermath of the war, Izvor established a book of the missing, collecting their pictures and their names, and working on a municipal database. Its representatives are proud of the truthfulness of their data and do not hesitate to contradict the Research and Documentation Center in Sarajevo: they prefer to reduce the number of casualties to prove the seriousness of their findings. Izvor representatives and members worked with the ICTY from its creation in 1993 and some have testified at The Hague. Indeed, the ICTY started its procedures with Prijedor crimes and targeted nearly twenty indicted perpetrators. In addition, given that Prijedor is located in the Republika Srpska, non-Serb victims needed the ICTY investigations to access the crime scenes and the mass graves.

In contrast, the Serb association for fallen soldiers and missing persons in Prijedor does not have a database or even a precise list of casualties. To every question concerning the quantity or quality of casualties (men, women, children and military/civilians), their representatives refer to a database in Banja Luka (the capital of the Republika Srpska), which they have not personally used. The Banja Luka database functions as a proof of authority, but not as a source of evidence that can be observed, checked and discussed. This association has never been in contact with the ICTY or the ICMP, has no relationships with non-Serb associations and does not celebrate the missing persons on 31 August, the international day of missing persons. This is particularly striking when considering the fact that the association of Serb missing persons from Krajina gathers victims from Operation Storm, carried out by the Croatian army against Serb forces in Croatia. Serbs from Croatia were reliant on the ICTY investigations to locate and access corpses in Croat territory and to prove that war crimes had been committed against their group. They have cooperated with the ICTY and the ICMP and have increased the precision of their evidence, demonstrating an attitude in line with that of other associations accustomed to working with international organizations.

Differences among Witnesses: A Relationship to an Event or to an Institution

What is true of victim associations is also true of individual witnesses. Some have been in regular contact with ICTY investigators. They may have testified several times, in the same or in different courts (the ICTY, Bosnia and Herzegovina state courts, and cantonal courts). Some may have done so due to their capacity to handle the judicial constraints of precision, coherence and steadiness when facing cross-examination or to their awareness of the court requirements. Aware that they might be called to testify in future trials, they also know that all of their statements or actions both inside and outside court can be used by defence lawyers to challenge and delegitimize their testimonies, and hence recognize the constant constraint that court testimonies cast on their entire lives. Indeed, being a credible court witness in the long term requires a considerable degree of quasi-professionalization.

These judicial procedures and court testimonies have created unexpected differences among eyewitnesses who have lived through similar wartime experiences, all being Bosniaks in the Prijedor area. There have been several trials for Prijedor since 1995, and many Bosniaks have testified, sometimes several times. In July 1992, men from the village of Biljani, located a few miles away, were rounded up and shot. The first trial specifically dealing with this massacre took place in 2007. For most of the Biljani witnesses, this was their first judicial testimony. When they were interrogated about their testimonies in court, the witnesses talked only about the Biljani massacre; testifying here was a relationship with an event. However, when I asked Prijedor witnesses about their testimonies in court, they mainly spoke about their ICTY experience; testifying was a relationship with an institution or with their performance in court as much as it was with an event.[27]

The case of Biljani also exemplifies a previously mentioned process of evidence selection. In Biljani, there is no difference between the discourse of the association and that of ordinary witnesses; indeed, the whole village was witness to the crime and the association remains at the local level. In contrast, a discrepancy between ordinary witnesses' accounts and their organized representatives is apparent for associations where the same individuals concentrate power and representation. In the small world of Bosniak associations, some stories circulate, while others are never mentioned. Some put forth radiant catharsis thanks to their court testimonies, but others were blatantly mistreated afterwards given their lack of protection. The stereotyped stories rarely correspond to the experiences of ordinary witnesses. They also overlook cases of Serbs who testified for the prosecution to accuse other Serbs of war crimes on non-Serbs, or cases of Bosniak victim witnesses who testified for the defence of Serbs.

Such selectivity of evidence and truth is common. Filtering processes in this way are stronger when association representatives become more institutionalized and unavoidable figures. The filtering process is also a side effect of the attendance of international organizations, such as the ICMP or the ICTY: the more these organizations favour contact with victim associations, the more their representatives acquire international legitimacy. Such an international legitimating effect also applies to media exposure. In fact, the same victim representatives represent the main sources for television and radio programmes, and academic researchers and journalists are typically drawn to them through the same channels (i.e. associations, NGOs and translators).

Other processes of selection and restriction in stimulating evidence gathering at the ICTY should also be stressed. The mobilization of victims and victim witnesses has its own biases. Some associations (especially those of Srebrenica) are over-researched, while others are neglected. There are also the more discreet mobilizations of defence witnesses and defence lawyers, which are even more neglected. Studies of defence witnesses remain inchoate and the ways in which defences at the ICTY are or are not the objects of mobilization, negotiation and pressure by political authorities, defendants and their lawyers remain unchartered territory. [28]

Concluding Remarks

The issue of the production of archives for or through international criminal proceedings is crucial for historians in particular and researchers in general. However, this is not solely an academic issue. The use (or lack thereof) of some ICTY archives by the ICJ in the genocide case of Bosnia and Herzegovina has triggered intense debates and violent polemics in the political and social arena as well.[29] The constitution of these archives of the war in Bosnia and Herzegovina cannot be separated from the state mobilization for the gathering of evidence, one that was primarily undertaken by the army, the police and the intelligence services.

The mobilization of victim associations is part of the same endeavour. The mobilization of victims and victim associations often continues the task of social movements in socialist Yugoslavia. State patronage remains central and the associations can also be a way of channelling and silencing protests against national and/or state authorities. Seeing their mobilization through Western lenses as signs of protest or dissidence against the authorities is misleading. So is a comparable interpretation of these mobilizations as proving the emergence of autonomous actors and of a new civil society, independent of political forces.[30] The paradigm of transitional justice as a process towards liberal democracy through (international) justice is also a form of wishful thinking.

Underlining how the mobilization of victims and victim associations for archive gathering also represents a form of state mobilization does not delegitimize them. The modest purpose of this chapter has been to oppose some misinterpretations of these mobilizations and to elucidate their complexities. It also calls for further research on processes that remain under-researched. In particular, too little is known about the work of state institutions (the intelligence services, the Army and the police) or defence witnesses or defence lawyers in this process of producing archives.

Isabelle Delpla is Professor of Philosophy at Jean Moulin Lyon 3 University. Her research on postwar and international justice has particularly focused on postwar Bosnia and Herzegovina. There, in the 2000s, she studied how the ICTY impacted and was perceived by victims and victim associations, prosecution and defence witnesses and some convicted persons. She is the author of *Le mal en procès: Eichmann et les théodicées modernes* (Editions Hermann, 2011); *La justice des gens; Enquêtes dans la Bosnie des nouvelles après-guerres* (Presses Universitaires de Rennes, 2014); and *Investigating Srebrenica: Fact, Responsibilities, Intelligibility* (Berghahn Books, 2014, coedited with Xavier Bougarel and Jean-Louis Fournel).

Notes

1. Wieviorka, *The Era of the Witness*.
2. For such a trend, see the television series *CSI: Crime Scene Investigation* [*Les experts*].
3. Lefranc and Mathieu, *Mobilisations de victimes*; concerning the mobilization of the mothers of Srebrenica, see also Nettlefield, *Courting Democracy in Bosnia and Herzegovina*.
4. This chapter focuses on my research on the reception of the ICTY in Bosnia and Herzegovina, especially by victim associations and witnesses, mainly published in a collection edited by Delpla and Bessone, *Peines de la guerre*; and Delpla, *La justice des gens* (especially Part IV).
5. Maupas, *Le Joker des puissants*.
6. See ICC, case ICC-01/04-01/07, case information sheet, retrieved 5 May 2021 from https://www.icc-cpi.int/CaseInformationSheets/katangaEng.pdf.
7. Branco, *De l'Affaire Katanga au contrat social global*.
8. 'ICTY Facts & Figures'. Retrieved 5 May 2021 from http://www.icty.org/en/content/infographic-icty-facts-figures.
9. For this procedure, see https://www.icty.org/en/cases/guilty-pleas; https://www.icty.org/en/features/statements-guilt (retrieved 5 May 2021); Combs, *Guilty Pleas in International Criminal Law*; Schweiger, 'Entre recherche de la vérité et pragmatisme', 151–65.
10. See Ruez, 'The ICTY Investigations'.
11. The term 'Bosnians' (*Bosanci*) refers to all inhabitants of Bosnia, while the term 'Bosniaks' (*Bošnjaci*) only refers to members of the nation that had until 1993 been described as a Muslim nation and distinct from the other constituent nations of Bosnia (i.e. Serbs and Croats).
12. Dean Manning (ICTY investigator), 'Summary of Forensic Evidence: Execution Points and Mass Graves, 16 May 2000. Retrieved 5 May 2021 from https://web.archive.org/web/20170425192611/http://abunodisceomnes.wellcomecollection.org/wp-content/uploads/2015/01/Manning-D.-16-May-2000-Srebrenica-investigation-Summary-of-forensic-evidence-Execution-points-and-mass-graves-ICTY-Investigator.pdf#page=69.
13. On this new role of forensic doctors, see Joyce and Stover, *Witnesses from the Grave*; Stover and Peress, *The Graves*; Lecomte, *Quai des ombres*; Koff, *The Bone Woman*.
14. See International Commission on Missing Persons, https://www.icmp.int (retrieved 5 May 2021).
15. For this international process, see Delpla, 'Incertitudes publiques et privées sur les disparus en Bosnie-Herzégovine', 287–301.
16. The Dayton Agreement of November 1995 made a territorial compromise, providing for the partition of Bosnia and Herzegovina between two constitutive entities: the Federation of Bosnia-Herzegovina (51 per cent of Bosnian territory) and the Republika Srpska (49 per cent).
17. Subotic, *Hijacked Justice*.
18. International Court of Justice (ICJ), Application of the Convention on the Prevention and Punishment of the Crime of Genocide (*Bosnia and Herzegovina v. Serbia and Montenegro*) (1996). Retrieved 5 May 2021 from https://www.icj-cij.org/en/case/91/judgments.
19. On the association of former camp inmates in Brcko, see Jouhanneau, *Sortir de la guerre en Bosnie-Herzégovine*.

20. These associations are organized at a municipal level; each municipality with wartime places of detainment has an association. The municipal associations are then reunited at a regional level and at a national level in the Federal Association of Former Camp Inmates.
21. For such an inflation process, see Revet, *Anthropologie d'une catastrophe*.
22. See ICTY press briefing, Office of the Prosecutor, 6 July 2005. Retrieved 5 May 2021 from http://www.icty.org/en/press/icty-weekly-press-briefing-6th-jul-2005. See also Tokaca, 'The Myth of Bratunac'. Retrieved 5 May 2021 from https://srebrenicamassacre1995.wordpress.com/tag/mirsad-tokaca.
23. For the demographic study of the ICTY Office of the Prosecutor, see Tabeau and Bijak, 'War-Related Deaths in the 1992–1995 Armed Conflicts', 187–215; and Tabeau and Zwierzchowski, 'A Review of Estimation Methods', 213 sq.
24. See Research and Documentation Centre Sarajevo, http://www.transconflict.com/gcct/gcct-members/europe/the-balkans/bosnia-and-herzegovina/research-and-documentation-centre-sarajevo (retrieved 5 May 2021).
25. A well-known case is that of the book *I Begged Them to Kill Me* about female victims of rape, published by the Federal Association of Former Camp Inmates: Dr Nedžib Šaćirbegović, Melika Malešević and Irfan Ajanović (eds), *Molila sam ih da me ubiju [I Begged Them to Kill Me:]*. Many women protested that their testimonies had been modified and published without their consent.
26. There are other important and sometimes unnoticed differences between victims and victim associations, which are less relevant here, and specifically municipal differences. See Delpla, 'In the Midst of Injustice', 211–34.
27. Such a contrast only holds for eyewitnesses – even when defence witnesses have testified for the first time, they tend to avoid the war's events.
28. To my knowledge, the only study is the one I conducted with defence witnesses in the Prijedor area; see Delpla, *La justice des gens*, Part IV.
29. The ICJ refused Bosnia and Herzegovina's request to order Serbia to furnish the ICJ with the minutes of the Supreme Defence Council, the body in charge of the Yugoslav Army. These minutes had been delivered to the ICTY within the framework of Slobodan Milošević's trial on the condition of confidentiality and were available to the judges when they decided to refuse to acquit Milošević of charges of genocide in several municipalities of Bosnia and Herzegovina. See Wilson, *Writing History in International Criminal Tribunal*, 42.
30. For such an interpretation, see Nettlefield, *Courting Democracy in Bosnia and Herzegovina*.

Bibliography

Branco, Juan. *De l'Affaire Katanga au contrat social global: un regard sur la Cour pénale international*. Paris: Institut Universitaire de Varenne, Collection des thèses, 2015.

Combs, Nancy Amoury. *Guilty Pleas in International Criminal Law: Constructing a Restorative Justice Approach*. Stanford: Stanford University Press, 2006.

Delpla, Isabelle. 'Incertitudes publiques et privées sur les disparus en Bosnie-Herzégovine', in Le Pape Marc, Johanna Siméant and Claudine Vidal (eds), *Crises extrêmes. Face aux massacres, aux guerres civiles et aux génocides* (Paris: La Découverte, 2006), 287–301.

————. 'In the Midst of Injustice: The ICTY from the Perspective of Some Victim Associations', in Bougarel Xavier, Elissa Helms and Ger Duijzings (eds), *The New Bosnian Mosaic: Identities, Memories and Moral Claims in a Post-War Society* (Farnham: Ashgate, 2007), 211–34.

————. *La justice des gens: Enquêtes dans la Bosnie des nouvelles après-guerres.* Rennes: Presses Universitaires de Rennes, 2014.

Delpla, Isabelle, and Magali Bessone (eds). *Peines de la guerre: La justice pénale internationale et l'ex-Yougoslavie.* Paris: EHESS Editions, 2010.

Jouhanneau, Cécile. *Sortir de la guerre en Bosnie-Herzégovine: Une sociologie politique du témoignage et de la civilité.* Paris: Karthala, 2016.

Joyce, Christopher, and Eric Stover. *Witnesses from the Grave: The Stories Bones Tell.* Boston: Little Brown & Co, 1991.

Koff, Clea. *The Bone Woman: A Forensic Anthropologist's Search for Truth in the Mass Graves of Rwanda, Bosnia, Croatia, and Kosovo.* New York: Random House Trade, 2004.

Lecomte, Dominique. *Quai des ombres.* Paris: Fayard, 2003.

Lefranc, Sandrine, and Lilian Mathieu. *Mobilisations de victimes.* Rennes: Presses Universitaires de Rennes, 2015.

Manning Dean. 'Summary of Forensic Evidence: Execution Points and Mass Graves, 16 May 2000. Retrieved 5 May 2021 from https://web.archive.org/web/20170425192611/http://abunodisceomnes.wellcomecollection.org/wp-content/uploads/2015/01/Manning-D.-16-May-2000-Srebrenica-investigation-Summary-of-forensic-evidence-Execution-points-and-mass-graves-ICTY-Investigator.pdf#page=69.

Maupas, Stéphanie. *Le Joker des puissants: Le grand roman de la Cour pénale international.* Paris: Editions Don Quichotte, 2016.

Nettlefield, Lara. *Courting Democracy in Bosnia and Herzegovina: The Hague Tribunal's Impact in a Postwar State.* Cambridge: Cambridge University Press, 2010.

Revet, Sandrine. *Anthropologie d'une catastrophe: Les coulées de boues au Vénézuela.* Paris: Presses nouvelles de la Sorbonne, 2017.

Ruez, Jean-René. 'The ICTY Investigations', in Isabelle Delpla, Xavier Bougarel and Jean-Louis Fournel (eds), *Investigating Srebrenica: Institutions, Facts, Responsibilities* (Oxford: Berghahn Books, 2014), 24–39.

Šaćirbegović Nedžib, Melika Malešević and Irfan Ajanović (eds). *Molila sam ih da me ubiju: Zločin nad ženom Bosne i Hercegovine* [*I Begged Them to Kill Me: The Crime against the Women of Bosnia-Herzegovina*]. Sarajevo: Savez logoraša BiH – Centar za iztraživanje zločina (CID), 1999.

Schweiger, Romana. 'Entre recherche de la vérité et pragmatisme. Le plea bargaining au TPIY et en Bosnie-Herzégovine', in Magali Bessone and Isabelle Delpla (eds). *Peines de la guerre. La justice pénale internationale et l'ex-Yougoslavie* (Paris: EHESS Editions, 2010), 151–65.

Stover, Eric, and Gilles Peress. *The Graves: Srebrenica, Vukovar.* Zurich: Scalo, 1998.

Subotic, Jelena. *Hijacked Justice: Dealing with the Past in the Balkans.* Ithaca, NY: Cornell University Press, 2009.

Tabeau, Ewa, and Jakub Bijak. 'War-Related Deaths in the 1992–1995 Armed Conflicts in Bosnia and Herzegovina: A Critique of Previous Estimates and Recent Results'. *European Journal of Population* 21(2–3) (2005), 187–215.

Tabeau, Ewa, and Jan Zwierzchowski. 'A Review of Estimation Methods for Victims of the Bosnian War and the Khmer Rouge Regime', in Taylor B. Seybolt, Jay D. Aronson and Baruch Fischhoff (eds), *Counting Civilian Casualties: An Introduction to Recording and Estimating Nonmilitary Deaths in Conflict* (Oxford: Oxford University Press, 2013), 213–43.

Tokaca, Mirsad. 'The Myth of Bratunac: A Blatant Numbers Game', 2006. Retrieved 30 May 2021 from https://srebrenicamassacre1995.wordpress.com/tag/mirsad-tokaca/.

Wieviorka, Annette. *The Era of the Witness*. Ithaca, NY: Cornell University Press, 2006 (original French edition Paris: Plon, 1998).

Wilson, Richard Ashby. *Writing History in International Criminal Tribunal*. Cambridge: Cambridge University Press, 2011.

CHAPTER 10

INTERNATIONAL LAW IN ACTION
THE ROLE OF THE LEGAL ADVISOR IN OPERATIONS IN THE TWENTY-FIRST CENTURY

Chris De Cock

Introduction

The nature of contemporary military operations reflects the complexities of their environment. First, the nature of military operations changed dramatically following the Second World War. Since the fall of the Berlin Wall in 1989, armed forces became increasingly engaged in military operations other than war, including traditional peace support,[1] law enforcement,[2] counterterrorism[3] and counterinsurgency.[4] Second, military operations are often conducted within the framework of an international organization, such as the United Nations (UN) or the North Atlantic Treaty Organization (NATO). This has raised some questions in relation to the applicable legal framework.[5] For example, if military forces are engaged in peace enforcement operations, are their actions covered and regulated by international human rights law (IHRL)[6] or by the law of armed conflict (LOAC)?[7] In the context of UN peace support operations, this complexity can be illustrated by the discussions surrounding the applicability (or not) and the relationship between, on the one hand, the Secretary-General's (SG) Bulletin of 1999 on the observance of international humanitarian law (IHL) by UN forces[8] and, on the other hand, the 1994 UN Safety Convention.[9] Some scholars support the view that when UN forces are engaged in peace enforcement operations, the law of (international) armed conflict should apply, while other commentators argue that the LOAC only applies insofar as UN forces are engaged as combatants and hence lose their protection against direct attack.[10]

This discussion is not merely academic. As stated by Garraway:

> While all this is of great interest to academics, it does not assist the soldier on the ground faced with an instant decision on whether or not to open fire. Of course, his decision will be instinctive – it has to be – but that instinct will be based on hours of training carried out before deployment. Training staff has to think more deeply into these matters. What is the test that the soldiers need to apply? What questions should he be asking himself, almost certainly unconsciously, as he makes that split-second decision? It is here that the difficulties start to arise.[11]

For instance, it would be illegal for troops when responding to domestic riots to establish ambush positions with a view to killing those attempting to leave the area. On the other hand, when the situation has developed to the point that it has become an armed conflict, it would be legal so long as the engagement was authorized by the appropriate military authority and those persons targeted were positively identified as enemy combatants[12] or civilians taking a direct part in hostilities,[13] falling within the approved target set and in accordance with the rules of engagement (ROE).[14] For example, situations of internal disturbances involve situations:

> in which ... there exists a confrontation within the country, which is characterized by a certain seriousness or duration and which involves acts of violence. These latter can assume various forms, all the way from the spontaneous generation of acts of revolt to the struggle between more or less organized groups and the authorities in power. In these situations, which do not necessarily degenerate into open struggle, the authorities in power call upon extensive police forces, or even armed forces, to restore internal order. The high number of victims has made necessary the application of a minimum of humanitarian rules.[15]

In the Abella case, which involved an organized attack on the Tablada military base in Argentina, the Inter-American Commission on Human Rights concluded that this assault and the subsequent military reaction that resulted in several killed and wounded persons were not to be qualified as mere internal disturbances:

> What happened there was not equivalent to large scale violent demonstrations, students throwing stones at the police, bandits holding persons hostage for ransom, or the assassination of government officials for political reasons – all forms of domestic violence not qualifying as armed conflicts.[16]

It should also be recalled that the applicable legal framework can change during the military campaign. Situations of internal disturbances and tensions may escalate to a non-international armed conflict; non-international armed conflicts can internationalize and international armed conflicts can internalize.[17] Therefore, the tactics, techniques and procedures that are permissible in one operation may be prohibited elsewhere or perhaps even during the same operation if the legal framework changes. As perceptively noted by Carswell:

> Today's troops are assigned roles that range from riot control to domestic counter-insurgency to more traditional international armed conflict, and they are expected, and indeed required, to grasp the legal nuances associated with the sliding scale of conflict. Failing to do so may have drastic consequences for the implicated troops. [18]

In addition, a fairly significant number of such operations are conducted outside national borders, challenging the extraterritorial applicability of IHRL.[19] Finally, the presence of new actors on the battlefield, expanding their scope to more than one state, challenges the *acquis* of the LOAC.

Despite the complex environment in which military forces operate, especially in asymmetric warfare, military commanders are expected to conduct their military operations while upholding the law. Today, their actions are carefully scrutinised not only by nongovernmental organizations (NGOs), but also by national and/or international judges. As stated by Knoops, subsequent prosecutions have proven that 'the concept of individual and superior responsibility, under norms of international criminal law, has become pivotal for intervening military forces'.[20]

In this complex arena, the legal advisor (LEGAD) plays an important role and acts as a force multiplier. The LEGAD, as a member of the joint operational planning group (JOPG), is fully involved in all planning activities and acts as the commander's single point of contact for all legal matters affecting the operation. This requires that the LEGAD understands the (goals of the) mission, the tactical situation and the weapon systems the operational planners intend to use for mission accomplishment, allowing him or her to draft clear and unambiguous ROE within the confines of the law. In a subsequent phase, the LEGAD plays a crucial role in the dissemination of the ROE. If needed, these ROE may be translated into a more comprehensive 'soldier's card' for the deployed troops. Finally, the LEGAD assists the commander and his or her staff in interpreting the promulgated ROE and determining the existence of any need to adapt them accordingly, while supervising, where necessary, their (correct) implementation.

Common Article 1: Respect and Ensure Respect

According to common Article 1 to the Geneva Conventions (GCs) and Article 1 of Additional Protocol 1 (AP I), 'the High Contracting Parties undertake to respect and to ensure respect for the Conventions and the Protocol in all circumstances'. It is not a coincidence that the first article, common to the four GCs, reiterates one of the cardinal rules of international law, namely that states have legal obligations under the LOAC. At first sight, this provision seems superfluous with regard to the fact that treaties are binding instruments *in se* upon the parties to them and consequently must be performed in good faith.[21] In other words, why state the obvious again? In light of the importance of the provisions contained in this Geneva law, common Article 1 reflects and highlights its fundamentally humanitarian purpose by emphasizing that the LOAC is binding upon states in all circumstances.

According to the Commentaries of 1952, this provision was supposed to emphasize the fact that states have obligations not only vis-à-vis themselves, but also in relation to others.[22] This raises the question as to its precise scope and consequences. Indeed, the obligation to 'respect and ensure respect' can be divided into an internal and an external component. The former comprises those obligations that the state has in relation to its own conduct and behaviour. The latter, on the other hand, comprises those measures that a state must undertake in order to ensure that other states comply with their obligations under international law.

Although the provision to 'respect and ensure respect' is directly addressed to states as high contracting parties, it should be recalled that the duty to respect implies ensuring respect by civilian and military authorities.[23] The primary addressee of this (internal) obligation is the armed forces as the de jure organs of the state. As stated by the International Military Tribunal (IMT) in Nuremberg: 'Crimes against international law are committed by men, not by abstract entities, and only by punishing individuals who commit such crimes can the provisions of international law be enforced.'[24]

For military commanders, this obligation is explicitly enunciated in Article 87 of AP I:

1. The High Contracting Parties and the Parties to the conflict shall require military commanders, with respect to members of the armed forces under their command and other persons under their control, to prevent and, where necessary, to suppress and report to competent authorities breaches of the Conventions and of this Protocol.

2. In order to prevent and suppress breaches, High Contracting Parties and Parties to the conflict shall require that, commensurate with their level of responsibility, commanders ensure that members of the armed forces under their command are aware of their obligations under the Conventions and this Protocol.

3. The High Contracting Parties and Parties to the conflict shall require any commander who is aware that subordinates or other persons under his control are going to commit or have committed a breach of the Conventions or of this Protocol, to initiate such steps as are necessary to prevent such violations of the Conventions or this Protocol, and, where appropriate, to initiate disciplinary or penal action against violators thereof. [25]

It includes positive (i.e. acting) and negative (i.e. abstain from acting) obligations, meaning that the armed forces must do everything feasible and reasonable to implement the LOAC at all stages, that is, from the strategic to the tactical level, and both during the planning and the execution phases of their military operations.[26]

The Internal Component: Preventive and Corrective Measures

The approach taken by AP I comprises two steps: prevention and repression. It is the responsibility of military commanders to ensure that their subordinates and other persons under their command or control are trained in the LOAC (i.e. prevention).[27] The dissemination and training of the LOAC are two sides of the same coin, but are not interchangeable notions. The dissemination aspect is primarily taken care of in the military academies and aims to instruct officer cadets, noncommissioned officers and privates on the LOAC.[28] Training, on the other hand, is undertaken in the respective units of the different branches (Army, Navy, Air Force, Special Forces) and should be integrated during the exercise periods (generically) and during 'mission oriented trainings' (specifically).[29] The ultimate goal is to ensure that all members of the unit, according to their respective roles and spheres of responsibilities, are aware of their obligations under the LOAC and are able to implement these provisions correctly in the conduct of (simulated) exercises. It also allows military commanders to assess whether the unit is capable of applying the relevant LOAC rules and to take the reasonable and necessary measures to identify shortcomings and, if and when required, to rectify them.

In addition to this more generic LOAC training, it is also necessary to integrate and train LOAC aspects that are specific to any given operation or mission in which the unit will participate. Indeed, each mission or operation is covered by a specific set of (legal) rules and procedures. Given that these rules vary from one operation to another, it is crucial that all members of the national contingent are aware of them. To illustrate this point, one can refer to the International Security and Assistance Force (ISAF) operation in Afghanistan and Operation Unified Protector (OUP) in Libya, in which Belgian F-16s were deployed. When Belgium decided to participate in OUP, air assets from Afghanistan were flown into Europe in order to participate in the Libya air campaign. However, the mandate and the ROE from OUP differed significantly from those in Afghanistan. Consequently, the ISAF ROE and subsequent practice could not be blindly 'copy-pasted' into the Libya engagement. The latter was framed according to another mandate, other ROE and other procedures. In other words, the units to be deployed had to undergo predeployment training sessions in which mission-specific or tailored LOAC and ROE issues were integrated into the scenario.

At this stage, the aim is to ensure that the unit is mission- or combat-ready, meaning that everyone is able to apply the aforementioned LOAC rules within the specific setting of the mission or the operation. The importance of this should not be underestimated. Based on the applicable mandate and the legal framework identified, the defence staff will develop an operational order in which the applicable rules for that particular operation are identified, particularly on the use of force, detention and targeting.

Military commanders must ensure the application of the LOAC by taking the necessary disciplinary or penal actions when (grave) breaches have been committed. An illustration can be found in the judgments by the IMT for the Far East regarding the treatment of prisoners of war (POWs) and civilian internees, in which the Tribunal stated that it was the duty of those responsible to ensure that prisoners were well treated, that ill-treatment was avoided, and to establish and guarantee an effective and permanent system for this purpose. If these groups fail to take the requisite measures or if, having taken them, they do not ensure their constant and effective application, they fail in their duties and incur responsibility.[30] Commanders who know or should have known that their subordinates committed or were about to commit war crimes and did not take the necessary and reasonable measures in order to prevent the commission thereof or to punish the perpetrators are criminally liable under the doctrine of command responsibility (i.e. repression).

The duty of commanders to prevent and repress breaches of the LOAC directly follows from definitions of 'combatant' and 'armed forces'. To be granted combatant status (and POW status in the event of capture by the enemy) under GC III, the following conditions must be fulfilled: '*to be commanded by a person responsible for his subordinates*, to have a fixed distinctive emblem recognizable at a distance; to carry arms openly, and to conduct their operations in accordance with the laws and customs of war' (emphasis added). In the same way, Article 43(1) of AP I provides that the armed forces 'shall be subject to an internal disciplinary system which, inter alia, shall enforce compliance with the rules of international law applicable in armed conflict'.

The relative importance of this disciplinary component of the commander's responsibility in military operations can be illustrated by the following incident. During the UN mission in Somalia in 1993, a sixteen-year-old unarmed civilian was taken into custody by the Canadian contingent and tortured to death. During the national investigation that followed, a lack of discipline and leadership errors were highlighted as crucial factors that led to the commission of the crime of torture. It follows that breaches of the LOAC are more likely to occur in a context of systemic violence. When crimes are committed on such a scale, the question of criminal responsibility does not solely rest upon the actual perpetrators of those crimes. Superiors in a position of effective control who failed to prevent the commission thereof when they could have done so may be held accountable under the doctrine of command responsibility.[31] The roots of this doctrine have been traced to Sun Tzu and his *Art of War* manuscript. Nevertheless, precedents may be found in the ordnance issued in 1439 by King Charles VII of France and the trial of Peter von Hagenbach, who was sentenced to death for crimes committed during the occupation of the city of Breisach. Although he committed no crime himself, he was convicted for crimes he had the duty to prevent as a knight.

External Component: To Respect and Ensure Respect for the LOAC

The external component of the requirement to 'respect and ensure respect' has engendered some controversy. The question raised pertains to the extent to which states have a formal legal obligation to take measures against other states when the latter are not respecting the LOAC. What is the precise scope of this obligation? Does it suffice that states take feasible and reasonable measures to ensure that the parties to an armed conflict abide by their LOAC obligations, such as exercising influence, or does it require more from them?

Let us first start with the obligation 'to respect' the LOAC vis-à-vis other states. This raises the issue of legal interoperability in the context of multinational operations. What is the impact of such operations when military forces from State A are engaged in multinational operations with the armed forces of States B and C, which are not (necessarily) bound by the same legal obligations or do not have the same interpretation of particular LOAC provisions? This can be demonstrated by the following two examples stemming from the Ottawa Convention (banning anti-personnel mines) and the Oslo Convention (banning cluster munitions).

According to Article 1 of the Ottawa Convention, each State Party 'undertakes never under any circumstances ... to use anti-personnel mines'. Furthermore, it is prohibited from assisting, encouraging or inducing 'in any way, anyone to engage in any activity prohibited to a State Party under this Convention'.[32] This raises some questions in relation to the obligations of states bound by the Ottawa Convention when they engage their forces in coalition operations with non-States Parties. In order to tackle these issues, several states have clarified their national positions through interpretive declarations at the time of depositing their instrument of ratification, such as Canada,[33] Australia[34] and the United Kingdom,[35] while other states such as Norway did so before ratification in Parliament.[36]

Controversy still exists on the definition of the terms 'assist', 'encourage' and 'induce'. According to the United Kingdom, 'assisting' includes the following activities: planning with others for the use of anti-personnel mines, training them for the use of anti-personnel mines, agreeing ROE permitting the use of anti-personnel mines, agreeing

Operation Plans permitting their use in combined operations, and providing security or transport of anti-personnel mines.[37] Other states demonstrate a more liberal interpretation of the Convention, such as Norway, which considers that it is not contrary to the Convention 'that mines are transported over Norwegian soil in connection with rotation of the stocks, or if Norwegian forces are protected by minefields laid by others'.[38] Moreover, Norway considers that the definition of the term 'use' in the Convention 'will not include pure participation in combined military operations where use of mines that are contrary to the Convention can be relevant for non-Convention parties'.[39] Insofar as the planning phase is concerned, Canada holds the position that 'while Canadians may participate in operational planning as members of a multinational staff, they may not participate in planning for the use of anti-personnel mines'.[40]

Whereas the restrictions of the Convention are clear during the planning phase of combined operations, problems may still emerge during the execution of the operation, especially when the ground forces of a signatory state request or receive close air support (CAS) from a nonsignatory state. Most commentators would agree that States Parties cannot (actively) request the use of anti-personnel mines. This is certainly true for CAS in the case of deliberate targeting, but is difficult to sustain in a more dynamic setting. In the latter case, ground forces probably require CAS when under attack or imminent attack. It would be unreasonable or even impossible to verify the payload of the aircraft. A further problem that may arise on the battlefield is the problem of mixed units, such as embedded Joint Terminal Attack Controllers (JTAC) in a foreign unit. Is the JTAC authorised to request CAS from an aircraft carrying anti-personnel mines if both the aircrew and the supported ground forces are not bound by the Convention?

Cluster bomb units are another example. When dropped, cluster bombs spin in flight before opening at a predetermined height and rate of spin. Each canister disperses many, sometimes hundreds, of smaller submunitions over a long and wide area of ground. One of the problems with cluster bombs is their so-called 'dud' rate, namely the number of submunitions that fail to detonate because of fuse or detonator failure. These weapons obviously present problems of distinction and proportionality, and continue to cause numerous civilian casualties after the end of hostilities. The use of cluster munitions and the consequent humanitarian concerns about their effects on civilian populations led to the 2008 Oslo Convention on Cluster Munitions. According to Article 1(c) of the Convention: 'Each State

Party undertakes never under any circumstances to assist, encourage or induce anyone to engage in any activity prohibited to a State Party under this Convention.'[41]

This provision must be linked to Article 21 of the Oslo Convention on interoperability. Indeed, Article 1 may affect interoperability functions if the personnel of a State Party to the Convention engage in Headquarter functions (mission or other planning activities while embedded with the personnel of non-States Parties), call in CAS from nonstate forces, relay intelligence to target nonstate personnel, or even provide logistics or conduct joint training exercises.[42] According to Article 21(2) of the Convention, States Parties shall make their best efforts to discourage non-States Parties from using cluster munitions. This raises questions pertaining to the joint planning of coalition operations and the establishment of ROE for that particular operation. When permissible ROE on the use of cluster munitions are developed, States Parties must issue national restrictions.

Article 21(3) of the Oslo Convention reads as follows: 'Notwithstanding the provisions of Article 1 of this Convention and in accordance with international law, States Parties, their military personnel or nationals, may engage in military cooperation and operations with States not party to this Convention that might engage in activities prohibited to a State Party.' In other words, States Parties can engage in coalition operations with non-States Parties, provided they do not 'assist', 'encourage' or 'induce' others to engage in activities prohibited under the Convention. At this stage, it remains unclear which activities are precisely covered by the term 'engage' in Article 21(3) of the Convention. With regard to Article 21(4) of the Convention, which states that nothing in paragraph 3 authorises a State Party to develop, produce or otherwise acquire cluster munitions, to stockpile or transfer cluster munitions, to use cluster munitions or to expressly request the use of cluster munitions in cases where the choice of munitions used is within its exclusive control, it follows that any activity falling outside the scope of Article 1 and Article 21(4) of the Convention is permissible. In practice, when the armed forces of a State Party request CAS from a non-State Party, this would not result in a breach of the Convention as long as they do not exercise exclusive control over the decision following such a request.

Challenges to legal interoperability are not insurmountable and military legal advisors are essential to the process of achieving interoperability and identifying potential points of friction, such as differences in ROE or the employment of weapons in order to resolve such differences during the planning of the operation.[43] With regard

to the complexity of modern military operations, several states have
created 'operational law' departments within their military legal systems to fulfil this responsibility.[44] The 1952 Commentaries to the GCs
explicitly referred to the fact that 'it is not sufficient for a State to
give orders or directives to a law civilian or military authorities, but
to the (positive) obligation of the State to supervise the execution of
aforementioned orders or directives. No reference was made to specific
obligations vis-à-vis other States'. In its more recent Commentary of
2016, the International Committee of the Red Cross (ICRC) identified
two different approaches:

> The interpretation of common Article 1, and in particular the expression
> 'ensure respect', has raised a variety of questions over the last decades. In
> general, two approaches have been taken. One approach advocates that
> under Article 1 States have undertaken to adopt all measures necessary
> to ensure respect for the Conventions only by their organs and private
> individuals within their own jurisdictions. The other, reflecting the pre-
> vailing view today and supported by the ICRC, is that Article 1 requires
> in addition that States ensure respect for the Conventions by other States
> and non-State parties.[45]

According to the ICRC, this second approach was already supported
by the 1952 Commentaries and was subsequently confirmed by customary international law.[46] However, there is no clear obligation for
states in international law to take all possible and imaginable measures capable of inducing transgressor states to comply. As Focarelli
has observed, 'to read Article 1 as imposing an obligation to ensure
respect, results in 193 breaches of common Article 1 every time the
Conventions are breached – which is not the practice of States and
seems implausible'.[47] Kalshoven, the author of an extensive paper on
this provision, has similarly concluded that 'Article 1 creates a moral
obligation, rather than a legal one'.[48] Only in those cases where the
Conventions and the Protocol explicitly require states to act can it be
said that an obligation to 'ensure respect' exists.

As an example, one can refer to the provision relating to the transfer of POWs in international armed conflicts. According to Article 12
of GC III:

> Prisoners of war may only be transferred by the Detaining Power to a
> Power which is a party to the Convention and after the Detaining Power
> has satisfied itself of the willingness and ability of such transferee Power
> to apply the Convention. When prisoners of war are transferred under such
> circumstances, responsibility for the application of the Convention rests
> on the Power accepting them while in custody. Nevertheless, if that Power

fails to carry out the provisions of the Convention in any important respect, the Power by whom the prisoners of war were transferred shall, upon being notified by the Protecting Power, take effective measures to correct the situation or shall request the return of the prisoners of war. Such requests must be complied with.

If the fundamental rights of transferred POWs are violated, the transferring state has a positive obligation to take 'effective measures to correct the situation' because the use of the word 'shall' clearly demonstrates that there is no discretionary power.[49]

However, the question at stake is the precise scope of this provision 'to ensure respect' (by other states). In our example, what is required of states to ensure respect for the GCs in case of transfer? This brings us to the distinction between, on the one hand, obligations of result and, on the other hand, obligations of conduct. For the purposes of this chapter, it suffices to say that states can only be asked to do what is feasible or possible – in other words, to make reasonable efforts to achieve a result. The obligation to 'ensure respect' is therefore an obligation of conduct. Stating otherwise would lead to unreasonable and absurd results.

The Incorporation of Legal Advisors

When negotiating the Additional Protocols to the GCs, it became clear that military commanders could not be expected to master the entire corpus of increasingly complex and legal rules, applicable to the different aspects of military operations, in the same way that they have to master different areas of military expertise. The need for a division of tasks led to the proposal to create a post of LEGAD to military commanders.[50] This suggestion was made at the beginning of the preliminary discussions preceding the Diplomatic Conference[51] and resulted in the adoption of Article 82 of AP I to the GCs of 1949, which reads:

> The High Contracting Parties at all times, and the Parties to the conflict in time of armed conflict, shall ensure that legal advisors are available, when necessary, to advise military commanders at the appropriate level on the application of the Conventions and this Protocol and on the appropriate instruction to be given to the armed forces on this subject.

Under this provision, LEGADs have a dual role: they advise military commanders on the application of the Conventions and the Protocol, and on how to disseminate the LOAC to the armed forces. In this respect, the availability of LEGADs in the LOAC is part of the general obligation to disseminate the LOAC.[52] However, the absence of LEGADs can never be an excuse for any violation of the LOAC by any party to any armed conflict.[53]

Based on the use of the expression 'shall ensure' in the wording of Article 82, there can be no doubt surrounding the *obligation* for states to adopt all appropriate regulations to ensure that LEGADs are available to the armed forces and that these legal advisors receive the appropriate training. The question of whether the obligation for states to provide a LEGAD is a customary law obligation has been answered in the affirmative by the ICRC. Indeed, in its customary LOAC study, the ICRC dedicates a specific rule to this obligation, applying to both international and non-international conflicts,[54] according to which: 'Each State must make legal advisors available, when necessary, to advise military commanders at the appropriate level on the application of international humanitarian law.'[55]

However, different states may use different methods to fulfil this obligation, in particular with regard to the conditions for the use of these LEGADs, the level in the military command structure at which they are deployed and the choice of methods of training them.[56] It is essential that these LEGADs, regardless of their qualifications, have a sound knowledge of the LOAC in order to be able to provide commanders with adequate and appropriate advice. Therefore, specific training on the subject appears to be necessary,[57] especially given that legal advice is no longer solely limited to the GCs and their Protocols, considering the growing number and complexity of relevant legal instruments.[58]

It should be noted that the customary law rule, which is a corollary to the obligation to respect and ensure respect for the LOAC,[59] is broader in scope than the treaty rule in Article 82 of AP I, as it refers not only to the application of the GCs and their protocols, but also to 'the application of international humanitarian law'. According to many states, current practice goes even beyond that point. Given the growing legal implications of military operations, states have a particular interest in deploying LEGADs in peacetime and in times of armed conflict.[60] In short, the intervention area of the LEGAD extends to different issues of operational law. There is no doubt that as a result of the intricacies of contemporary operational law, the presence of LEGADs in the theatre of operations has become indispensable.[61] They can contribute to military decisions being made in accordance with international law.[62]

Before examining how Belgium has implemented this legal obligation, it should be noted that the objective pursued by LEGADs is comparable to that of military commanders, namely mission accomplishment.[63] Therefore, it is important that the LEGAD understands the goal of the mission and that he or she has specific knowledge of the military forces, tactics and arms used. However, the LEGAD must in no case provide a flexible or broad interpretation of the applicable law to ensure the accomplishment of the mission at any price, or give advice to meet the military commander's needs; on the contrary, his or her role involves setting as precisely as possible the limitations and restrictions imposed on the commander and his or her team by operational law.[64] The LEGAD should also draw the attention of the commander and his or her team to the 'grey areas' of operational law,[65] provided that having been duly informed, the commander will ultimately make the decisions and assume responsibility within the decision-making process.

The Belgian Perspective

In order to comply with its obligations under Article 82 of AP I, the Ministry of Defence (MOD) created 'Advisers on the Law of Armed Conflict' in all military units, up to the level of battalion/independent company and the equivalent unit within the Defence Staff in 1987, as well as in the respective military academies and training centres.[66] These LOAC advisors were responsible for advising commanders on LOAC and ROE issues.

However, it became clear that they were not legal professionals. Consequently, the need emerged to entrust the post of advisor to legal professionals in order to meet the requirements of Article 82 of AP I. An apparently essential prerequisite for the implementation of that provision was the subsequent creation of a division or service devoted to international law applicable in armed conflict.[67] Within the Belgian MOD, this service became integrated into the Directorate General Legal Support and Mediation of the Ministry of Defence (DGJM), composed of military and civilian legal experts. The DGJM is responsible for giving advice on the basics of the LOAC as well as more broadly on the different issues of operational law.

With regard to the latter, the Legal Advice Division of the DGJM has developed an 'operational law concept', including but not limited to developments of operational law at the Belgian MOD, the training of the LEGADs in operational law issues and the provision of legal advice to the Operations and Training Staff Department (ACOS Ops & Training) as well as to other staff departments.

LEGADs can be deployed during operations conducted in one's national territory or abroad and in peacetime or times of armed conflict. As mentioned above, unlike the LOAC advisors, LEGADs are legal professionals, whether civilians or servicemen or servicewomen on the active or reserve list. Although the LEGAD as a member of the special staff of the commander is responsible to the latter, he or she does not belong to the operational chain of command. For all legal matters, he or she remains subject to his or her hierarchy within the legal department. Before deployment, the LEGAD will receive additional legal training and/or briefings, as well as mission-oriented training.

With regard to the reduced number of available LEGADs, it will not always be feasible to permanently send a LEGAD in support of every contingent.[68] In practice, deployment takes place according to need: continued presence according to the rotations of the detachments (in the case of the ISAF), in the case of a new mandate or in the case of an exceptional occurrence such as an accident. A LEGAD can also be asked to be on 'standby', meaning that he or she is not permanently present, but is ready to be deployed if necessary. Incidentally, the permanent presence of the LEGAD can be cancelled when this is no longer justified by the workload. In any event, when the LEGAD belonging to a mission or an exercise is not deployed, he or she needs to be permanently accessible and reachable (24 hours a day) by phone in Belgium.

The mission of the LEGAD consists in advising the commander and his or her team to ensure that the mission complies with national and international law. In practice, the operation order describes the terms of deployment of the LEGAD (periodic presence, geographical indication and so forth) and the outlines of his or her mission.[69]

During the planning of the operations, the advice provided by the LEGAD generally covers the full spectrum of legal matters of an operation relating to, *inter alia*: the use of force and the rules of engagement; targeting; intelligence; the negotiation, layout and interpretation of international agreements, Memoranda of Understanding and any other technical arrangements; general international law, the LOAC or international human rights law issues; domestic law issues (the application of either the law of the host state or the Belgian law, in particular with regard to criminal law or criminal proceedings); treatment of the wounded and sick, of civilians and refugees; if necessary, all legal matters with respect to the detention, treatment and transfer of detainees; liaising with LEGADs of higher echelons and other sending states to optimize legal support to the operation; the procurement, transfer or use of goods or services and any contractual issues; and the environmental aspects of the operation and compliance with the legal and international provisions in this field.

Furthermore, the LEGADs are generally in charge of supervising the handling of all claims within the area of operations relating to incidents involving damage to property or injury or loss of life to third parties arising from the operation or activities taking place after the deployment of forces. In addition, the LEGAD should ensure that all plans, orders, ROE, policies and directives are consistent with the applicable national and international law.

The LEGAD also liaises with the Federal Prosecutor and the federal police[70] on criminal matters affecting Belgian personnel – military and assimilated personnel – within his or her area of responsibility. During the conduct of European Union Naval Force Somalia (EUNAVFOR) ATALANTA the EU-led counterpiracy operation in the Horn of Africa, this liaison also concerned the prosecution of alleged pirates in Belgium.

Finally, the LEGAD submits occasional and/or periodical reports to the DGJM. In the postdeployment phase, he or she submits a final report and holds a briefing focusing on the lessons learned from the mission.

Conclusion

With regard to the complexity of the modern battlefield, it is clear that the presence of LEGADs in advising military commanders when planning and conducting military operations is essential to accomplishing the mission while upholding the law. The incorporation of LEGADs is a direct and logical consequence of the more general obligation to respect and ensure respect of the LOAC, provided in common Article 1 of the GCs and particularly as a result of Article 82 of AP I. As a member of the special staff of the commander, the LEGAD must ensure that all assigned tasks and missions comply with both domestic and international law. In the context of multinational operations, the LEGAD advises the military commander on interoperability issues that may affect the accomplishment of the mission, as not all partners of the coalition will necessarily be bound by the same treaty obligations. In such a complex environment, the LEGAD acts as a force multiplier.

Chris De Cock has been a senior lecturer in the fields of humanitarian law and operational law at the Royal Military Academy in Brussels since September 2020. He has participated in several operational deployments as legal advisor in Afghanistan, during counterpiracy operations and counternarcotics operations with the Navy, during Operation Unified Protector and more recently during Operation Inherent Resolve. He previously served as Head of the Operational Law Section and Chief of Staff at the Legal Department of the Belgian Armed Forces. From 2017 to 2020, he served as the legal advisor to the Director of the Military Planning and Conduct Capability within the European External Action Service.

Notes

The views expressed in this chapter are those of the author in his personal capacity and do not intend to reflect the views of the EU, the European External Action Service (EEAS) or the Military Planning and Conduct Capability (MPCC).

1. Peace support operations can be divided into two main categories: peacekeeping operations (Chapter VI of the UN Charter) and peace-enforcing operations (Chapter VII of the UN Charter). On the evolution of peace operations generally, see Thakur, *The United Nations, Peace and Security*, 27–47.
2. Examples of law-enforcement operations include counternarcotic or counterpiracy operations, such as European Union Naval Force Somalia (EUNAVFOR) ATALANTA, the EU-led counterpiracy operation in the Horn of Africa.
3. Counterterrorism comprises 'all offensive measures taken to neutralize terrorism before and after hostile acts are carried out'. Such measures include those counterforce activities justified for the defence of individuals as well as containment measures implemented by military forces or civilian organizations. Anti-terrorism, on the other hand, comprises 'all defensive and preventive measures taken to reduce the vulnerability of forces, individuals and property to terrorism'. It should be noted that NATO makes a clear distinction between anti-terrorism and counterterrorism. Whereas anti-terrorism comprises 'all *defensive and protective* measures taken to reduce the vulnerability of forces, individuals and property to terrorism', counterterrorism means 'all *offensive* measures taken to neutralize terrorism before and after hostile acts are carried out' (emphasis added). See 'NATO's Military Concept for Defence against Terrorism' (2016), https://www.nato.int/cps/en/natohq/topics_69482.htm (retrieved 8 May 2021).
4. Bard E. O'Neill argues that: 'Insurgency may be defined as a struggle between a non-ruling group and the ruling authorities in which the non-ruling group consciously uses political resources (e.g. organizational expertise, propaganda and demonstrations) and violence to destroy, reformulate, or sustain the basis of one or more aspects of politics'; O'Neill, *Insurgency and Terrorism*, 47. On the other hand, according to Beckett, counterinsurgency is 'far from being a purely military problem ... coordination of both the civil and military effort must occur at all levels

and embrace the provision of intelligence'; cited in Hammes, 'Countering Evolved Insurgent Networks', 18–26.

5. The first authoritative ruling on the relationship between these two branches of law was enunciated by the International Court of Justice (ICJ) in its Nuclear Weapons Advisory Opinion. The Court ruled that protection of the International Covenant on Civil and Political Rights does not cease in times of war, except by operation of the derogation clause. Recognizing that the right to life provision continues to apply, even in the case of derogation, the Court stated that it also applies during hostilities: 'The test of what is an arbitrary deprivation of life should than be determined by the applicable *lex specialis*, namely the law of armed conflict, designed to regulate the conduct of hostilities and not deduced from the Covenant itself' (Advisory Opinion on the Legality of the Threat or Use of Nuclear Weapons, [1996] *ICJ Rep.* 226, 256 (hereafter 'Legality of the Threat or Use of Nuclear Weapons'), para. 25). In other words, the LOAC defines what IHRL means in times of war. In its Wall Advisory Opinion, the Court reiterated its previous statement, albeit with different wording, when stating that: 'As regards the relationship between international humanitarian law and human rights law, there are three possible situations: some rights may be exclusively matters of international humanitarian law; others may be exclusively matters of human rights law; yet others may be of both branches of international law' (ICJ, *Legal Consequences of the Construction of a Wall in the Occupied Palestinian Territory*, Advisory Opinion of 9 July 2004, *ICJ, General List* N°. 131, para. 112). See also Porretto and Vité, 'The Application of International Humanitarian Law'; Guellali, '*Lex specialis*, droit international humanitaire et droits de l'homme', 545.

6. Quénivet, 'The History of the Relationship between International Humanitarian Law and Human Rights'.

7. The term 'law of international armed conflict' is used in a generic way and is synonymous with other terms such as 'international humanitarian law' and 'law of war'. According to the ICJ, 'these two branches of the law applicable in armed conflict have become so closely interrelated that they are considered to have gradually formed one single complex system, known today as international humanitarian law. The provisions of the Additional Protocols of 1977 give expression and attest to the unity and complexity of that law' (ICJ, 'Legality of the Threat or Use of Nuclear Weapons'). The complexity of this body of law is also due to the merging of provisions of international humanitarian law and disarmament or weapons control issues in treaty law.

8. Secretary-General's Bulletin: 'Observance by United Nations Forces of International Humanitarian Law', 6 August 1999, UN Doc. ST/SBG/1999/13.

9. Convention on the Safety of United Nations and Associated Personnel, 1994, 34 *ILM* 482 (1995).

10. On this particular issue, see Naert, *International Law Aspects*, 491–92. This author supports the latter view, namely that the LOAC only applies insofar as UN troops are engaged as combatants in situations of armed conflict. See Ruys and De Cock, 'Protected Persons', 417–19.

11. Garraway, 'To Kill or Not to Kill?, 499–510.

12. According to the Geneva Conventions, the following conditions are required to have combatant status: being commanded by a person responsible for his or her subordinates; having a fixed distinctive sign recognizable at a distance; carrying arms openly; and respecting the laws and customs of war. See Art. 4(A)(2) of GC III, Art. 13(A)(2) of GC II and Art. 13(A)(2) GC I. Article 44 of AP I extended the scope of combatant status to include situations in armed conflict where, owing to the nature of the hostilities, an armed combatant cannot distinguish himself or herself as

such. This person shall retain his or her status as combatant provided that in such situations, he or she carries his or her arms openly during each military engagement and during such time as he or she is visible to the adversary while he or she is engaged in a military deployment preceding the launching of an attack in which he or she is to participate.

13. The protection from attack afforded to civilians by Art. 51 of AP I is suspended when and for such time as they directly participate in hostilities.

14. Mandsager, *Rules of Engagement Handbook*, 1: 'Rules of Engagement are designed to ensure that application of force is carefully controlled. ROE are directives to military forces that define the circumstances, conditions, degree and manner in which force, or actions which might be construed as provocative, may or may not be applied. Although commanders may delegate authority for operations, they remain responsible for the conduct of the forces under their command. Ideally, there should just be one common set of ROE, agreed by the competent authority and all troop contributing nations. In general, the operational plan (also known as OPLAN) will contain the approved ROE and the political policy indicators governing the operation.' See also *NATO Glossary of Terms and Definitions*, AAP-6 (2010), 3-R-7; *Operational Law Handbook*, (US), 2009, p. 73; Joint Publication 1-02, Department of Defense, *Dictionary of Military and Associated Terms*, 8 November 2010, p. 317. Compare with the Canadian definition of ROE: 'Orders issued by competent military authority, which delineate the circumstances and limitations within which force may be applied by the CF to achieve military objectives in furtherance of national policy' (*Law of Armed Conflict at the Operational and Tactical Levels*, Joint Doctrine Manual, B-GJ-005-104/FP-021, 2003, p. 17).

15. Sandoz, Swinarski and Zimmerman, *Commentary on the Additional Protocols*, para. 4475 (hereinafter *Commentary AP I*).

16. The intensity of the violence and the degree of organization of the parties involved seemed to be decisive in distinguishing situations of internal disturbances from non-international armed conflicts. See Tablada Case, *Inter-American Commission on Human Rights*, Rep. No. 55/97, Case No. 11.127: Argentina, OEA/Ser/L/V/II.97, Doc. 38, 18 November 1997, paras. 154–55; ICTY, *Prosecutor v. Tadic*, Opinion and Judgment, Case No. IT-94-1-T, 7 May 1997, para. 562, ICTY, *Prosecutor v. Delalic, Mucic, Delic and Landzo*, Judgment, Case No. IT-96-21-T, *T.Ch. II*, 16 November 1998, para. 184; ICTR, *Prosecutor v. Kayishema and Ruzindana*, Judgment, Case No. ICTR-95-1-T, *T.Ch. II*, 21 May 1999, paras. 170–72; ICTR, *Prosecutor v. Rutaganda*, Judgment and Sentence, Case No. ICTR-96-3-T, *T.Ch. I*, 6 December 1999, paras. 378–82.

17. Solis, *The Law of Armed Conflict*, 154–55; see also Milanovic and Hadzi-Vidanovic, 'A Taxonomy of Armed Conflict', 292–302.

18. Carswell, 'Classifying the Conflict', 144.

19. In its reading of Art. 2(1) of the International Covenant on Civil and Political Rights, the UN Human Rights Committee found that the aforementioned obligation means that: 'A State party must respect and ensure the rights laid down in the Covenant to anyone within the power or effective control of that State party, even if not situated within the territory of the State party' (UN Committee on Human Rights, 'General Comment No. 31: The Nature of the General legal Obligation Imposed on State Parties to the Covenant', 2004, UN Doc. HRI/GEN/I/Rev.7, 12 May 2004, 192, para. 10). In its Advisory Opinion on the *Legal Consequences of the Construction of a Wall in the Occupied Palestinian Territory*, the ICJ observed that: 'While the jurisdiction of States is primarily territorial, it may sometimes be exercised outside the national territory. Considering the object and purpose of the International Covenant on Civil and Political Rights, it would seem natural

that, even when such is the case, States parties to the Covenant should be bound to comply with its provisions' (para. 109). See also the abundant jurisprudence of the European Court on Human Rights on the extraterritorial application of the Convention in *Loizidou v. Turkey*, Application No. 15318/89, judgment of 18 December 1996; ECtRM (Grand Chamber*)*, *Vlastimir and Borka Banković*, Živana *Stojadinović, Mirjana Stoimenovski, Dragana Joksimović and Dragan Suković* v. Belgium, *the Czech Republic, Denmark, France, Germany, Greece, Hungary, Iceland, Italy, Luxembourg, the Netherlands, Norway, Poland, Portugal, Spain, Turkey and the United Kingdom*, Application No. 52207/99, decision of 12 December 2001, Reports of Judgments and Decisions 2001-XII; Milanovic, *Extraterritorial Application of Human Rights Treaties.*

20. Knoops, *The Prosecution and Defense of Peacekeepers*, 20.
21. Convention on the Law of Treaties, *ILM* (1969) 689, Arts. 31, 46 and 69. See also ICJ, *Case Concerning Military and Paramilitary Activities in and against Nicaragua (Nicaragua v. United States of America), Merits, 27 June 1986, Gen. List No. 70*, pp. 392 and 418; ICJ, 'Legality of the Threat or Use of Nuclear Weapons', para. 102.
22. Pictet, *Commentary on Geneva Convention I* (1952), 25: 'The use of the words "and to ensure respect" was, however, deliberate. They were intended to emphasize and strengthen the responsibility of the Contracting Parties. It would not, for example, be enough for a State to give orders or directives to a law civilian or military authorities, leaving it to them to arrange as they pleased for the details of their execution. It is for the State to supervise their execution.'
23. *Commentary AP I*, para. 41.
24. UN General Assembly, *The Charter and Judgment of the Nürnberg Tribunal – History and Analysis: Memorandum submitted by the Secretary-General*, Doc. A/CN.4/5, 1949, p. 41.
25. AP I, Art. 87.
26. However, it should be noted that the obligations enshrined in the different LOAC conventions are not confined to the Ministry of Defence and its armed forces. Although much will depend on the way in which the state is organized, other departments such as the Justice Department or the Department of Foreign Affairs will have to implement the relevant provisions of the LOAC within their spheres of responsibility.
27. Henckaerts and Doswald-Beck, *Customary International Humanitarian Law* (hereinafter *Customary LOAC Study*), Rule 139: 'Each Party to the conflict must respect and ensure respect for international humanitarian law by its armed forces and other persons or groups acting in fact on its instructions, or under its direction and control.'
28. GC I, Art. 47; GC II, Art. 48; GC III, Art. 127; GC IV, Art. 144; AP I, Art. 83; AP II, Art. 19; Hague Convention for the Protection of Cultural Property and its Second Protocol, Arts. 25 and 30; Convention on Certain Conventional Weapons, Art. 6; *Customary LOAC Study*, Rule 140.
29. As stated in the LOAC Manual of South Africa: 'In the circumstances of combat, soldiers may often not have time to consider the principles of the LOAC before acting. Soldiers must therefore not only know these principles but must be trained so that proper response to specific situations is second nature' (reprinted in the *Customary LOAC Study*, 503).
30. *Commentary AP I*, para. 3548.
31. Article 28 of the Statute of the International Criminal Court (ICC) (Responsibility of commanders and other superiors): 'In addition to other grounds of criminal responsibility under this Statute for crimes within the jurisdiction of the Court:

(a) A military commander or person effectively acting as a military commander shall be criminally responsible for crimes within the jurisdiction of the Court committed by forces under his or her effective command and control, or effective authority and control as the case may be, as a result of his or her failure to exercise control properly over such forces, where:

   (i) That military commander or person either knew or, owing to the circumstances at the time, should have known that the forces were committing or about to commit such crimes; and

   (ii) That military commander or person failed to take all necessary and reasonable measures within his or her power to prevent or repress their commission or to submit the matter to the competent authorities for investigation and prosecution.

(b) With respect to superior and subordinate relationships not described in paragraph (a), a superior shall be criminally responsible for crimes within the jurisdiction of the Court committed by subordinates under his or her effective authority and control, as a result of his or her failure to exercise control properly over such subordinates, where:

   (i) The superior either knew, or consciously disregarded information which clearly indicated, that the subordinates were committing or about to commit such crimes;

   (ii) The crimes concerned activities that were within the effective responsibility and control of the superior; and

   (iii) The superior failed to take all necessary and reasonable measures within his or her power to prevent or repress their commission or to submit the matter to the competent authorities for investigation and prosecution.'

32. Convention on the Prohibition of the Use, Stockpiling, Production and Transfer of Anti-Personnel Mines and Their Destruction, Art. 1 (1)(c).

33. Canada declared that 'in the context of operations, exercises or other military activity sanctioned by the United Nations or otherwise conducted in accordance with international law, the mere participation by the Canadian Forces, or individual Canadians, in operations, exercises or other military activity conducted in combination with the armed forces of States not party to the Convention which engage in activity prohibited under the Convention would not, by itself, be considered to be assistance, encouragement or inducement in accordance with the meaning of those terms in article 1, paragraph 1 (c)'.

34. 'It is the understanding of the Government of Australia that, in the context of operations, exercises or other military activity authorized by the United Nations or otherwise conducted in accordance with international law, the participation by the Australian Defense Force, or individual Australian citizens or residents, in such operations, exercises or other military activity, conducted in combination with the armed forces of States not party to the Convention which engage in activity prohibited under that Convention would not, by itself, be considered to be in violation of the Convention.'

35. 'It is the understanding of the Government of the United Kingdom that the mere participation in the planning or execution of operations, exercises or other military activity by the United Kingdom's Armed Forces, or individual United Kingdom nationals, conducted in combination with the armed forces of States not party to the [said convention], which engage in activity prohibited under that Convention, is not, by itself, assistance, encouragement or inducement for the purposes of Article 1, paragraph (c) of the Convention.'

36. Dahl, 'Observance of International Humanitarian Law', 350.

37. 'United Kingdom Intervention on Article 1', Statement of the Standing Committee on the General Status and Operation of the Convention, Geneva, 16 May 2003. Retrieved 8 May 2021 from https://www.apminebanconvention.org/fileadmin/APMBC/IWP/SC_may03/speeches_gs/UK_Art_1.pdf.
38. Dahl, 'Observance of International Humanitarian Law'.
39. Ibid.
40. Office of the Judge Advocate General, *The Law of Armed Conflict at the Operational and Tactical #Levels* (2013), s. 5.10. annex A.
41. Compare with Art. 1(1)(c) of the Ottawa Convention.
42. Nystuen and Casey-Maslen, *The Convention on Cluster Munitions*, 553.
43. The requirement to incorporate legal advisors to advise military commanders is set forth in Art. 82 of AP I and provides that: 'The High Contracting Parties at all times, and the Parties to the conflict in time of armed conflict, shall ensure that legal advisors are available, when necessary, to advise military commanders at the appropriate level on the application of the Conventions and this Protocol and on the appropriate instruction to be given to the armed forces on this subject.' On the role of the military legal advisor, see Rogers and Stewart, 'The Role of the Military Legal Advisor', 538–64.
44. Operational law is defined as 'the body of domestic, foreign and international law that impacts specifically upon the activities of U.S. Forces in war and operations other than war ... It includes military justice, administrative and civil law, legal assistance, claims, procurement law, national security law, fiscal law, and international law' (International and Operational Law Department, the Judge Advocate General's Legal Center & School, *Operational Law Handbook A-1*, 1994). See also Voetelink and Walgemoed, 'De totstandkoming van het hedendaags Militair operationeel recht', 195–212.
45. Dörmann, Lijnzaad, Sassoli and Spoerri, *Commentary on the First Geneva Convention* (2016), para. 120.
46. Ibid.
47. Focarelli, 'Common Article 1 of the 1949 Geneva Conventions', 167.
48. Kalshoven, 'The Undertaking to Respect and Ensure Respect in All Circumstances', 3, 4, 60.
49. The same obligation exists in relation to the transfer of detainees in non-international armed conflicts. In Afghanistan, troop-contributing nations concluded memoranda of understanding with other nations in order to ensure that the fundamental (human) rights of transferred detainees were satisfied.
50. *Commentary AP I*, paras. 3342–43.
51. Ibid.
52. David, *Principes de droit des conflits armés*, 639.
53. *Customary LOAC Study*, 659.
54. Practice also indicates that states often deploy and use legal advisors within the framework of peacekeeping operations and military operations that do not reach the threshold of armed conflict; see Rogers and Stewart, 'The Role of the Military Legal Advisor', 540.
55. *Customary LOAC Study*, Rule 141. For an opinion questioning whether military powers such as the United States or Israel that are not parties to Protocol I but have long had legal advisors available to their forces are deemed to be bound by a legal obligation, see Rogers and Stewart, 'The Role of the Military Legal Advisor', 539. The study of customary international humanitarian law conducted by the ICRC seems to plead in favour of such an obligation: *Customary LOAC Study*, 658.
56. Ibid., paras. 3344–45.
57. Rogers and Stewart, 'The Role of the Military Legal Advisor', 538.

58. Examples include international armament and international criminal law treaties.
59. Common Art. 1 of the GCs; Rule 139 of the *Customary LOAC Study*.
60. Rogers and Stewart, 'The Role of the Military Legal Advisor', 540.
61. With regard to the increasing complexity of the tasks of legal advisors and the contributing factors, see McLaughlin, '"Giving" Operational Legal Advice', 103.
62. In this sense, see Dickinson, 'Military Lawyers on the Battlefield', 3.
63. Voetelink and Walgemoed, 'De totstandkoming van het hedendaags Militair operationeel recht', 198.
64. McLaughlin, '"Giving" Operational Legal Advice', 120.
65. Examples with regard to these areas of legal uncertainty include the consequences of international human rights law on operations and the accurate definition of the rules of AP I to the GCs that have become customary law rules.
66. General Order of 7 July 1987.
67. *Commentary AP I*, para. 3348.
68. The post of LEGAD is indeed a permanent post within the DGJM.
69. Annex AA to the operation order (legal affairs) generally includes a description of the specific mission of the LEGAD.
70. The DJMM is the unit subordinate to the federal judicial police in charge of specialized judicial assignments in the military environment. It works under the supervision and authority of the Federal Prosecutor.

Bibliography

Published Sources

Carswell, Andrew J. 'Classifying the Conflict: A Soldier's Dilemma'. *International Review of the Red Cross* 91(873) (2009), 143–61.
Dahl, Arne Willy. 'Observance of International Humanitarian Law by Forces under the Command of International Organizations', in Stanislas Horvat and Marco Benatar (eds), *Legal Interoperability and Ensuring Observance of the Law Applicable in Multinational Deployments* (Brussels: Printing House of Defense, Recueil XIX, 2013), 345–63.
David, Eric. *Principes de droit des conflits armés*, 5th edn. Brussels: Bruylant, 2012.
Dickinson, Laura A. 'Military Lawyers on the Battlefield: An Empirical Account of International Law Compliance'. *American Journal of International Law* 104(1) (2010), 1–28.
Dörmann, Knut, Liesbeth Lijnzaad, Marco Sassoli and Philip Spoerri. *Commentary on the First Geneva Convention, Convention (I) for the Amelioration of the Condition of the Wounded and Sick in Armed Forces in the Field*. Cambridge: Cambridge University Press, 2016.
Focarelli, Carlo. 'Common Article 1 of the 1949 Geneva Conventions: A Soap Bubble?' *European Journal of International Law* 21(1) (2010), 152–71.
Garraway Charles. 'To Kill or Not to Kill?: Dilemmas on the Use of Force', *Journal of Conflict & Security Law* 14(3) (2009), 499–510.
Guellali, Amna. '*Lex specialis*, droit international humanitaire et droits de l'homme : leur interaction dans les nouveaux conflits armés'. *Revue Générale de Droit International Public* 111(3) (2007), 539–74.
Hammes, Thomas X. 'Countering Evolved Insurgent Networks'. *Military Review*, July–August 2006, 18–26.

Henckaerts, Jean-Marie, and Louise Doswald-Beck. *Customary International Humanitarian Law. Volume I: Rules*. Cambridge: Cambridge University Press, 2005.

Kalshoven, Frits. 'The Undertaking to Respect and Ensure Respect in All Circumstances: From Tiny Seed to Ripening Fruit'. *Yearbook of International Humanitarian Law* 2 (1999), 3–61.

Knoops, Geert-Jan. *The Prosecution and Defense of Peacekeepers under International Criminal Law*. Ardsley: Transnational Publishers, 2004.

Mandsager, Dennis. *Rules of Engagement Handbook*. International Institute of Humanitarian Law, San Remo, November 2009.

McLaughlin, Robert. '"Giving" Operational Legal Advice: Context and Method'. *Revue de Droit Militaire et de Droit de la Guerre* 50 (2011), 99–126.

Milanovic, Marko. *Extraterritorial Application of Human Rights Treaties*. Oxford: Oxford University Press, 2011.

Milanovic, Marko, and Vidan Hadzi-Vidanovic. 'A Taxonomy of Armed Conflict', in White Nigel and Christian Henderson (eds), *Research Handbook on International Conflict and Security Law: Jus ad Bellum, Jus in Bello and Jus Post Bellum* (Cheltenham: Edward Elgar, 2013), 256–314.

Naert, Frederik. *International Law Aspects of the EU's Security and Defence Policy, with a Particular Focus on the Law of Armed Conflict and Human Rights*. Antwerp: Intersentia, 2010.

Nystuen, Gro, and Stuart Casey-Maslen. *The Convention on Cluster Munitions: A Commentary*. Oxford: Oxford University Press, 2010.

O'Neill, Bard E. *Insurgency and Terrorism: From Revolution to Apocalypse*. Washington DC: Potomac Books, 2005.

Pictet, Jean. *Commentary on the Geneva Conventions of 12 August 1949*. Geneva: International Committee of the Red Cross, 1952.

Porretto, Gabriele, and Sylvain Vité. 'The Application of International Humanitarian Law and Human Rights Law to International Organizations'. *Research Paper Series n. 1/2006*, Geneva: University Centre for International Humanitarian Law, 2006. Retrieved 9 May 2021 from http://www.iihl.org/wp-content/uploads/2018/03/Application_of_IHL-and-H-rights-law.pdf.

Quénivet, Noëlle. 'The History of the Relationship between International Humanitarian Law and Human Rights', in Roberta Arnold and Noëlle Quénivet (eds), *International Humanitarian Law and Human Rights Law: Towards a New Merger in International Law* (Leiden: Nijhoff, 2008), 1–13.

Rogers, A.P.V. and Darren Stewart. 'The Role of the Military Legal Advisor', in Terry D. Gill and Dieter Fleck (eds), *The Handbook of the International Law of Military Operations* (Oxford, Oxford University Press, 2010), 538–64.

Ruys, Tom, and Chris De Cock. 'Protected Persons in International Armed Conflicts', in Nigel White and Christian Henderson (eds), *Research Handbook on International Conflict and Security Law: Jus ad Bellum, Jus in Bello and Jus Post Bellum* (Cheltenham: Edward Elgar, 2013), 375–420.

Sandoz, Yves, Christophe Swinarski and Bruno Zimmerman. *Commentary on the Additional Protocols to the Geneva Conventions*. Geneva: Martinus Nijhoff Publishers, 1987.

Solis, Gary D. *The Law of Armed Conflict, International Humanitarian Law in War*. Cambridge: Cambridge University Press, 2010.

Thakur, Ramesh. *The United Nations, Peace and Security*. Cambridge: Cambridge University Press, 2006.

Voetelink, J.E.D., and G.F. Walgemoed. 'De totstandkoming van het hedendaags Militair operationeel recht'. *Militair Rechtelijk Tijdschrift* 102(5) (2009), 195–212.

List of Relevant Decisions

ICJ, Case Concerning Military and Paramilitary Activities in and against Nicaragua (Merits), [1986] *General List* No 70, 27 June 1986.

ICJ, Advisory Opinion on the Legality of the Threat or Use of Nuclear Weapons [1996] General List No. 95, 8 July 1996.

ICJ, Advisory Opinion on the Legal Consequences of the Construction of a Wall in the Occupied Palestinian Territory [2004] *ICJ General List* No. 131, 9 July 2004.

ICTY, *Prosecutor v. Tadic*, Opinion and Judgment, Case No. IT-94-1-T, 7 May 1997.

ICTY, *Prosecutor v. Delalic, Mucic, Delic and Landzo*, Judgment, Case No. IT-96-21-T, *T.Ch. II*, 16 November 1998.

ICTR, *Prosecutor v. Kayishema and Ruzindana*, Judgment, Case No. ICTR-95-1-T, *T.Ch. II*, 21 May 1999.

ICTR, *Prosecutor v. Rutaganda,* Judgment and Sentence, Case No. ICTR-96-3-T, *T.Ch. I*, 6 December 1999.

CONCLUSION

Pieter Lagrou and Ornella Rovetta

This book is the outcome of a long-running engagement with trial archives and of the intellectual encounter of two scholars working on the International Criminal Tribunal for Rwanda (ICTR) and the Belgian military tribunals after the second World War, respectively. Trial archives across time and space share many features, produced as they are by rather stable administrative routines, legal traditions, methods of investigation and, maybe most of all, a common sense of purpose that drives the people who produce them: to bring the authors of heinous crimes to justice. When these crimes are sponsored by state authorities, the scale of the atrocities and the number of victims and offenders surpass the reach of national judicial systems. They require vast operations of judicial cooperation and are somehow accountable to the international legal opinion and the moral conscience of humankind. The timeless nature of much of their sources is one of the most striking features of judicial archives of mass crimes. Burning down a village and killing its inhabitants in Belgium in 1914, in Volhynia in 1943 or in Taba in 1994 might be part and parcel of very different conflicts, with different dynamics, sources and outcomes. Yet, in judicial terms, they produce comparable types of evidence and are submitted to comparable procedures of investigation, vetting and legal qualification.

The first outcome of this encounter was the *Jusinbellgium* project, which produced a digital and online archive of Belgian case law in international crime, ranging from the German invasion in 1914 to the genocide in Rwanda in 1994, and thus trials initiated between 1919 and today. The *Jusinbellgium* project set itself the same objective as this book: to cherish the record of the fragmentary but pioneering attempts of the Belgian judiciary to bring war criminals to trial by digitizing them and making them freely accessible online.[1] Of the approximately 130 trials *in absentia* held in 1924 and 1925, as mentioned by Thomas Graditzky and Arnaud Charon in Chapters 1 and 2, we could trace back and digitize eighty-six complete trial records, totalling almost 8,000 pages of original documents. This is no mean accomplishment if we recall that the files had been confiscated by an *Einsatzkommando* of the German *Abwehr* in May 1940 and brought to Berlin. From there, they ended up in Moscow and only came back to Brussels in 2003. The fight against impunity is always intrinsically also a fight against the destruction and loss of evidence. Of the thirty-five war crime trials held in Belgium between 1948 and 1951 mentioned by Marie-Anne Weisers in Chapter 6, we could retrace and digitize thirty-four complete trial records, totalling almost 150,000 pages of original documents. The one trial missing was either lost or destroyed earlier on.

We attempted to document the constant effort to defeat impunity, from local municipal authorities gathering evidence of German atrocities in the summer of 1914 to the fundamental contribution of Belgian judicial investigations in the Rwanda Tribunal in Arusha. This century of judicial experiments has produced a unique heritage that urgently needed to be made available to scholars working on mass crimes and practitioners of international justice. Much of this material was unknown to researchers, difficult to access and very much underused. The 158,000 pages of records not only offer new insights into the challenges facing international justice today, but hopefully also provide a new understanding of past judicial policies. They contain the details of fathomless violence and suffering, sometimes in their crudest form and sometimes in shockingly distant bureaucratic language. But they also constitute a monument to the dignity of victims who detail their ordeal before the court, to the tenacity and inventiveness of investigating police officers, magistrates, defence attorneys and ordinary citizens. The complete collection of these records is now available in the database of the International Criminal Court (ICC).[2]

Belgian case law accumulated into an exceptional archive for several reasons, most of which not of its own doing. Belgium was invaded and occupied twice by its German neighbour. Its colonial adventures in Central Africa (1885–1962) turned it into a central actor in a spiral of violence of which genocide in Rwanda in 1994 was but one of many sequels.[3] With the *Digicoljust* project, together with our colleagues Amandine Lauro and Benoît Henriet, we are currently extending the reach of our digital online archive into the records of colonial military tribunals dealing with cases involving Congolese, African and Belgian soldiers.[4] These courts also held extended powers during both world wars and in times of 'special military regimes' (in the course of colonial expansion and war). As a tiny country sandwiched between powerful neighbours, Belgium did not have many alternatives to pleading the cause of a European and, much later, a global order based on international law and international treaties, from the foundation of the Institute of International Law in Ghent in 1870 to its unfortunate experimentations with universal jurisdiction in the 1990s.

The history of international justice and the quest to defeat impunity for international crimes cannot be captured in a single narrative. If we want to understand some of the central challenges facing international justice today, we need to diversify our sources of inspiration. One challenge stands out, over time and space. International justice might well be a universal language but it systematically runs into the cornerstone of the global legal order, that is, the sovereign nation state. International justice depends on the willingness of sovereign states to extradite suspects, to share information, and to allow access to the field to rogatory commissions and forensic expertise. Supranational jurisdictions depend on judicial cooperation by national judiciary authorities to conduct their investigations, to bring witnesses and defendants to their courts and to establish judgments that are accepted as legitimate first and foremost by the offending states.

This book has therefore offered to tell an alternative tale and an alternative genealogy to the dominant narrative that dates the birth of international justice from the start of the Nuremberg trial and positions it as a somehow unmatched model to emulate. Nuremberg as a foundational moment and yardstick brings with it manifold problems for the challenges of international justice today. In 1945, the sovereign German nation had been dissolved in total defeat and unconditional surrender. The Allies could do as they saw fit: seize archives and apprehend, extradite, exchange, judge, hang or imprison leading Nazis. Ultimately, the major accomplishment of Nuremberg was that it was considered legitimate by the German population, but it did not always look that way, certainly not in the 1940s and 1950s. Victor's justice generally suffers from a legitimacy problem. The Tokyo trials have never fully acquired the legitimacy in Japan that Nuremberg found in Germany. Allied policy was admittedly more half-hearted, leaving Emperor Hirohito, the man in whose name Japanese war crimes were committed, on his throne, and this in spite of the American insistence on unconditional surrender that ultimately justified the Hiroshima and Nagasaki bombs.[5]

If it takes a defeat on the scale of that of Germany in May 1945, if it takes crimes on the scale of magnitude of the Nazi Holocaust, and if it takes terrifying destruction and weapons like the atomic bombs dropped in August 1945 for international justice to succeed, its prospects definitely do not look good. One might even wish the preconditions for its success are never again met. The Istanbul trials of 1919–20 judging the authors of the Armenian genocide are a case in point. They were organized under foreign occupation, when the Sublime Porte was in the hands of the Entente powers, under the humiliating conditions of the Treaty of Sèvres. As the work of Vahakn Dadrian and Taner Akçam shows, the trials organized by the rump state, the remnant of the Ottoman Empire, constituted a crucial contribution producing a unique record of the Armenian genocide.[6] The regime that had compromised itself by the humiliating acceptance of the Treaty of Sèvres, including the obligation to bring the authors of the genocide to trial, did not survive for long and was overthrown by the military rebellion of Mustapha Kemal. Through military might, Kemal was able to renegotiate the postwar settlement in the Treaty of Lausanne, which drew new borders and no longer contained any mention of war guilt and trials. This was a powerful source of inspiration for nationalists and revanchists in Weimar Germany and beyond.[7] The rejection of the legitimacy of the Istanbul trials thus became a foundational act of the sovereignty of the Turkish Republic. Sadly, many Turks came to confound their rejection of the legitimacy of the ottoman courts of the Istanbul trials of 1919–20 with their rejection of the reality of the crime under judgment.

The current crisis of the ICC is the best illustration of the dead-end in which international justice finds itself without judicial cooperation. The ICC is not and can never be some permanent version of the Nuremberg trial. With the creation of the ICC in 1998, international criminal justice returned to the challenges of the 1920s: problematic access to evidence, uncertain international cooperation, asymmetric support and contested legitimacy. In 2020, eight defendants have been convicted and four acquitted since the ICC's beginnings. Unlike France and Belgium in the 1920s, the ICC does not allow trials to be held in the absence of the defendants and it keeps the proceedings against fifteen accused fugitives on hold. Today, governments of some of the major world powers and the electorates that voted them into power have largely abandoned the idea of international justice and the institutions that embody them. The disastrous record of the ICC does little to contradict the sceptics in this respect. Yet, there is even less reason to acclaim the untrammelled exercise of national sovereignty as an alternative solution. In December 2020, Donald Trump's presidential pardon of four Blackwater private contractors sentenced in 2015 for their role in the random killing of fourteen unarmed civilians on Nisour Square in Baghdad in 2007 is a stark reminder of how sovereignty rhymes with cynicism and sanctions impunity for even the most blatant violations of the law of armed conflict.

This book has therefore endeavoured to unearth some lesser-known attempts to defeat impunity. Over the one hundred years covered in this volume, defeating impunity has been connected with issues of sovereignty, intellectual and legal activism, public opinion and the changing politics of memory. In the 1920s, diplomats and experts who had put together the Peace Treaties of Versailles and Sèvres experienced how difficult it was to bring individuals to trial for war crimes. And this was despite the fact that most of the belligerents had signed The Hague Conventions before the start of the war and despite Article 227 of the Treaty of Versailles, which explicitly stated that 'the German Government recognizes the right of the Allied and Associated Powers to bring before military tribunals persons accused of having committed acts in violation of the laws and customs of war'.[8] Twenty years later, as Kerstin von Lingen and Guillaume Mouralis show in Chapters 3 and 5 respectively, the definition of crimes against humanity was clouded by domestic and strategic considerations. The trials of war criminals in Belgium in the aftermath of Nuremberg (1948–52), analysed by Marie-Anne Weisers in Chapter 6, reveal how difficult it was to integrate the pioneering definition of 'crimes against humanity' into domestic law. It is baffling to record that crimes against humanity and genocide were only included in Belgian law in 1999 through the amendment of the 1993 law on extraterritorial jurisdiction, the so-called 'universal jurisdiction' legislation. This means that the first suspects prosecuted in Belgium in 2001, 2005, 2007 and 2009 for their role in the genocide against the Tutsi in Rwanda in 1994 were tried on charges of war crimes (breaches of the Geneva Conventions of 1949) and not of genocide, since the law was, again, not applied retroactively.[9]

In the 1960s, the debate on the nonapplicability of statute of limitations to war crimes and crimes against humanity took place in the context of a 'past that does not pass'[10] in Germany and France. As Rebecca Wittmann underlines in Chapter 8, watershed trials in Germany were intended to trigger a debate in the public space about the past. This was the case in 1963 with the Frankfurt Auschwitz trial and with the Majdanek trial in 1975. In the 1960s, Germany had faced the problem of statute of limitations for Nazi criminals, especially because they were prosecuted according to the German Criminal Code, which did not permit the use of international charges, even though genocide had been integrated in the meantime into German law. In France too, the law of 1964 declared crimes against humanity – but not war crimes – imprescriptible in French law, in a formulation that was careful enough to prevent the law from ever being applied to French state crimes in Algeria. In 1968, these initiatives converged in an international convention. During the Cold War era, important trials – many of which were 'historical trials' – took place in Israel, Germany and France, with considerable effects on state policies of memory and on historical research.[11] However, the project of a permanent international criminal court proved to be impossible as long as the Cold War lasted. The forerunners of this permanent international court were the ad hoc tribunals created by the United Nations (UN) in the 1990s and early 2000s for the former Yugoslavia, Rwanda, Sierra Leone and Cambodia.[12]

This book has limited its scope to case studies and alternative tales concealed in twentieth-century European history. This is not an indication of a Eurocentric bias of its editors and contributors, but merely of the focused ambition to show that even the sole experience of the European continent should inspire us to go beyond the foundational tale of the road from Nuremberg to The Hague. The history of international justice is a global tale. Many of its most important chapters have been written far from Europe's shores.[13] We are convinced that their contribution deserves more than one or two chapters in this volume to exonerate ourselves from Eurocentrism. They deserve several comparable volumes in their own right. The intellectual challenge ahead for scholars of international justice is to continue to explode and expand our chronological and geographical boundaries.

The case of the ICTR, to which one of the editors of this book has devoted a recent monograph, connects to many of the central topics addressed in this book. Contrary to 1944, no new qualification or word was needed to describe what was occurring in Rwanda from April to July 1994. However, the word 'genocide' was charged with fear and reluctance, for it had a strong moral dimension and implied the commitment of the international community to stop the massacres. While the massacres continued, killing between 800,000 and more than a million people by July 1994,[14] the debate on international justice was taking place in two different arenas: that of diplomacy and that of transnational civil society. On 8 November 1994, the UN created the

ICTR to prosecute the 'perpetrators of the crimes of genocide and serious violations of international humanitarian law committed in Rwanda in the spring of 1994'.[15] This creation is often described as an act of contrition of the international community for having failed to fulfil its mission of protection and prevention. The framing of post-genocide justice policies in the Rwandan case echoes the key questions that animated both the interwar years and the post-Second World War period. The first remarkable observation is that the question of justice became central while the massacres were taking place in April 1994. Thus, very early on, the issue of accountability was raised – however, too late to stop the massacres. Experts at the time insisted on the fact that the perpetrators of the episodic massacres that Rwanda had experienced since the late 1950s and independence in 1962 had enjoyed impunity. They pointed this out as one of the causes of the ongoing genocide. In the end, by November 1994, only international crimes committed during the year 1994 would fall within the juris-diction of the ICTR, a decision that disappointed the new Rwandan authorities. The second important debate was about the scope and scale of the mechanism to be established. While the idea of a truth and reconciliation commission was quickly dismissed, the distribution of the judicial agenda was planned for an international court, followed – once its work would be completed – by national trials in Rwanda and elsewhere. Such a chain of trials, from the international level to the national level, proved unworkable and was not implemented. Instead, a simultaneous process of justice was pursued until 2015, when the ICTR closed its doors. Back in 1994, nongovernmental organizations (NGOs) massively advocated the creation of an international court, relying not only on the Genocide Convention but also on the risk of 'double standards', since a tribunal had been set up for the former Yugoslavia just one year earlier. They were important actors gather-ing evidence in the first weeks and months after the genocide. Third, today, perhaps one of the most frequent criticisms made against the ICTR is that the Tribunal did not prosecute members of the Rwandan Patriotic Front (RPF), which is still in power today and defeated the genocidal government in July 1994. This political movement and its armed branch at the time are accused of war crimes and crimes against humanity. According to these critics, the absence of trials against the RPF before the ICTR fundamentally calls into question the independence of international justice and its impartiality. Yet, looking back at the context and discussions of the summer of 1994, we can see quite clearly that those who would be at the heart of the upcoming prosecutions were the leaders of the Rwandan government, army and militias who organized and carried out the genocide from April to July 1994. This is especially so since, at one point, it was considered to give jurisdiction to the ICTR only for the period from April to July 1994. Finally, all this makes it difficult to understand why there was such a total lack of international coordination to arrest the members of the government and the army in June and July 1994 when they were clearly located both in the French humanitarian zone (Zone de l'Opération Turquoise) and in neighbouring countries. At the time, a draft proposal for an international tribunal was pending at the UN and a commission of experts was working on the project. Political reluctance – concealed behind a veil of an insufficient legal basis[16] – led to the decision to not proceed with any arrests before the creation of the court. This missed opportunity burdened the ICTR for a long time, as it never possessed a police force of its own and consequently had to rely on international cooperation, which would prove particularly difficult to secure from the states in the Great Lakes region.

Despite the obstacles that had to be overcome in order to arrest the alleged *génocidaires*, to collect evidence and to find witnesses, trials before the ICTR started in January 1997. Fifty years after the adoption of the Genocide Convention, an international court, established in Arusha, Tanzania, composed of three judges – a Senegalese, a Swedish and a South African – convicted a Rwandan mayor of genocide, crimes against humanity and public incitement to commit genocide. Thus, in September 1998, for the first time, an international court, set up by the UN Security Council, sentenced an individual based on the legal definition of genocide.

With over fifty-two trials and seventy-four people tried (including one defendant who died before the end of his trial), the ICTR established a judicial truth that unequivocally affirms the reality of the genocide against the Tutsi.[17] The tribunal, which has been the subject of considerable criticism but little public attention aside from key decisions, has produced essential case law and documentary material on Rwanda. The massive documentary legacy of the postwar trials of the ICTR and the ICTY – as Isabelle Delpla shows in Chapter 9 – has been available almost in real time to researchers. These two tribunals remain the most extensive projects of international justice conducted at the international level since Nuremberg and Tokyo.

If we look at the Rwandan case from a global perspective, we can also consider that it is probably the most judged genocide in history, both in terms of the scope of the proceedings (more than a million persons prosecuted at different levels) and its duration. The ICTY and the ICTR operated far from the usual postwar justice processes

(1918–1925 and 1945–56). For more than twenty years, trials have been going on before local (Rwandan *gacaca* courts, 2001–12)[18] and national (Rwandan, but also Belgian, French, German and Swiss) courts to bring to justice those responsible for the massacres. While the ad hoc courts, the *gacaca* courts in Rwanda and the ICTR, closed their doors in 2012 and 2015, national courts do still proceed with prosecutions. Not all national jurisdictions have surrendered to impunity, as the conviction of Fabien Neretse for genocide and crimes against humanity before the Cour d'Assises (jury trial) of Brussels in 2019 shows, twenty-five years after the genocide against the Tutsi in Rwanda.

On 16 May 2020, Félicien Kabuga, one of the ICTR's most wanted fugitives at the point when the tribunal closed its doors, was arrested near Paris. His arrest and future trial in Arusha or The Hague provide proof of the imprescriptible character of international crimes today. Indeed, international justice, through the successive and insistent attempts to defeat impunity, has not been a victorious march forward, but today no less than in 1919, it is the only project that carries the hope for a world in which offenders cannot totally discount the possibility that one day, in some place, they might be held accountable for their crimes. This may not be much in itself, but every single conviction is a small brick in the edifice of justice. Every single investigation, regardless whether it leads to a trial and regardless whether it sends even a single criminal to prison for even a single day, is proof that the world does not disarm in the face of wanton violence and injustice, that it does not sentence the victims to oblivion and that there is a place, a language and a voice in which to tell injustice and thereby to uphold the standards of law, justice and truth. As historians, we follow the tracks left by investigations and trials. In doing so, we come across personal experiences and encounters with the constantly developing institutions of international criminal justice. The German officers Jeanne recognized on a postcard before the military tribunal of Namur (Belgium) in 1925 and Assumpta's[19] testimony when she was first heard by the ICTR investigators in the Rwandan village of Taba help us to question, write and rewrite the narrative of a century of violent injustice that is a source of anguish, but also of the timid attempts at international justice that can be a source of hope.

Pieter Lagrou has taught contemporary history at the Université libre de Bruxelles since 2003. He has published on the legacy of the Second World War in Europe, on war crime trials and European contemporary historiography. He is currently working on the histories of popular sovereignty since 1789.

Ornella Rovetta is a postdoctoral researcher in contemporary history at the Centre de Recherche Mondes Modernes et Contemporains (Université libre de Bruxelles). Her research interests include the history of international criminal justice and of Rwanda. She has published *Un génocide au tribunal. Le Rwanda et la justice internationale* (Belin, 2019) and coauthored a radio documentary on the ICTR.

Notes

1. See https://jusinbell.hypotheses.org (retrieved 10 May 2021).
2. legal-tools.org: on the left-hand scroll bar, tick successively National Criminal Jurisdictions, Belgium, Core International Crimes and Case Law (retrieved 10 May 2021).
3. See in particular the chapter 'The Empire of Law' in Mazower, *Governing the World*; and on the Congo, see Goddeeris, Lauro and Vanthemsche, *Le Congo colonial*; Bevernage, 'The Making of the Congo Question'; Burroughs, *African Testimony in the Movement for Congo Reform*.
4. See https://digicoljust.hypotheses.org (retrieved 10 May 2021).
5. On the Japanese surrender, see Hasegawa, *Racing the Enemy*.
6. Dadrian and Akçam, *Judgment at Istanbul*.
7. See Ihrig, *Atatürk in the Nazi Imagination*.
8. Article 227 of the Treaty of Versailles (1919).
9. Meire and Vandermeersch, *Génocide rwandais*, 156–57; Rovetta, 'La compétence universelle'.
10. 'Un passé qui ne passe pas', following the title of the book by Conan and Rousso, *Vichy, un passé qui ne passe pas*.
11. Rousso, *Face au passé*; Hilberg, *Politics of Memory*; Bloxham, "'The Trial That Never Was"'; Brayard (ed.), *Le génocide des Juifs entre procès et histoire*; Priemel, *The Nuremberg Trials and German Divergence*.
12. Schabas, *The UN International Criminal Tribunals*; Cryer, *Prosecuting International Crimes*; Clarke and Goodale, *Mirrors of Justice*; Clark and Kaufman, *After Genocide*; Dumas, 'Rwanda : comment juger un génocide ?'.
13. On postwar justice in Asia and the origins of international criminal law, see, for instance, von Lingen, *Transcultural Justice at the Tokyo Tribunal*; Totani, *The Tokyo War Crimes Trial*; Crowe, *War Crimes, Genocide, and Justice*; Bergsmo, Cheah and Yi, *Historical Origins of International Criminal Law*; von Lingen, *Justice in Times of Turmoil*; Tanaka, McCormack and Simpson, *Beyond Victor's Justice?*; Cohen and Totani, *The Tokyo War Crimes Tribunal*.
14. Depending on the estimates. The UN retains the estimate of 800,000 victims, while the Rwandan government's estimate is 1,074,017 reported victims and 934,218 counted victims.
15. United Nations, Security Council, Resolution 955, 8 November 1994.
16. Department of State Archives, 'Consultations with France on Rwanda War Crime Issues', cable no. 19216, 13 July 1994, para. 4-7.
17. For a history of the ICTR, see Rovetta, *Un genocide au tribunal*, Chapters 1, 5, 6, 7 and 8; see also Kaufman, 'The United States Role', 229–60.

18. *Gacaca* courts are local customary arbitration instances reinstalled and transformed by law in 2001–2 to judge the massive number of suspected *génocidaires* in prison at the time in Rwanda.
19. The original name has been changed.

Bibliography

Bergsmo, Morten, Wui Ling Cheah and Ping Yi (eds). *Historical Origins of International Criminal Law*, 2 vols. Brussels: Torkel Opsahl Academic E-Publisher, 2014.

Bevernage, Berber. 'The Making of the Congo Question: Truth-Telling, Denial and "Colonial Science" in King Leopold's Commission of Inquiry on the Rubber Atrocities in the Congo Free State (1904–1905)'. *Rethinking History* 22(2) (2018), 203–38.

Bloxham, Donald. '"The Trial That Never Was": Why There Was No Second International Trial of Major War Criminals at Nuremberg'. *History* 87(285) (2002), 41–60.

Brayard, Florent (ed.). *Le génocide des Juifs entre procès et histoire. 1943–2000.* Brussels: Éditions Complexe, IHTP CNRS, 2000.

Burroughs, Robert M. *African Testimony in the Movement for Congo Reform: The Burden of Proof.* New York: Routledge, 2018.

Clark, Philip, and Zachary D. Kaufman (eds). *After Genocide: Transitional Justice, Post-conflict Reconstruction and Reconciliation in Rwanda and Beyond.* New York: Columbia University Press, 2009.

Clarke, Kamari Maxine, and Mark Goodale. *Mirrors of Justice: Law and Power in the Post-Cold War Era.* Cambridge: Cambridge University Press, 2010.

Cohen, David, and Yuma Totani. *The Tokyo War Crimes Tribunal: Law, History, and Jurisprudence.* Cambridge: Cambridge University Press, 2018.

Conan, Eric, and Henry Rousso. *Vichy, un passé qui ne passe pas.* Paris: Fayard, 1994.

Crowe, David. *War Crimes, Genocide, and Justice: A Global History.* New York: Palgrave Macmillan, 2014.

Cryer, Robert. *Prosecuting International Crimes: Selectivity and the International Criminal Law Regime.* Cambridge: Cambridge University Press, 2005.

Dadrian, Vahakn N., and Taner Akçam. *Judgment at Istanbul: The Armenian Genocide Trials.* New York: Berghahn Books, 2011.

Dumas, Hélène. 'Rwanda: comment juger un génocide?' *Politique étrangère* 4 (2015), 39–50.

Goddeeris, Idesbald, Amandine Lauro and Guy Vanthemsche (eds). *Le Congo colonial. Une histoire en questions.* Waterloo: La Rennaissance du livre, 2020.

Hasegawa, Tsuyoshi. *Racing the Enemy: Stalin, Truman, and the Surrender of Japan.* Cambridge, MA: Belknap Press, 2005.

Hilberg, Raul. *Politics of Memory: The Journey of a Holocaust Historian.* Chicago: Ivan R. Dee, 1996.

Ihrig, Stefan. *Atatürk in the Nazi Imagination.* Cambridge, MA: Belknap Press, 2014.

Kaufman, Zachary D. 'The United States Role in the Establishment of the United Nations International Criminal Tribunal for Rwanda', in Philip Clark and Zachary D. Kaufman (eds), *After Genocide: Transitional Justice, Post-conflict Reconstruction and Reconciliation in Rwanda and Beyond* (New York: Columbia University Press, 2009), 229–60.

Lewis, Mark. *The Birth of the New Justice: The Internationalization of Crime and Punishment, 1919–1950.* Oxford: Oxford University Press, 2014.

Mazower, Mark. *Governing the World: The History of an Idea.* London: Penguin, 2013.

Meire, Philippe, and Damien Vandermeersch. *Génocide rwandais : le récit de quatre procès devant la Cour d'Assises de Bruxelles*. Brussels: La Charte, 2011.

Priemel, Kim Christian. 'Consigning Justice to History: Transitional Trials after the Second World War'. *Historical Journal* 56(2) (2013), 553–81.

———. *The Betrayal: The Nuremberg Trials and German Divergence*. Oxford: Oxford University Press, 2016.

Rovetta, Ornella. 'La compétence universelle', in Aude Musin, Aude Hendrick, Xavier Rousseaux and Nathalie Tousignant (eds). *Les mots de la justice* (Brussels: Mardaga, 2017), 156–57.

———. *Un génocide au tribunal. Le Rwanda et la justice internationale*. Paris: Belin, 2019.

Rousso, Henry. *Face au passé: Essai sur la mémoire contemporaine*. Paris: Belin, 2016.

Schabas, William. *The UN International Criminal Tribunals: The Former Yugoslavia, Rwanda, and Sierra Leone*. Cambridge: Cambridge University Press, 2006.

Tanaka, Yuki, Timothy L. H. McCormack and Gerry Simpson (eds). *Beyond Victor's Justice? The Tokyo War Crimes Trial Revisited*. Leiden: Brill, 2011.

Totani, Yuma. *The Tokyo War Crimes Trial: The Pursuit of Justice in the Wake of World War II*. Cambridge, MA: Harvard University Press, 2008.

Von Lingen, Kerstin. *Justice in Times of Turmoil: War Crimes Trials in Asia, 1945–1954*. New York: Palgrave Macmillan, 2016.

———. (ed.). *Transcultural Justice at the Tokyo Tribunal: The Allied Struggle for Justice, 1946–48*. Leiden: Brill, 2018.

INDEX